JOURNEY
through the
VALLEY
of the
SHADOW

PATRICIA C. SHELTON

www.xulonpress.com

In memory of
Jack D. Shelton

Introduction

⚜

¹The LORD *is* my shepherd; I shall not want. ² He makes me to lie down in green pastures; He leads me beside the still waters. ³ He restores my soul; He leads me in the paths of righteousness for His name's sake. ⁴ Yea, though I walk through the valley of the shadow of death, I will fear no evil; For You *are* with me; Your rod and Your staff, they comfort me. ⁵ You prepare a table before me in the presence of my enemies; You anoint my head with oil; My cup runs over. ⁶ Surely goodness and mercy shall follow me all the days of my life; And I will dwell in the house of the LORD forever (Psalm 23 NKJV).

In analyzing the verse above, I have come to realize that: ^{1.}He *is* my shepherd. He *does* lead me. He has been with me every step of the way. ^{2.} He does give me quiet times and puts me in a place of comfort so I can rest. ³ He does restore my soul. He is leading me in the right way to handle what I am going through so I can bring glory to His name. ^{4.}Even though I am facing the death of a loved one, He is there with me; I am not alone. He has sent comfort through His Word, through people and through things that have happened. ^{5.}He has prepared a place for me to dwell while in the presence of the enemy (death). It is with Him; He has anointed me with the oil of His presence, His love, His mercy. The cup of my peace overflows. I know it is because He walks with me on this journey. ^{6.} His goodness and mercy will follow me when these days are done and when my own journey is over, I know I will dwell in His house forever.

When I was considering a title for this book, the only one that would come to me is the one I eventually chose. Jack was a truck driver, so calling it a journey seemed appropriate. Because we were definitely going to be in the valley of death, that fit also. Then I realized that Psalm 23 had become more real to me during this journey. I have paraphrased that Psalm, and I trust that is okay. It is what God had been speaking to me since the journey began. Each verse had, and has, a special meaning. Someone told me you can't have a shadow without light. That really comforted me as I traveled the dark valley. Knowing that His light was casting the shadow, I had no fear.

Because of how that Psalm had spoken to me, I've thought long and hard about putting my journal writings in book form and then decided I must—to help anyone going through something similar. My prayer is that this will encourage someone, give helpful insights, and make the journey a little less daunting. No, I do not have all the answers—sometimes I don't have any answers. I only have my experience, and while it may be different from someone else's, there will be some similarities.

My pastor always asks if anyone has had any "God sightings." Some people might wonder what that means. No, he's not being weird, and he's not looking for a physical apparition; he's asking if we see God in things that happen in our lives. You can call it coincidence, fate, karma, nonsense, or whatever you want. Me—I'll call them "God sightings," and you can agree or disagree, but too many things in this journey were well beyond my control or happened in a way I never would have planned. And, you know what? What God has done was far and away better than anything I would have thought would work.

Here, then, is my story.

Friday, November 23, 2012—The Diagnosis

That Friday morning (the day after Thanksgiving) I was working on my laptop, finishing up a scrapbook journal I was doing for my grandson, Ryan. Ryan and his sister, Destiny, had spent the month of June 2012 at our farm helping me with yard work, building work, house work, and other work. They also had plenty of time to swim, fish, and play. I was doing a scrapbook journal for both of them. Destiny's was done; Ryan's was almost finished.

I needed a break, so about 9:00 A.M. that morning I started reading *The Circle Maker*, a book my pastor had given to all the people on his prayer team. As a part of that prayer team, I met monthly with others and most Sundays stood on our back balcony at church and prayed over one of the two morning services. Pastor Mick wanted us to read this book and use it as a tool in our prayer life.

I had not gotten very far into the book when I realized that the ideas presented were right up my alley, so to speak. I do better praying when I can focus, I mean really focus, as in picturing what I am praying about. In *The Circle Maker* the author was describing how to put someone or something in a circle and focus the prayer on him or her or the situation. That resonated with me. In my mind, I immediately put my husband Jack in that circle and began to pray for him to give his heart to Christ—something I had done for years, but now was focusing that into a circle. That request was in the center, and around it were other prayers—for restoration of relationships (ours, for one, as we were at odds about a few things lately), for him to quit smoking (I had been praying this for years but now it was in the circle and focused on), and for his health issues (most of which I felt were caused by smoking).

The main focus was for him to accept Christ—everything else was secondary. I kept reading and that one focus kept coming back. I knew if he got that right the other things would follow. I was picturing a 3x5 index card with a circle on it and writing in that circle. In my mind I could see that index card, and it was easy to focus on what I was praying about. That is how my mind works, and that day I put it all in that circle and offered it up to the Lord. I knew once I had it in the circle, I could leave it there, and when I returned to that prayer, my focus would be there. For me, that really worked!

While I was alternating reading the book and working on Ryan's album, my granddaughter Amber had been pestering her sister Brittany about taking her to get her check from work. It was her first check, and she was so excited she bounced around the house all morning. Around noon Brittany finally gave up trying to do anything and said she'd take her. She asked if I wanted to go for the ride, and I decided I needed a mental break, so I went with them.

When we got to where Amber worked, Chuck E. Cheese's, she panicked and didn't want to go in unless one of us went with her. Brittany threatened to push her out of the car if she didn't get out. I told her if she didn't hurry and get out, we'd push her out and lock the doors so she'd have to go in. She was so nervous it was actually funny. Then Amber asked how she should ask for her check. Exasperated, Brittany told her to go tell them she was there for her paycheck. She had earned it; she didn't need to be afraid to ask for it. She finally went in and came back out smiling. Her first paycheck! One more step in the growing up process!

The rest of the afternoon was quiet as everyone was off doing something to work off the big meal we had the day before. I was off and on reading the book and working on the journal for Ryan. I wasn't interested in any movies that Friday. My focus had changed to getting the gift done and reading the book and praying.

About 4:00 P.M. Chicago time everything changed. That was when my son Charlie called me. He had been getting ready to make a trip to Chicago the next day. His wife, Josette, was working, so they had to wait until Saturday morning to leave. Because his dad hadn't answered the phone since late Thanksgiving night and he was concerned, he decided to check on him one more time before he left town. He was calling me to tell me that on Thanksgiving his dad had been wobbly and seemed a little confused. He said his dad told him he might have had a mini-stroke. Since he seemed okay other than that, Charlie had told him goodbye and he'd see him the next day.

He was on the way to the farm when he called me to tell me all this and that he would probably be taking his dad to the hospital if he was worse. Charlie was sure something was wrong because a friend had called him and said he saw one of our ducks in the road; it was dead, and the other ducks were wandering around. He knocked on the door, but no one answered although Jack's pickup was in the driveway. That concerned Charlie because of how his dad had acted the day before at dinner. Since his dad had not answered the door, Charlie was afraid he had gotten worse. He tried calling, but his dad didn't answer the phone. Now he was really concerned. He was pretty sure his dad had had a mini-stroke and would let me know what was going on when he got to the house.

When I got that call, my oldest son Dave was out running errands, and Rob, my other son, was down the street at a neighbor's. I could not settle down as I waited for them to return. I paced the floor trying to decide how to tell them the news. How did I tell them when I had so little information? How did I tell them when I was still in shock myself? What would I tell them? When they returned, I called them together with my daughter-in-law, Tracy, and told them I had something to tell them. They knew immediately something was wrong, but no one was prepared for what I had to say.

They had questions, of course, but I could not answer them. I had only the most basic information that Charlie had given me, and I was waiting for more information. Something had happened for sure, but I had no idea what. I knew for sure though that Dave and I would be heading home that day because even if it was just a mini-stroke, I had to get back home.

Charlie called again and told us that when he got to the house, he was shocked by what he saw. Jack was sitting in the living room in just his underwear, very confused and not able to coherently tell him what he wanted. As I said, Jack was a smoker. Charlie said he was trying to light a cigarette using another cigarette as a lighter. He was so stunned by that he did not know what to think. All he could think to do was get his dad to the hospital. He helped his dad get dressed and took him to the ER. Because of the way Jack was acting, Charlie was sure it was a stroke and called to tell me that.

Now at last we had some idea of what was going on. He was sure it was "only a mini-stroke" and they were running tests. I told him Dave and I would be leaving to drive home immediately. He kept saying it wasn't that serious, that he was pretty sure it was just a mini-stroke and to wait till morning to start back. I told him there was no way I would sleep worrying about it and that we would be starting back right away. Here I am in Chicago, over 300 miles from home, getting news like that, and he expects me to wait until morning? Like that was really going to happen!

The decision was made to leave as soon as we could pack, regardless of what they found out. I knew it was serious from what Charlie had described, but I could tell them no more than that he suspected a mini-stroke and what the symptoms were.

In addition to confusion and an obvious problem with dressing and walking, Charlie said his left eye was drooping and almost closed, and his left side seemed weak. He had all the classic symptoms of a stroke.

Dave and I began packing immediately. We knew we would lose an hour heading home due to the time change and would be getting in very late at night or very early in the morning. Both of us were too keyed up to worry about falling asleep at the wheel though. I doubted I'd sleep at all thinking about what we would face when we got home. We were still in a state of shock. Trying to absorb what is happening long distance is twice as hard as facing it when you are there when it happens—you just don't know for sure what is going on.

Rob asked if he should come with us and take a train back to Chicago later that weekend. Charlie kept insisting it wasn't that bad and Rob did not need to come with us. At that time, while we were packing and leaving, we were all thinking mini-stroke, and I was already planning how to take care of him while he recuperated. I knew his first thought would be how long before he could return to work.

One of the first people I called that evening was our pastor and good friend Pastor Garry Beecher. I felt so bad calling him. He was on the way home to Michigan from Indiana where he had just had his mother's funeral. He was still in mourning, and here I was calling him with my troubles. I apologized for calling but told him I needed some urgent prayer. After I told him what I knew, he told me not to worry about having called them and that he and his wife Martha would be praying as they drove home. He also told me if we needed anything or needed him to come to the hospital, to call immediately. I promised to do that but told him I might not have any information before the next day, which was Saturday. We hung up, and I went back to trying to process what I had heard.

We were well into Michigan when Charlie sent me a text that said, "Not stroke. Brain tumor." That cryptic message was a total shock. I sent a text back and said, "Call me—NOW!" I could not believe he sent that message and no explanation. Dave asked me what was going on, and I didn't know what to tell him. I read the message to him and said I did not understand why Charlie would send such a message and not call to explain. I found out much later that he could not talk about it right away because he had gone into another area of the hospital and cried before he could call me and tell me about it.

At first I was so angry that he would not give me more information. Here I am in a car trying to get home and all I get is a short text message. I was beside myself. I needed to know what was going on— now! Later, when I realized what he had been through, I could no longer be angry with him. In fact, I felt really bad that he had been all alone getting all this bad news. He was by himself at the hospital for more than eight hours dealing with all that was going on. At least I had Dave to talk to.

Charlie called soon after the text and gave us the information. I put my phone on speaker so I would not have to repeat everything to Dave. Charlie told us that the doctor said for sure it was not a stroke. The CAT scan they had done right away showed two brain lesions. Because of the lesions, they immediately x-rayed his lungs. The x-ray showed a mass in the right lung also. I found out later that many times tumors in the brain have metastasized from the lung, which is why they immediately ran the x-ray.

I was in such shock I didn't know what to say. After we hung up, I told Dave I didn't want to tell the others what we had heard until the next day. I knew they would have questions, and I just did not have any answers. Not only that, I was still reeling from the news. I had no idea how to tell the others what we had just heard. Dave and I discussed waiting until morning after everyone had a chance to sleep and we had a chance to process what we had heard. That changed when we found out Charlie's daughter Rica had called her cousin Destiny to tell her what happened to Papa. Rica had heard her mom talking to her dad on the phone. Because Destiny and she were close, she immediately contacted her.

When Rob heard what Rica had told Destiny, he called us to find out what was going on. I really didn't want to talk about it, but now I had no choice. While Rob was calling us to see what was going on, Josette was giving Rica a hard time for calling her cousin. Rica had no idea that no one else had been told. She felt bad for contacting Destiny and was upset because her mom had yelled at her. The kids were having a hard time dealing with the news also, so I could not be too hard on them. I had just wanted to wait till morning to tell everyone else.

Dave and I spent most of the rest of the trip across Michigan talking to Rich in Arizona, Rob in Illinois, and Charlie in Michigan. We never did reach Karen in Toronto and found out the next day they had been in an ER in Rochester, New York. Her son Riley had been injured in a hockey game and had a concussion. Karen did not find out about her dad until later that weekend.

Dave and I reached the hospital about midnight that Friday. Jack had finally fallen asleep, and Charlie was exhausted from the emotions of the day and the stress of being at the hospital for seven hours trying to get answers and then trying to process all the information. We decided we all needed to get some sleep and would come back in the morning. There was nothing we could do this night. After hugging Charlie and saying good night, we split up and went home. And so began our journey.

September to November, 2012—Backtracking

I was going to start this story with the events of Thanksgiving 2012 and go forward, but in thinking about it I realized there were indications before that day that something was amiss. I wasn't sure how far back I should go because some things happened so far apart I was never sure if they were related to the cancer. I decided to start with September, 2012 even though there were warnings long before then that something was wrong.

From July until September Jack kept talking about going to his fifty-seventh high school reunion (scary isn't that?) in Tennessee in October. He even went out and bought new clothes to wear. In late September he was on a trip to California when I talked to him and offered to go with him to the reunion and take the three grandkids that we watch three or four days a week. I thought he'd like the company, and the kids could see their aunt and uncle, who lived in Murfreesboro, Tennessee.

When he got home from that trip on October 8, he said he decided to go to Tennessee alone. He had some truck accessories he was building and wanted to visit several places along the way to talk about selling them. He thought the kids would be bored waiting in the pickup while he talked with people. So he packed up the pickup and headed out. I figured he'd be gone at least five days. I was shocked when he pulled back in the driveway a few hours later.

I thought maybe he had forgotten something or had decided we should go along after all. What he had decided was to not go at all. I was surprised because that is all he had talked about for two months.

When he came in the house I asked, "What are you doing here?" His answer was, "I live here don't I?" Well, yes, but that's not what I meant and he knew it. He then told me he was tired and didn't feel good and he didn't feel like driving all that way just to see people he hadn't seen in many years. That should have been an indication to me that something wasn't quite right. This is a man who had just driven to California and back hauling a huge boat behind his semi without batting an eyelash. Driving to Tennessee seemed like too much effort? I should have really questioned that because it made no sense.

We've all done this—missed things that should be a warning that something is not quite right. Have you been there, done that? Are you on a guilt trip because you missed something and then later thought "If I had only . . ." I'm here to tell you to get off the guilt trip. Park that guilt train in the station. You can't second guess yourself. You can't live on "what if" or "I should have" because you will drive yourself crazy. We have ALL done it. Don't waste energy you need to handle things on regretting things in the past that you can't change.

And for me—I didn't just miss the one—I missed more than one. Through September, October and even into November Jack was coughing a lot, and his coughing was getting worse. In fact, it was so bad he almost could not catch his breath when he coughed. He had been a heavy smoker all his life, and I just chalked it up to the smoking—or possibly emphysema. In fact, Charlie and I talked about it a lot. We were sure that was his problem, and he was always saying it was a cold or the weather. He was living in denial, according to us.

The coughing, and now wheezing, were getting so bad I told Charlie he should "encourage" (another word for nag) his dad into going to the doctor. I had tried and met with much resistance. I was sure the doctor would find something to indicate his lungs were beginning to suffer the effects of smoking for so many years. I was also sure that is why he would not agree to see the doctor—he just didn't want to face it. The reason I asked Charlie to be the one to ask him to do it is because I was sure if I brought it up again he'd get defensive and argue with me.

He would not go, and I was frustrated and angry. I told Charlie it is hard to have sympathy for someone who will not take steps to take care of an obvious problem. I knew there was a problem. Charlie knew there was a problem. Jack knew there was a problem—he just wouldn't face it.

I wasn't getting much sleep either because his coughing at 4:30 in the morning would wake me out of a sound sleep. I was actually relieved when, late in September, he had the trip to California to pick up a boat. I counted the days he would probably be gone and planned to sleep in till about 6:00 A.M. as often as I could. That probably sounds heartless, but I was not sleeping well and would be exhausted by mid-afternoon. I really needed several good nights' sleep.

He made the trip to California without incident. He did complain of being tired and came back coughing even more. It was after this trip he was supposed to go to Tennessee but canceled. Since he didn't go to Tennessee, I booked him for a short trip across Michigan. He made that trip in October.

If I had been checking his log books like I am supposed to for the company, I would have seen that he logged October 18 and 19 correctly, but on what should have been October 20 to October 31 (or 10/20/12—10/31/12), he dated it 9/20/12—9/31/12. Anyone can make a mistake, but this error was so out of the ordinary for someone who spent his life filling in log books. In all the years I had to review his log sheets, I had never seen an error like this.

His coughing kept getting worse, and by November it was so bad I was afraid he would not be able to catch his breath when he was coughing. It was really unnerving. I didn't know what I would do if he stopped breathing, so I'd lie awake in bed to make sure he continued breathing after the coughing spell; then I'd try to get some more sleep. By then it was not just in the morning; he'd have sessions like that throughout the day.

About that time I began to have a problem with one of my teeth. I knew it was loose because I could feel it move. I didn't have any pain, but I knew something would have to be done. I have a friend who is a dentist, and I told him about the problem and said I needed to get in to see him as soon as I could. My insurance, which was completely messed up, did not cover him. In fact, I could not find if I had coverage at all. In the meantime, the tooth got worse. I still didn't have any pain, but I knew it was getting more wobbly because I would wake up in the middle of the night and feel myself grinding my teeth, making it sore.

Early in November we talked about going to our son Rob's house in Illinois for Thanksgiving. It was always hard to make plans because we never knew when he would get a load. It looked like there would be nothing coming up this time, and then Hurricane Sandy changed things for us. The other driver had been scheduled to go south to drop a boat and then head up to New York to pick one up going to Ohio. We were told to put that on hold as they could not get at the boat because of all the mess from the hurricane. The boat was at a marina on the Hudson River, north of New York City.

The other driver called and asked Jack if he could pick that one up and drop it in Ohio. He would then pick one up near his drop off point in Ohio and take it to the west side of Michigan.

Jack did not want to go. He kept complaining he didn't feel well, but he still would not go to the doctor. I remember telling a friend I was having a hard time being sympathetic toward him because he refused to go to the doctor when he was obviously sick. He was cranky, and I was cranky right back, which didn't make for a peaceful home. We weren't fighting because we weren't speaking. I was so aggravated with him it was hard to have a conversation because it always came back to the fact that he should see the doctor.

He did take that trip in mid-November. Again, I missed something—actually a couple of things. He called me one day while on the trip and told me he had been really sick the night before with the flu. When he woke up he was sweating, had a headache, and was disoriented. He said he didn't know where he was or what direction he was heading. He had to sit a while and "wake up" so he could think about where he was. He said it was the worst flu he ever had.

He *never* called me from the road, and he never would tell me how sick he really was. I should have known it was really bad. He kept insisting it was the flu and said when he got home he just wanted to sleep. The fact that he woke up and did not know where he was going or where he was should have been a huge red flag for me. He carried his own mental GPS in his head, and that I knew of he had never had a time when he didn't know where he was.

He also told me he would have gone to the hospital but they told him the hospital was about five miles away and the ambulance would cost $300. He said forget it, he'd go when he got home. He was at a truck stop, and the staff there would not take him because of liability. Looking back, I'm glad he didn't go. I don't even want to think about what it would have been like trying to get him and the truck home with what was going on. I believe that was God's provision.

This all happened when he was in Ohio, near the Pennsylvania border. He hadn't even picked the boat up yet, and he was having problems. He continued on the trip, loaded the boat, and headed for

Ohio. It was not until later that I heard what he did when he loaded the boat. I shudder to think of what would have happened if the men in the yard had not been there to stop him. God's protection at the marina was so obvious.

He never did tell me what happened until after the marina called and reported damage to a boat. Even then he didn't fully explain what had happened. Looking back, I realized he really didn't know all of what happened that day. He knew he "bumped" into a boat. I'm not sure he ever knew what almost happened. I knew because I talked to the marina owner. It was so scary. It wasn't until after we had the diagnosis that I even knew about the accident because the marina did not call to tell us about the damage until after Thanksgiving, and it was the day after Thanksgiving that we found out what was going on with him.

But back to the boat. He told the people at the marina he had the flu and he was pretty weak. They let one of their men assist him with loading it and getting everything set up. Because of liability and insurance, marinas are not allowed to assist once the boat is on the carrier's trailer. It then becomes the liability of the carrier. He has never, ever, that I know of, asked for assistance. I didn't know about this at the time or it really would have been a red flag. But then, would I have really picked up on it? It's hard to say because I was just labeling everything going on as "side effects" so to speak of what I was convinced was emphysema.

The damage to the boat he scraped was minor, under $500. I breathed a huge sigh of relief because after talking to the marina owner I found out how much worse it could have been. It was a pretty tight spot where he loaded the boat. He has been in tight spots before but this was different. He was backing up, trying to make a really tight turn. He did not know it, but he was scraping along the edge of a boat parked in the yard. The marina owner told me he ran all the way across the lot, jumped up on the steps on the side of Jack's truck, and was banging on the door of the truck, screaming at him to stop. The men in the yard had also been screaming, waving, and trying to get his attention, but he did not hear or see them. Another few feet and he would have knocked over a fifty-foot, $100,000 boat that was sitting on a cradle.

All of what happened there made sense later when we found out what was going on with Jack. But at the time he was not aware, and neither were we, that he did not have peripheral vision on his left side.

By the time he loaded the boat he said he was exhausted and needed to rest. From the marina to where he unloaded in Ohio was less than a day's drive. Because of his extreme exhaustion it took him almost two days. Looking back, it's a wonder he made it at all. The entire trip should have been a disaster given what was going on with him. It's only God's protection that kept this trip from being a major nightmare.

The second thing I missed was the amount of time he spent "off duty" on such a short trip. Again, I did not look at the log books until much later. In fact, the log books show the following:

On Nov 10 he left home at 1:00 P.M. and stopped for the night at 7:00 P.M. He had driven four-and-one-half hours and 264 miles. Since he was unloaded, he could have driven much further and normally would have gone almost 500 miles.

On Nov 11 he started driving at 8:30 A.M. He spent a total of five hours driving that day, stopping for the day at 6:00 P.M. He drove 300 miles. This was the morning he woke up disoriented.

By this time, normally he would be at his destination, having driven at least 500 miles each day. This was unheard of for him.

On Nov 12 he arrived at his destination, having driven for one-and-one-half hours. He loaded the boat and drove another one-and-one-half hours, stopping for the night at 4:30 P.M. He had driven about 100 miles after loading the boat.

On Nov 13 he drove seven hours for a total of 376 miles. He stopped for the night at 4:00 P.M. Normally, he would have almost been to his destination.

On Nov 14, he drove two hours total time and 109 miles. He dropped the one boat and drove to a truck stop near the next marina, about 50 miles from the first one. He stopped for the day at 2:00 P.M.

On Nov 15, he drove a half hour to the next marina and loaded. Then he drove another two-and-one-half hours for a total of 172 miles. He stopped by 3:30 P.M. On a normal trip, he could have easily driven another 150 or so miles and still stopped before dark, well into Michigan. He would have been within an hour or so of his destination. This was not a normal trip. In fact, in a normal trip, he would have almost been at his destination.

On Nov 16, he drove four-and-one-half hours for a total of 257 miles, arriving at the second destination at 11:30 A.M. He was unloaded by 2:00 P.M. He could have headed home right then as he was unloaded. He would have been home before dark. He stopped for the day at 3:00 P.M.

On November 17—at 8:00 A.M. he started driving and arrived home early in the afternoon.

So why am I putting all this detail in here? Because this trip was the last one he drove, and all the indications are there that something serious was going on and we totally missed it.

He said the flu had wiped him out and he could only drive for a few hours at a time and had to rest. For something to wipe him out to that extent should have raised a red flag and he should have immediately gone to the doctor. As I said, I didn't look at the log book until weeks later, so I never saw how little he actually drove and how much he spent "off duty" on what should have been a relatively short trip.

Here again, it was his responsibility to take care of himself, but I also should have realized how serious this was and should have done whatever I could to get him to a doctor. He kept saying it was the worst case of the flu he ever had and that he needed to get a flu shot. I kept saying it was from his smoking and he had emphysema and I didn't want to hear about it. Yep, I've had to eat humble pie *and* my words. Neither tasted very good.

He arrived home from that trip the Saturday before Thanksgiving. We were scheduled to leave Tuesday night to drive to Illinois, giving us Wednesday to shop and prep for Thanksgiving dinner at Rob's. He said he was too tired to go and would stay home and rest. He said to go ahead with our plans and he'd have Thanksgiving with Charlie before Charlie left for Chicago on the Saturday after Thanksgiving. If he felt better, he might ride with Charlie to Chicago where they were going for a baby shower for Charlie's wife's cousin. We would meet them and bring him to Rob's for the weekend.

19

Dave and I packed up and left Tuesday evening for Rob's. Jack was tired, still coughing and wheezing, but saying he just needed to rest from having the flu so bad. He also said that trip to New York had worn him out. I remember thinking he must be feeling bad if a short trip like that made him feel so exhausted. Normally a trip like that is about four days. It had taken him nearly twice that long, and he was still worn out.

That Wednesday before Thanksgiving at Rob's, I alternated between watching movies and working on the journal for Ryan that I mentioned earlier. It's what I worked on most of the time I was in Illinois. Doing this was my downtime, and for me it was relaxing.

Dave and Rob were shopping, prepping, and cooking for Thanksgiving. Tracy was doing homework and studying for classes she was taking at the nearby community college. The others were sleeping, watching movies, playing with friends, or texting friends.

Thanksgiving was quite an affair. Dave and Rob had cooked enough food to feed an army, and we ate like one! We ate just about all day long. First there was breakfast. I thought that was enough to keep me until Friday, but later when dinner was ready I found room for the feast.

It was again a movie marathon day. Those who weren't sleeping or off somewhere were with me curled up on the couch watching movies. There were plenty of movies to choose from, and I was content just to relax and watch or doze, something I didn't often get to do. I was enjoying being lazy and not having any responsibilities. It was good to have someone else do all the holiday cooking and cleaning.

I had no idea until later that this Thanksgiving Day back home was quite different. Jack had called Charlie and they had decided to get together and go to Cracker Barrel for Thanksgiving dinner. Jack liked going there; it was one of the few places open, and Charlie had no other plans for the day. He was planning to leave Saturday morning for Chicago where his wife Josette was to attend the baby shower.

Charlie later said his dad was acting quite odd and seemed a bit "wobbly" as he was walking. Looking back, he said he should have pushed to take him to the hospital that day as something was obviously wrong, and he was pretty sure it wasn't the flu. Jack mentioned to him that he thought he had had a mini-stroke. Because his dad seemed to be okay, and because he had his whole family there and they were distracted, Charlie didn't push too hard to take him in. Later he said he regretted not being more aware of what was happening. Like I said, though, we can miss things because of other things happening at the same time. You cannot live with "I should have"; it will drive you crazy.

The next day was the day that changed our lives completely. It's not that what happened just came about that day—it obviously had been building for quite a while. It's just that the events of that day put things in place that brought to our awareness a situation that was far worse than we thought at first. So, now, we will pick up where we left off, after Thanksgiving.

Saturday, November 24, 2012—Getting the News

I didn't think I would sleep much that Friday night, but exhaustion took over, and I got about four hours of sleep. I called Charlie Saturday morning when I got up and told him not to go to the hospital until I met up with him at his house and we would go together. I said I'd leave my vehicle at his house and get a ride there later to pick it up. Dave said he would come down to the hospital later and bring anything we would need at that time.

Before I go further, I need to relate another "God provision." Charlie has a severely autistic son. He had lined up caregivers from Friday, November 23, 2012 at 4:00 P.M. until bedtime on Monday, November 26, 2012 because they were supposed to join us in Chicago that weekend and were not taking Josiah with them. With his son already taken care of, he was able to spend all that time with his dad and me without having to worry about who would take care of Josiah. With Josiah taken care of, Charlie had one less stress on his mind.

That Saturday morning we were still in a state of shock and were not even able to talk about what was happening to anyone other than immediate family members and a few very close friends. When Charlie and I were driving to the hospital, I asked if he slept at all. He said he did sleep some, after he had cried half the night.

Charlie wasn't sure how much of what had been said had been understood by his dad. He said as foggy as he had been, he didn't know if he realized the doctor told him he had cancer. When the doctor came in that Saturday and asked Jack if he knew, or remembered what had been told to him the day before, Jack said he remembered being told he had two brain tumors and one in his lung. We weren't sure how he would react to that information, but initially he seemed to take it pretty well.

The doctors that came in kept saying it could be an infection. Charlie finally asked one of them what the chances were that it was something other than cancer. One of them finally admitted they were ninety-eight percent sure it was cancer. I wasn't glad to hear that diagnosis but I was getting tired of the game playing. Just say what you think it is and let's go from there. That was my thought.

One of the doctors explained what his treatment options were. At first Jack said he would have no treatments—no radiation and no chemo and no surgery. When the doctor told him he would have maybe two months if he did no treatments, he relented and said he'd try the radiation (for the brain tumors) and see what happened. He said absolutely no surgery on his brain. He had heard and seen too many problems with that surgery and wanted no part of it.

He kept insisting if it didn't work or if the side effects were so bad that he would be incapacitated, he would stop the treatments. I told him I understood and fully agreed with that decision because I would feel the same way.

Charlie and I spent most of the day at the hospital. To say we were overwhelmed is an understatement. If there was a word more powerful than overwhelmed, I'd use it. We were given so much information I could not keep it all straight. In fact, I am sure there is a lot I have forgotten because I just could not absorb all of what we were told. I don't even remember how many different doctors we saw. I do remember the doctor who admitted that it was probably cancer and one that was a neurosurgeon. There was another doctor that was the hospital counterpart of his primary doctor.

We knew immediately with the change in diagnosis (from stroke to cancer) that there would be much more to be done than we had initially thought. I went from thinking about how to help him recoup from a stroke to thinking about all the legal, medical, and work decisions that would have to be made. I just could not put it all together and think about it. I had to take small steps and thoughts to try to keep things straight in my mind. We eventually had notebooks to put our thoughts in because, as I said, we were overwhelmed with all that we had heard.

Dave came down later with a change of clothes, a newspaper, and a Coke for his dad, and some items for me. Jack was obviously having difficulty with his left side. Dave had brought him the Coke since that was his favorite drink besides coffee. He was sitting in the bed with the Coke in his left hand. He said, "Where's that Coke you brought me, Dave? Did I drink it already?" Dave pointed to his left hand and said, "It's in your hand." He turned to look at the Coke, totally surprised. That was the first time I had seen what the tumors were doing to him, and it was unnerving.

We took turns going to eat in the cafeteria and walking the halls, calling family and some close friends. The phone calls were never short. It took a lot of explaining to everyone we contacted about what was going on. Also, it was hard to talk when we had to keep stopping to let our emotions settle down. We still hadn't told more than a half dozen close friends and, of course, family. Even with that few people, we were on the phone for hours, although not all at once. At one point Jack asked Dave why Charlie and I kept disappearing. We didn't want to discuss what we had learned while we were in his room, and each call took considerable time.

Later that day Charlie met his wife and in-laws at a nearby mall. When he came back, he stepped in the doorway and told his dad he had filled a prescription for him but it was so big he could not carry it in. Then he pulled our youngest grandchild, Elisha, into the room. Jack's face lit up when he saw him. Elisha hung on his dad though and would not go near Papa. He did not know Papa looking like that. This was another indication to me that the kids were going to have a hard time dealing with this.

After a while Elisha got over being bashful and crawled up on the hospital bed next to his Papa. While we were talking, Jack looked around and then asked Charlie, "Where is Elisha? He's not running down the halls is he?" Charlie pointed to his left side and told him, "He's sitting right next to you, where he's been for the past five minutes."

The loss of the peripheral vision on Jack's left side was quite obvious. The fact that he could hold a Coke or crackers or anything else in his left hand and not be aware that he was holding something indicated that his cognitive ability was impaired or at least his sensory nerves. We had no idea if either would ever be regained.

We spent the day and evening at the hospital, leaving his room only to go to the cafeteria to eat. By the time we left, he was asleep and we were exhausted. I still had to drive home from Charlie's house and took back roads because I was in no shape to pay attention to traffic. I fell into bed immediately and although I was exhausted, I had a restless night and not much sleep.

Sunday, November 25, 2012—Information Overload

Again, we saw many doctors this day. Some we had already seen, and some were new. All the doctors that came in to talk to us kept telling Jack that he had not had the flu. They kept saying to him, "When you had the flu-like symptoms . . ." He had all the symptoms of a stroke or the flu but those symptoms were all caused by the brain tumors. It took Jack a while to realize that what he thought was the flu were the brain tumors beginning to affect his body.

They had run tests and had ruled out both the flu and a stroke. There were two tumors in the brain. The one in the cerebellum (back of the head) was the one that had caused the problems with the stroke-like and flu-like symptoms. That part of the brain is the area controlling motor movement and cognitive skills. The other tumor was on the top of the head. If they told us, I don't remember what that one was affecting. He also had weakness in his left side. A body CAT scan showed no tumors in any major organs but some "irregularity" in lymph nodes, kidney, and colon. Those were so small they never mentioned them to us—we just saw them on the written report.

They gave him steroids to help with edema (swelling) in the brain. They said that was more of an issue than the tumors at the moment because the edema was pressing on nearby brain cells and that was causing the problems. He was walking and talking much better and wanted to go home, but they wanted to run another test. This test was to be a biopsy on his lung. That biopsy would tell them what type of cancer they were dealing with. The doctor explained that if the brain tumors were from the lung tumor, they would know what treatment to try. If the brain tumors had started in the brain, it would be a different issue. They were pretty sure which one it was but needed the biopsy before they could discuss or offer any type of treatment.

When they explained that there would be no charge for the test while he was still in "in-patient" status, he agreed to stay "one more night" if I would stay with him. I agreed. If he were to come back on Monday as out-patient we would incur a charge for the room as well as a co-pay for the procedure. It was Sunday so actually at that time nothing could be scheduled for the next day. However, they assured us that the procedure would be set up—they'd see to that. I'm not sure what strings they had to pull, but early Monday morning they did get the order in for that day.

Jack finally settled down, and one of the nurses got me a blanket and some pillows. I made myself as comfortable as I could on the chair beside his bed. The chair was not comfortable, so he told me to crawl into bed with him to sleep. I tried that but after a few hours it was impossible for either of us to get comfortable so I went back to the chair for the rest of the night.

While we were talking that evening, he said we needed to invite his spiritual advisors out to the house as soon as he got home. I knew he meant the pastor I mentioned earlier—one of our pastors and good friend, Garry Beecher. He wanted Pastor Garry and his wife Martha to come out and talk to him. I knew if he was asking for a spiritual advisor, he had something spiritual in mind. I was elated and went back to my "circle" and the prayer in the middle. I zeroed in on that prayer for the next few days. I also called some of my siblings and a few close friends and asked for specific prayer for that meeting, whenever it would be.

Monday, November 26, 2012—Going Home

Jack was antsy in the morning, wanting to get the procedure done so he could get out of there. He also admitted later he was quite nervous about what they would be doing in the procedure. I tried to tell him I had something similar done and it was not a big deal. But to him it was an unknown, and he was understandably nervous about it.

We had to wait for the procedure, though, because it could not be scheduled until the scheduling crew arrived in the morning. They were able to get him on the schedule and did the lung biopsy early in the afternoon.

While they were doing the procedure, Charlie and I walked down to the cafeteria to get something to eat. On our way back, we ran into Pastor Garry Beecher, who was there to visit another member of the church that was in the hospital. We asked if he had a minute, and he said yes. I felt this meeting was not accidental but orchestrated by God. I had wanted Pastor Garry to visit, and Charlie kept saying to wait. Now it was taken out of our hands—here he was!

We walked him down to where Jack was in recovery after the procedure. The curtain was pulled around his bed, so Charlie and I went in and Charlie told him that we had found something in the hallway he might like to see. Jack asked what he was talking about. Charlie pulled the curtain aside and Pastor Garry walked over to the bed. As groggy as he was from the anesthetic, Jack all but jumped off the bed he was so excited. He grabbed Pastor Garry and hugged him so hard we thought Jack would make him fall. He kept saying how glad he was to see him and how much he appreciated him stopping by. We left them alone for a few minutes and drew the curtain around the bed again. I told Charlie I was so glad that we had run into him.

Then, because they could do nothing further, they said they would release him. They sent him home late Monday afternoon. Jack was hungry, and since we were leaving before they served dinner at the hospital, he wanted to go to his favorite place, Cracker Barrel, to eat.

Charlie had left the hospital earlier to pick Josiah up from a respite house he had been at and had to arrange for a caregiver to meet him and take Josiah home. Josette would meet him, and they would bring the other kids and join us at Cracker Barrel. Dave was working on something and could not get away, so he did not join us. By the time we ate dinner it was late, and once we arrived home we both were more than ready to go to bed. It was well after 10:00 P.M.

Tuesday, November 27, 2012—A Night to Remember

The first thing I did after we got up and had breakfast was to call Jack's primary doctor and make an appointment. Usually it is weeks before you can get in, but when I told them what was going on and that we were told to see him as soon as possible, they said they would get us in that week.

We scheduled the appointment for Friday morning. Since Jack wanted to leave for Tennessee as soon as we could arrange it, I had been pushing for an appointment before the end of the week. I was glad when we were able to get in so soon. We still had not told very many people what was going on. It was still too new, too fresh, too overwhelming.

I had asked Pastor Garry and Martha to come to dinner Tuesday night and spend some time with Jack. They readily agreed. We had already told them everything we knew about his condition and what the prognosis was (not good). Now it was Tuesday and another problem was rearing its ugly head.

That morning for the first time I had real pain with the tooth that had been bothering me for several weeks. I was so glad I had already made an appointment to have the tooth removed that afternoon. The pain kept getting worse, and I was not feeling up to par. X-rays at the dentist showed the tooth was loose and also abscessed.

Because of the abscess, Novocain, and antibiotic I was not feeling very well when Pastor Garry and Martha joined us for dinner; but I was not about to cancel the evening. I just ate a little and let the others talk for a while. My mouth was still numb, and I could barely talk. I had to leave the room a couple of times because my stomach was upset. While I was gone from the room, Pastor Garry prayed with him, and Jack committed his heart to Christ. I was not upset that I was not in the room; I was too happy to hear what happened to care where I was. It did not matter to me if I missed the actual words—it was enough to know they were said!

Pastor Garry and Martha talked for a while after that but it was getting very late, and I knew they both had to work the next day so we thanked them for bringing dinner and for coming over to spend the evening with us. For me, it was not only an answer to prayer, it was the best night I had ever had since we had been married. It was the culmination of nearly forty years of prayer!

Wednesday, November 28, 2012—Decisions and Plans

When we got up, Jack told me that he knew he was on his way to heaven and that he was ready to face whatever was to come. There are not words to describe how you feel when someone you have prayed for nearly forty years makes that commitment. I could write a book on just that emotion alone! To me, that was more than a "God sighting"; it was a "God visitation!"

The next thing Jack said was that he wanted to visit family in Tennessee to say goodbye. He wanted to go as soon as possible. He felt that once he started treatment he would not have the energy to make the trip. As it turned out, he was right.

At this point I was overwhelmed with all the decisions I knew we must make, appointments to schedule, homeschool prep for two of the grandkids, normal housework, the office work I needed to complete before the end of the year, and all the things that go into daily living. Thinking about trying to schedule a trip in the middle of all of this was almost more than I could handle. I knew it was important to Jack though, so I began the process of writing things in a notebook that I knew needed to be done before we left.

We spent part of that day talking about the urgent need to see an attorney to do a will or trust, deciding what treatment he wanted to do, and trying to take care of the daily routine like laundry, fixing dinner, and cleaning the house.

Our lives were forever changed, and yet there had to be a normal routine. It's just not possible to go through a crisis on a continuing basis without some normal activity to keep your balance. I knew also that it was time to start letting other friends know what was going on. I needed a prayer team and people needed to be able to come alongside of us.

Thursday, November 29, 2012—Making a List, Checking It Twice

I began the process of checking things off my list. The first thing I had to do was to call a good friend who was a CPA. I asked him for a recommendation for an attorney who handled wills and trusts. He gave me the name of someone to contact.

The next thing I did was search the State of Michigan website to see if there was any possibility of getting a partial refund on Jack's license plate for the semi. Since the official diagnosis was terminal cancer (even without the biopsy results) we knew he would not be driving again. This was actually the hardest thing for him to face. Giving up his ability to drive was more devastating to him than hearing he had cancer.

The site did show that there was a refund available for certain conditions. I called to request the paperwork based on what I felt was a condition we met—a terminal health condition. Making that decision and requesting the information was one more step in coming to grips with the reality of the situation. It wasn't that we were living in denial; it's just that each thing we had to do made it seem so . . . final.

I also spent part of the day searching RV rental sites and calling for information, prices, and availability. If we were going to make the trip I had to make a decision soon so we could rent one before the weekend.

Friday, November 30, 2012—It's Official; Now What?

We had the appointment with Jack's primary doctor, and he confirmed what we pretty much already knew. The official biopsy report said Jack had "small cell lung cancer" or SCLC. We discussed the options with his doctor, and he told us he could do nothing except recommend we seen an oncologist. I googled it as soon as I had time. All the sites listed two stages—we were already in the second stage because it had metastasized to the brain. Everything I read said the prognosis was poor. Almost every site said maximum time even with treatment was six months. I think I visited over a dozen sites trying to find if any gave a better prognosis or any longer time span. None did. It was time to make plans to enjoy what time we had left and take care of some urgent matters.

Since we were planning to leave to go to Tennessee over the weekend, or as soon as I could rent an RV, I decided to wait and call from Tennessee once we arrived there to try to schedule an appointment with an oncologist. The doctors at the hospital had all said surgery was probably not an option, and certainly not on the brain tumors, so we might consider radiation for the brain tumors and chemo for the lung. The next step they said, if he wanted to take it, was radiation. We were expecting to hear the same suggestions from the oncologist whenever we could get the appointment.

When we got back from the doctor's office I started to check out some more RV sites. I had checked a couple on Thursday and was trying to find something large enough at a decent enough price that we could afford for the week we would be using it. The actual trip was going to be about four to five days, but we wanted to rent for a least a week to give us some leeway in traveling.

This is the next "God provision." Since we had decided we needed to make plans even before we started the rounds of doctor visits, I had begun to make calls to try to rent an RV. It made sense to get something he could relax in. Also, since Charlie and three of his kids were going, we needed the extra room. We felt Charlie's van would not be comfortable enough for Jack to ride in, and with the kids and all the luggage it would be too crowded for all of us on such a long trip.

As I was checking things out and calling to get prices and availability, Charlie called and said to call his father-in-law, George, before committing to anything. Thinking George may know someone in the industry, I gave him a call. To my utter surprise and shock, what he said was, did we want to meet him at his house and go look at the RV he was renting for us? I didn't know how to answer. How do you even respond to such generosity?

I told Jack what George had said and asked if he was up to the trip across town to look at it. He was also in shock but readily agreed. We had to be at George's house in an hour to make it to the RV rental place before they closed. To say we hurried is putting it mildly. We raced to his house!

Once at the RV rental place we were again surprised. He was renting a 2012 RV with less than 10,000 miles on it. To us it was a luxury we didn't expect. It slept eight, had a bathroom, a full mini-sized kitchen, including microwave, two (count them—two)

TVs with DVD players (the kids loved it!), and either heat or air, depending on how warm it was where we were going.

We had to do a walk through while they explained how to use everything. I was glad Jack was along because most of it was over my head, and I knew he would understand a lot of it from having driven a truck for so many years.

It was truly a blessing. Jack was able to stretch out on the full–sized bed in the back for most of the travel time. That was good because sitting for long periods was hard on him. The kids were able to watch movies, read, eat, and play during the trip.

This day, though, we were again overwhelmed. It wasn't just the generosity of George; it was also the unit itself—to us it was such luxury to be able to travel like that. I kept thinking it was a dream and I'd wake up and be disappointed. It wasn't a dream though, and when they gave us the paperwork to be able to pick the unit up the next day, Saturday, I realized this was for real. I had no idea how to thank George for making this trip so special for us.

Charlie, who was going to be driving this thing, was not able to go with us for the walk-through so he didn't see it except through the picture I took with my phone and sent to him by text message. Charlie said it would be no problem. I'm not so sure he realized how big it really was.

Saturday, December 1, 2012—Getting Ready to Travel

Today was George's birthday, and we were the ones getting a gift. Somehow that seemed so weird. George said not to worry about it; it was a gift to him to see how much we appreciated it and how it would make our trip so much easier.

Charlie, Jack, and I drove over to the RV rental place. After looking it over Charlie said, not quite as confidently, that it would be no problem. I think the size of it was a bit more than he expected. He drove it to his house without a problem, though, and parked it in his driveway. It took up the entire driveway and was hanging over the sidewalk. I wondered what his neighbors thought of all this.

Jack and I went home, packed all our stuff, and brought it to Charlie's. We did some grocery shopping, packed it all in, and spent the night in the RV so we could leave as soon as possible Sunday morning.

When Rob found out we were going to Tennessee, he told us he had asked for time off work and said he would meet us there. Tracy was studying for exams but would come with him. Brittany and Amber were working and could not get away. Destiny wasn't working but could not take more time off school. That left Ryan, and rather than leave him with his sisters, they decided to bring him (and his schoolwork) on the trip. Rob said they would leave on Saturday because they needed to start back by the following Wednesday. He called while we were getting the RV and said they were on their way and would be at his Aunt Joyce's that evening. He was very anxious to see his dad.

Sunday, December 2, 2012—Another Surprise Gift

We were packed and ready to go when George and Luz came by to see us off. While the others were walking around, prepping the RV and talking, Luz came over and pressed something into my hand. I looked down and saw it was a wad of money. I started to say something, and she pushed my hand away and said, "It's to help with the gas or food, whatever you need most." When I checked later, it was $500. How do you say thank you to such generosity? I just pray God's blessing on them tenfold.

To say the kids were excited to go is an understatement. They could not wait until that thing pulled out of their driveway—with them in it! At first it was very difficult for Charlie to drive. It was windy, and the RV kept wanting to drift. Also, drafts from passing trucks tended to make us want to pull us in toward the truck. He was exhausted from driving, but I could not help him because with the rheumatoid arthritis acting up, I could not manage to hold the wheel and fight the wind and the pull of other vehicles.

We had bought some Cracker Barrel gift cards so we could stop and eat at least once on the way down and once on the way back. The rest of the time we'd eat the food we brought along. By getting the gift cards, we got "fuel points" where we shop so it helped in two ways.

Our first stop was at the Cracker Barrel that was less than thirty minutes from Charlie's. We were off to a slow start. Then, after a quick stop at a nearby store, we were finally, officially on our way. The trip was hard on Charlie, and it rained almost three-quarters of the way, so it was all he could do to concentrate on the road. I was worried he would be stressed out because he had spent a lot of time making sure Josiah was taken care of while we were gone and had not had much sleep for several days. He also was still trying to process all of what we had heard about his dad's condition.

We pulled into Don and Joyce's drive just before midnight. Well, I say "we" but really it was Rob and Charlie who had to figure out how to get that huge RV into their driveway without taking out the mail boxes across the street. Eventually it was parked and set up. There was no way I was sleeping in it—I could not wait to get into a comfortable bed!

Monday, December 3, 2012—Family Time

Joyce outdid herself with her usual southern breakfast of bacon, sausage, eggs, and biscuits and gravy. She made enough to feed an army—and we ate like an army. I would have tried to help her, but I am no match for her Southern cooking, so I just had a cup of coffee and talked with her while she fixed the food.

Since we dawdled over breakfast, it was too late to go anywhere. Jack's brother Aubrey said he would come out in the afternoon to visit. Jack, Charlie, and Rob got ready to run some errands. As they were talking, Jack was smoking (he hadn't quit even with the diagnosis). He knew his sister and I weren't happy about it. As he lit one, he said, "What does it matter? I'm dying anyway."

That did not sit well with me. My thought was, "What about me? Don't you care enough to help me to deal with this?" I didn't say anything because they left the house then. I just went into the bedroom and cried for half an hour. I called Pastor Garry, and he prayed for me on the phone, and within an hour I calmed down. I was sure there would be more times like this.

After I calmed down, I went into the kitchen where Joyce was preparing dinner. I told her what I thought of Jack's statement and how it affected me. She was very sympathetic. I told her I was so angry at him for talking like that. I also explained I knew he was having a hard time dealing with it, but so was I, and it was hard to want to help him when he had such an attitude. She told me she understood how I felt and agreed with me. We talked for a while, and I calmed down even more. We eventually agreed between the two of us that we still needed to do all we could to make him comfortable, even if we disagreed with his choices and decisions.

I called the oncologist's office and whoever I talked to there got us an appointment for 3:00 P.M. that day before I could tell her we were out of town. I had to apologize for not telling her up front we were not home. She said no problem and made an appointment for Thursday at noon in Novi.

When Jack got back and I told him about the appointment he was angry and said he wasn't ready to leave on Wednesday and they would have to wait. I told him getting an appointment with a specialist wasn't easy and we had to take what they had. I also reminded him that he said he only wanted to be gone for two or three days. Leaving on Wednesday would be the third day and would give us time to get back for the appointment. He finally relented but kept grumbling about it. I really did not want to wait another week for an appointment, and that was the earliest we'd be able to get in if we didn't take this one. I also reminded him that we had to get back because Charlie needed to get back to work and he had only scheduled helpers for Josiah until then. He still fussed about it, but eventually he let it go.

The kids did some schoolwork in the RV while Jack and his brother visited. Ryan, Rica, and Reina loved the opportunity to do schoolwork in the RV. For recess, they were running barefoot in the yard. It was the first week of December, and this was something they could not do at their cold northern homes. They thought it was a wonderful way to have a recess. In fact, it was hard to get them back in the RV and back into their schoolwork.

Late that afternoon Charlie, Rob, and Tracy took the kids to Nashville to show them the sights while the older folks stayed home and visited. They had a good time, and it was good for the guys to get away and have a little fun after being under so much stress for the past couple of weeks.

Rob needed to see his dad physically so he could relax a bit. Having left him behind when we left Chicago so quickly, he had never had time to process what was happening to his dad like we did. Being long distance and getting the updates just wasn't the same as being there. This trip helped him to come to grips with it.

That evening while the others were out, two of Jack's nieces stopped by to visit with us. There are three in the area, and two were able to stop by while we were there. One lives out of state, and we were not able to see her this trip.

Tuesday, December 4, 2012—Down Memory Lane

The weather was beautiful, warm enough to go without a jacket. Not bad for December. After breakfast our first trip was to see the cemetery where his parents and many ancestors and other relatives are buried. Then we drove to where their childhood home had once stood. Jack and Joyce reminisced the whole time. I told Charlie later we should have thought to take a tape recorder with us so we could have captured that conversation.

On the way back, Charlie spotted an antique store that he couldn't pass up. We wandered around in there for a while and finally found a couple of things we thought his mother-in-law would like as a thank-you gift. They were small in comparison to what they had provided, but we both thought they were things she would like, which is what was important.

Back at the house, we spent the evening together just talking. Joyce fixed a good Southern dinner, and we spent the evening relaxing.

Wednesday, December 5, 2012—Saying Goodbye

Rob had already planned to return home today and with the scheduled appointment for tomorrow, we had to leave also. We had everything loaded and were ready to go right after breakfast. It was hard to leave knowing it was the last time they would see Jack.

When we were ready to go out the door, Jack hugged his sister and told her, "Well, you know I won't be able to come back down here, but I'll see you on the other side." That statement had everyone within ear shot crying, especially his sister. For her, this was a very hard goodbye. I was wishing we could have stayed longer but getting started with any treatment he was going to do was important.

We had decided we could travel together until we got to where Rob had to head west to Illinois and we had to head east to Ohio and Michigan. Since we planned to eat together at a Cracker Barrel on the way, Ryan rode with us until then. The kids had a good time watching movies and playing in the RV.

When we left Cracker Barrel, Ryan was still with us. We planned to make a quick stop for ice cream as dessert so we weren't too worried. However, because of miscommunications, we had to miss the dessert stop and actually pull off the highway to find a place we could stop with the RV so he could get out and get in the van with his parents. Then, finally, we were on our way.

After we split off, the trip was pretty quiet and uneventful. We had hoped to get in fairly early, but it was nearly midnight when we arrived at Charlie's, and we had to be at the doctor's office the next day at noon. We left everything in the RV in Charlie's driveway and drove home so we could take a shower and find clean clothes in the morning.

Thursday, December 6, 2012—More Overwhelming News

We saw the oncologist at noon, and we were, in a word, overwhelmed. Not just because of what he said but all of it just piled up—it had only been two weeks since we had started this journey. Not much sleep for the past ten days was catching up to me. It was hard to focus and process all of what the doctor said. Dave and Charlie went with us because I felt they might have questions that I might not think of, and I knew I would not retain most of what was said.

So first of all—"No, we didn't have an answer" to "How much time does he have?" That was what I told everyone after the appointment. I knew that was what everyone wanted to know, but I simply couldn't answer that, and neither could the doctor. In fact, in reality, only God knew the day he would call Jack home. I told everyone that I could only tell them was what the doctor had told us, and that wasn't much. At this point, I was doing this via email because I just could not make that many phone calls, and text messages just did not work.

The doctor did not sugarcoat anything. He was pretty up front about the diagnosis, the treatment, and the results. He said if Jack were to refuse all treatment, he would have maybe two to four months. It's an aggressive cancer. That said, according to the doctor, it responds well to radiation and chemo that could possibly give him a year or more. Jack had said right from the start he would take no treatment. The doctor's explanation of what he would face changed his outlook. He decided to at least try the radiation, and if all went well, he'd try at least the first chemo session.

The radiation was an immediate need. We scheduled an appointment for Monday, December 10, 2012 at 3:00 P.M. to see a doctor at Henry Ford Macomb Hospital to consult and possibly even begin that day. If we could not set it up that day, then as soon as possible after that. The radiation was for the brain tumors and was critical. Without it, his time was very limited. The radiation would specifically target the tumors. We had been told while he was in the hospital that there was one treatment for the back of the brain that was a one shot deal. This doctor said that would not work for his tumors. He had more than one tumor, and the treatment they had talked about only worked on one tumor. What they would do was radiation over a short span of time—ten days. Chemo has no effect on the brain tumors and would be used to address any tumors in other parts of the body.

They also wanted to make sure it had not metastasized to the bones so a bone scan was set for 8:00 A.M. at Henry Ford West Bloomfield Hospital. That trip was a forty-five to sixty minute drive. We needed to be out of the house by 7:00 A.M. at the latest and would have three grandkids with us. Monday would be a challenge.

Friday, December 7, 2012—Decorating for Christmas and a Christmas Program

We were behind on Christmas decorating this year. I usually had it done by Thanksgiving weekend. Because we had been out of town and coming back to having to deal with all the appointments and other obligations, decorating took a back seat.

The kids wanted at least some things put out, so I let the girls get the tree and decorations down from our attic and a small village that we usually set up in the living room. They also brought down some garland from the attic and decorated the house. We were trying to make things as normal as possible at a time when normal had gone out the window, and we now had a "new normal."

Our church had a Christmas dinner scheduled for this night with a gospel singer we had known for a long time. I asked Jack if he wanted to go and hear Rob Mills and family, and he readily agreed. It was a great evening. He enjoyed the concert, and it put us in the mood for the holiday.

It was a good way to end a very hectic week.

Saturday, December 8, 2012 — Getting Ready for the Holidays

I wasn't sure how the holidays would play out this year. The kids (the ones that lived out of town) kept calling and asking if they should come home before Christmas. They all planned to be here Christmas Day for sure. I told them to wait. There was no indication at the moment that their dad would not survive until the holidays. I didn't know that for sure, of course, but indications were that he was stable and would be okay for a while. He was alert while in Tennessee and responded to questions at the doctor's office, so I was sure we didn't have to panic at this time.

I was way behind on gift shopping so I decided I would have to get gift cards for the older grandkids at least. The young ones would not know what to do with gift cards, so I had to do some gift shopping. I had the albums for Ryan and Destiny. The push now was to assemble them in time for Christmas. Fortunately, I had a good portion of the albums done already and just needed to print the stories and put them in with the photos.

I also had to think about what to have for Christmas dinner and for breakfast, lunch, and dinner while everyone was in town. Dave would do most of the cooking, but we had to decide what to fix that would work for a crowd. Since I would be gone a lot with doctor appointments and radiation treatments, my time was going to be limited. I had to get as much done as I could as quickly as I could because I knew I'd be stressed later if I didn't do it now.

So, why did I even care? Because Christmas is a special time for me and always has been. I was not going to let this cancer diagnosis cause us to lose sight of our family traditions at Christmas. Besides, Jack wanted it to be as normal as possible since he said it would more than likely be his last one with us. He also wanted no gifts, but I could not see him not opening anything at all on Christmas morning, so I told everyone to get him a box of chocolate candy or a six-pack of Coca Cola in small glass bottles, which were his favorite things.

I knew next week would be hectic, so I got done what I could, and we called it a day. I had so much stuff rolling around in my head that it was hard to concentrate. I knew I had to try to keep some things organized, and it was critical that I get proper rest. Getting sick for me was not an option, so I paced myself, ate as best I could, and tried to get plenty of rest.

Sunday, December 9, 2012 — More Planning

I started the day by going to church. We had not yet told a lot of people, but I told Charlie it was time. I needed to share what was going on, I needed prayer support, and I needed to be able to talk about this to people rather than keeping it inside.

At church that morning I told several friends what was happening and the diagnosis we had received. They were shocked. I knew they would be. It was hard to verbalize it without tears, but all my friends were understanding and hugs were plentiful.

I needed to hear the Christmas message to set the tone for the rest of this month because Christmas has always been a special time for me, and I didn't want that to change just because we were dealing with a cancer diagnosis. The message was good, and it helped me to focus on something other than what we were dealing with.

The rest of the day was spent trying to get things ready for what would be a very busy ten-day period of appointments—and then Christmas would be upon us! Because of our early appointment and Charlie's and Josette's work schedules, we would be taking the kids with us in the morning. I told them the kids needed to spend the night. That would make it easier for me than to try to go get them early in the morning.

Monday, December 10, 2012 — A Full Day of Appointments

Getting Jack and three kids ready to leave for the hospital by 7:00 A.M. was a major task. He was not the issue — getting the kids awake was. I fixed Jack a quick breakfast at 6:00 A.M. and then got the kids up. Fortunately, we did not have any snow storms at this time. Before 8:00 A.M. we were at Henry Ford West Bloomfield Hospital for the bone scan. Since we were actually a few minutes early, I got coffee for Jack and me and hot chocolate for the kids.

They told us the scan would take approximately five hours. I settled the kids in the lobby and signed Jack in for his appointment. Once they took him back for the scan, the kids and I sat in the lobby, and they did schoolwork. Jack was more than hungry by the time we were done there, but we had an appointment at 3:00 P.M. at Henry Ford Macomb Hospital, which was across town, to meet with the doctor who would be doing the radiation. We were barely going to have time to get across town as it was, so stopping to eat was out of the question, or so I thought.

On the way, Jack insisted we stop for a quick lunch, and then we stopped at Cold Stone Ice Cream to get dessert. Because of all the rushing and pressure, I felt like we needed a treat. We were short on time but stopped anyway. Jack said he didn't want any ice cream but agreed to try a bite of mine. He liked the one I got so much that he shared it with me. I kept trying to get him to buy his own and he kept saying he "just wanted a bite." His bites were half my bowl!

We made it to the hospital with not much time to spare. This racing across town was beginning to wear me out, and we had just started. I could not even imagine what it would be like in the future.

Initially they had scheduled chemo to start December 18, 2012. The doctor scheduling the radiation treatments said that the chemo needed to be postponed until after the radiation was complete. She said he would not be able to do both at the same time because it would be too much for his system. So I had to cancel those appointments and reschedule. I could never make any plans for any more than one day because things like this kept coming up and changing my schedule. Learning to be flexible was going to be key to my not going crazy.

I was also waiting for a call to let us know when they would schedule the outpatient surgery to put a port in his chest for the chemo. We were now delaying the chemo until after the first of the year, so that surgery had to be rescheduled also. They scheduled the port for the week after Christmas because chemo was now to start the first week of January 2013.

We had talked to the oncologist and asked if we could schedule the radiation and chemo at Henry Ford Macomb because that was half the distance that it would be go to Novi for the treatments. He agreed, and I was ecstatic. That would save us so much time, mileage, and stress.

For now though, she was able to schedule the radiation to start the next day, Tuesday, December 11, 2012, and complete it on Christmas Eve, December 24, 2012. It usually takes several days to set up the schedule for a new patient, but we asked if she could push to get it started; otherwise we would have a gap of several days because of Christmas, putting us into the new year for finishing radiation and putting the chemo off still further. Fortunately, she agreed and pushed it through. We had no idea how she did it, and we did not care. It was enough that she was able to work it out. We were to be there every day at 8:30 A.M. except Saturday and Sunday. Tomorrow, though, we had to be there at 11:00 A.M. for a fitting for a face mask.

Now I had to again reschedule all appointments for follow-ups, surgeries, and chemo. David had put a calendar on his phone that updated on Charlie's and mine every time there was an appointment for the day. I was having trouble keeping it all straight. I don't know what I would have done without him.

Tuesday, December 11, 2012 – Starting Radiation

This morning at 11:00 A.M. Jack was fitted for the face mask that would protect him and help them to focus where the radiation was to go. On a side note, WOW! That room looked like the interior of a spaceship. The machine was huge and yet would zero a laser beam focused on one tiny part of the brain. It was amazing to see.

Usually it took a few days after the fitting to get the treatments started. But we were to come back later this day to start. Then after this day it would be 8:30 A.M. every morning. The sessions were short but with drive time and waiting, it was always two to three hours every day. Just getting it underway was such a relief, and I was so thankful to the doctor who pushed this through so we would not be delayed by the holidays that were coming up very fast.

I was now emailing many family members on a daily basis to keep them informed about what we were doing, what we were changing, how Jack was feeling, and what our life was now like. It saved me a lot of time because that many phone calls were more than I could handle. It was like one stop shopping where I could communicate with a multitude of people and keep them in the loop.

In response to one of my emails where I was trying to explain what we would be going through, my son David wrote the following note that I am including here because it is so well written.

If it wasn't evident from Mom's explanation: there are two wholly separate sets of treatments that have to be scheduled over a period of months and results monitored after they've taken place. Today's doctor (in Novi) was ONLY for the chemotherapy treatment plan. There were not any radiation therapy doctors at today's meeting, and they operate out of different facilities. There will be a lot of driving. The "port" that the chemo doctor will put in his upper chest to aid in the delivery of chemo is done in West Bloomfield, and then the scheduled rounds of chemo treatment will take place in Novi [that was changed to the Macomb hospital].

A rough schedule for this is that he will have to go for 3 straight days, take 2 or 3 weeks off, and then go for treatment on another 3 days. And then repeat over a course of four (?) months. That may not be exact but, as I remember, it's close to the process and length that the doctor described. Given that this doctor won't have any new information to give us until after at least one round of chemo treatment has occurred, it's possible that there isn't any additional info coming on the efficacy of the chemo until January; or later. Obviously, they're going to have to do more x-rays to find out if the tumors are still growing, reduced in size, or no change.

The information from the chemo doctor we visited today is partial (and the schedules for initial treatments isn't nailed down yet) because the chemo physician doesn't want to give information on radiation therapy outcomes/side effects/timelines. He only would say that the INITIAL radiation therapy visit and subsequent radiation treatments for that was something of a higher priority than the chemo treatments that he will be administering.

The second set of doctors will get the ball rolling after the December 10 appointment, and that will cover all of the radiation therapy issues. As Mom said, this branch of therapy is for the brain since the chemo won't help with the cancer in the head. It's still not clear where all of the treatments and appointments will take place for this branch of therapy but it appears that MOST of it will be closer to home. Still a lot of driving since there are many required days of therapy, but not having to go to Novi for all of it helps some.

For all we know now, the doctor teams (for chemo or radiation) may never volunteer specific timelines or prognoses for how much time Dad has left. But it's clear that there won't be ANY information about this forthcoming until a) we meet with the radiation team AND get those appointments well underway and b) probably a month or more of treatments will have to take place before they start scheduling new imaging scans to see how things are going.

And that's just the update on why more information from the doctors likely isn't coming anytime soon. The other thing to consider, and pray for guidance about, is Dad's mental state as all of this gets underway. The hope for undergoing this treatment at all is that it extends life. But he's made it pretty clear—and it's perfectly understandable—that length of life isn't everything. The quality of life must be maintained to make the suffering from the treatments worthwhile. It would be very beneficial if he found internal reasons to keep on going, and to fight through discomfort/fatigue/nausea when the side effects of treatment occur.

He doesn't have a lot of experience sitting around doing nothing and even less experience in being dependent on others for so much assistance. It's a heavy load to start carrying very suddenly when you've been both busy and independent for many decades. He needs to find something SATISFYING to fill his days, something that allows him to overlook the side effects and say "THIS is a reason it's worth living an additional 10 or 20 or 30 months." It seems, on the surface, like this might be an easier situation to take for someone that was a voracious reader, or someone who got enjoyment out of watching a lot of movies or surfing the Internet. Being present for the continued exploits of the grandkids is one of the reasons to keep going, obviously. But it might take something more. If you're talking to God and asking him to provide an additional 22 months of life (or 220, or whatever), you might also put in a request to have Dad find an activity or hobby that he really likes.

The people I've known that have done the best under adverse circumstances like this have done so because they had enough enjoyable things going on that they could sometimes forget they were ill. Having him invested in something to fill those additional months and years of life would make a big difference. All of the necessary treatment isn't medical.

A friend had told me about a website where I could post daily updates. That site helped me keep track of what was going on, although not all the emotion that went with it. It also helped me connect with people I had not seen in years but who now were keeping up with our journey and praying for us.

Wednesday, December 12, 2012—More Travel, More Decisions, More Stress

I said every day that I would be home right after therapy, and that did not happen. It seemed that every day when we left the radiation therapy, there was something else we had to do or some errand to run.

Jack did well during the treatments. They told us, however, that his feeling well might end as the radiation sapped his strength.

While all of this was going on, our ducks were using our back porch as their private toilet. I am not going to explain how bad that problem was—just know it became a huge issue. I posted them on Craig's list. Within a few days they were gone, much to my relief.

I called and rescheduled the surgery to implant the port on December 27, 2012 at 11:30 A.M. at Henry Ford West Bloomfield Hospital. They said it would be five to six hours, and since we expected all the kids to still be in town we planned to caravan over and spend the day together because most of them were leaving the next day to go home.

I had so many things to take care of it was overwhelming. I had many offers of assistance, and some people came out to help with what they could. At this point it really was one day at a time.

I had stepped down from our church's Stephen Ministry program right after we got Jack's diagnosis. When I heard a man from our church was going to speak this night about taking care of the elderly, I decided to attend the meeting. As Spencer started to talk, I knew the reason I was there. He had changed the topic and was now speaking on end-of-life care and pre-planning for funerals. After the meeting I met him in the hallway and told him, "We have to talk."

Spencer and I talked for a few minutes, and I briefly filled him in on what Jack's diagnosis was and that I would like more information on how to pre-plan a funeral. It seemed strange to be talking about something that serious when Jack was doing well for the moment. The doctor, though, had told us that this was a fast-growing cancer and most people did not last more than six to twelve months and that was with treatment and otherwise good health. Jack did not have the good health going for him, and we weren't sure how much of the treatment he could endure.

Spencer gave me his phone number and told me to call him as soon as I could set something up. I told him the kids were coming home for Christmas and I wanted them at the meeting, if at all possible. He understood and said if anything changed to let him know right away. I knew having this meeting was important and looked at the calendar to see when we could work it into an already overloaded schedule. I really felt it was important for all the kids to be in attendance and hoped we could arrange it during our already busy holiday week.

Thursday, December 13, 2012 — More Information Overload

We went to the radiation therapy session and then to Charlie's for breakfast. We had the morning off and had to be in Novi at 2:00 P.M. for patient chemotherapy training. David went with us because I knew I would be overwhelmed and not retain everything I learned. In fact, I would be lucky to retain anything at all.

To say it was information overload is an understatement. There was so much to try to grasp and understand; so many decisions to make; so much to consider. There was diet, exercise, side effects, family concerns and issues, procedures, and how it's done, etc., etc.

They had given us a notebook with information, and I kept adding sheets to it. I briefly read it and needed time to go back and try to absorb some more of it. I just wasn't sure when I would have that time.

When we returned from our appointments, I told Charlie's oldest, Rica, to journal her thoughts. Her note follows:

Written December 13, 2012, 5:33 P.M. by Rica Shelton

When I heard that my Papa had two brain tumors it totally shocked me. I didn't know what to think. To me Papa was one of my heroes. He helps load boats that weigh thousands of pounds up to his truck all the time! I never thought that he could get so weak in just a short amount of time. To me that was strange. Since I'm at my Papa's and Grandma's house nearly all the time (my Grandma homeschools me and my little sis and little bro) I have to help the both of them. Neither of them can open a bottle of water.

After Papa got out of the hospital we started making plans to go to Tennessee. A week later we were driving down in an RV! (Thanks to the generous donation of my other grandpa, George) It was lots of fun. Uncle Rob, Aunt Tracy, and Ryan came too. We stayed with Papa's sister (although us kids including Ryan slept in the RV). What's the point in taking one if you don't sleep in it? So now it seems that until Christmas Eve it will be mostly therapy for Papa. We will see what happens come Christmas. Thank you everybody who helped in prayer and donated to our Tennessee trip. Keep us in your prayers!

One of the things Spencer had said was that anyone that could write a letter or journal what they were feeling should do so as soon as possible. I also felt it was good for the kids and grandkids to journal their thoughts. Not only would it help them, it would be good to look back on it later and realize how many people came alongside them during this time.

Friday, December 14, 2012 — A Heartbreaking Decision

I knew there would be tough decisions down the road, but I didn't expect one so quickly. Jack was a truck driver, so he had a commercial driver's license. In September he bought his license plate for the semi for the year—$2144 (it always ran from October 1 to September 30). I had always heard that the plate was non-refundable but I checked the state website anyway. I found out we could get a refund, but he would have to surrender his driver's license.

We talked it over, and he knew he would never drive a semi again, but it was still a very tough decision, especially for a man, and especially for a man who had driven for over sixty years. The process was not hard. We needed to get a form from Secretary of State and have the doctor fill it out. Then we needed to get a "driver assessment" done. Because it is a commercial license, it was more complicated than just turning in your license. If I had known what a nightmare this would eventually become, I'm not sure I would have proceeded with it. But, since I didn't know at that time, we went ahead and picked up the paperwork to file.

It was one more step in giving up independence. He was already struggling with feeling "worthless and useless," and this was the hardest thing he had to do. Over and over Jack said giving up driving was worse than hearing he had cancer.

Saturday, December 15, 2012—A Break from Appointments

This morning we went to Cracker Barrel and had breakfast with a young lady who is our oldest "adopted daughter." Carol had started babysitting for us when she was eleven years old and Rob was three months. She's been part of the family ever since. We had two gift certificates left from our trip to Tennessee, and they were enough to get the three of us breakfast and have $3.50 left over. You can't beat that deal.

Carol asked why we were out having breakfast at Cracker Barrel. I told her we are doing it because it was Jack's favorite place to have breakfast, and down the road we probably would not be able to, so we were taking advantage of the good days.

By this time I knew it would be a stretch to get the rest of my Christmas shopping done. I could not have a gift for two grand-kids and not get something for the others, so I had decided to do two shopping days, and one would have to be a one-stop shopping where I would get gift cards for several of the kids and grandkids. I had gotten some gift cards the previous week and needed to finish up. It's not something I wanted to do, but under the circumstances it was the best I could do. At this point I had five gifts I had bought or completed. I wasn't stressed about it, but I wanted to get it done so I could enjoy the holidays and not be worried about having to get the shopping finished.

We were looking forward to the Arizona and Illinois portions of the family to arrive in one week. Our daughter from Toronto was scheduled to arrive by Christmas Eve.

Sunday, December 16, 2012—A Needed Break

It was a quiet day. We desperately needed a quiet day because we knew that before too long they would be history. The previous week of appointments, decisions, and errands left us both exhausted. I wanted a day to do nothing. After church I had to do some grocery shopping and fill the gas tank for the week. The next day would start another five days of 8:30 A.M. appointments for radiation. Each day would also hold other things that needed to be addressed or handled.

For now, though, it was get groceries, put groceries away, and do nothing else. Everything else was just going to have to wait.

The house desperately needed cleaning, and I was so thankful my niece Suzanne was scheduled to come on Tuesday. I told her to get rested and wear old clothes. I didn't even know where to tell her to start. I thought it needed to be the laundry so I would have clothes to wear. She had been coming out off and on to help with the kid's schoolwork and had offered to help with housework so I could get caught up on things. Having her come was such a blessing.

A combination of stress and other factors had caused an RA flare up. It was affecting my left hand, and the pain was causing me to have to use my right for most things. I couldn't grip anything with my left hand, which meant I was limited on what I could do. I had a ton of laundry, and folding it was out of the question. I was trying to keep the stress level down, but this coming week was going to be tough with all the things I had to handle in addition to getting ready for family to visit for the holiday.

Monday, December 17, 2012—Trying to Catch Up

My pain level Sunday night had been eight with almost no use of my left hand. When I woke up on Monday, the level was two, and I was able to do dishes without breaking any. I was so thankful for those who had prayed that the pain would subside. I was still sore by evening, but the pain was not as bad as it had been.

Adding doctors' appointments, hospital visits, and scheduling and rescheduling on top of getting ready for Christmas made this one of the most stressful holiday seasons I had ever been through. Fortunately, I was able to finish a Christmas gift and bought two. I still had more to do, and I was hoping to finish by Wednesday. I was running out of time.

Because I was on medication for the RA, I needed monthly blood tests done. I was trying to combine trips, so I planned to go after therapy on Tuesday. After that we hoped to have breakfast with a friend. I was also trying to get the kids caught up on schoolwork, but we were still behind a bit.

We had a call on Jack's Kenworth from someone who saw it listed on Craig's List. I was hoping this guy would make an offer Jack would agree to. The guy said he lived near Lansing and would like to see the truck after Christmas. I knew it would be very hard for Jack to part with it, but reality said it must go as we would need the money going forward, and he would never drive it again.

He kept saying the radiation treatment was useless and he should quit, but then he would admit his vision was better and he felt stronger on the left side. The downside was it left him very fatigued, and he hated not being able to do much. They had warned us that one of the side effects was extreme fatigue.

A friend had sent me a message and told me Jack would get a package on Monday. She told me it was quilt that a group from her church was sending. Diane is a cancer survivor. The quilt was made by The Piece Maker's Quilting Group in Nevada where Diane lives. A woman named Joyce Koontz began the group when she found out she had cancer. Her idea was to make quilts for women, men, and children with cancer. Her hope was that these quilts would wrap the warmth of God's Word around them and bring peace and comfort to family and friends. They are called Hope Quilts and are made with some of the pieces having Scripture printed on them.

Joyce is now with the Lord, but her work goes on. Every person who receives a quilt is added to the group's prayer list and prayed for every week. Their group is with Central Christian Church, Henderson, Nevada. I will probably never meet these women until we all meet in heaven, but my heartfelt thanks went out to them for this wonderful gift and ministry. When Jack saw the package, he said he would open it on Christmas Day. He had already said he didn't want any gifts, so he probably was expecting this to be the only one he would open.

Tuesday, December 18, 2012—Running Errands, Paperwork and Cleaning House

This was a busy day. I had to get the kids up at 7:15 A.M. to take them with us to therapy because they had spent the night. After that, I had already planned to get a blood test. After all that, we met their other grandmother, Luz, for breakfast and made a trip to the dollar store. We got back just before noon. I had been working with Luz at her home one day a week, helping her put her grades into the computer. She was a language professor at Oakland University in Rochester, Michigan. Luz had given me her laptop and paperwork to finish her class assessments for the four classes she had taught this semester. She also gave me a huge pot of chicken soup—not chicken noodle, just chicken and veggies since I am gluten-free and can't eat noodles. It was delicious.

While I worked on the paperwork, Suzanne cleaned the front bedroom, did some laundry, and folded a mountain of clothes. In addition to that, I had expected her to bring me a 20% coupon from Bed Bath & Beyond so I could get a hand warmer that I heard helped with RA. I was surprised to see, not a coupon, but the warmer—with a new box of paraffin. What a blessing. Thank you so much, Suzanne. She said she had this for a year and it was in a closet not being used so she brought it out for me.

By this time there were small indications the radiation was shrinking the tumors, or at least stopping them from growing. Jack's left side seemed to have a little more stability, and he said he could see better out of that eye. He was still extremely fatigued, which was the first side effect listed for the radiation.

Emotionally, he was up and down. He said he felt like such a burden. I asked him if he would consider me a burden if I was the one going through this. He said, "Of course not!" I said, "Well, it works both ways—you are NOT a burden so get that out of your head." I think we all can identify with how he felt though. If it was me, I would feel like a burden. It's funny how, when it's someone else, you don't feel that way at all.

Wednesday December 19, 2012—Trying to Drive Again

During all this we were not in denial as to what was happening. It seemed so surreal, though, to go through each day as normal as possible with the thought in the back of your mind that this won't last. Things had stayed relatively normal in our lives, which made it harder when something came up that brought reality right up front.

This day was such a day. Since the weather was beautiful, I told Jack it would be a good time to back the trailer he had been using into the lot with the others (we have a section of land behind the house where the trucks and trailers for the business are parked) and pull the semi up by the barn so we could finish cleaning it out. When he came home from that last trip he had parked the truck and trailer in the drive close to the house. We needed to get the trailer parked in the area where we kept the other trucks and trailers because it wasn't ours; it belonged to the company. I knew it needed to be unhooked so we could try to sell Jack's semi, so I called a friend of his to see if he could come and help him.

At first Jack was irritated that I had asked for help and said he would have no problem backing it up but then admitted he might need help unhooking it. It was a surprise and discouragement to him when he realized he could not back it into the lot. He could not judge where the other trailer was. His depth perception was off, and the vision on his left side was still not good. In fact, he said if he hadn't stopped and let his friend move it for him, he might have driven it into the field. It scared him to realize how much his sight and depth perception were off.

Later he told me, "Well, if I ever thought I might drive again, today changed that for sure. I can't believe I couldn't tell where I was in that lot." This from a truck driver who could back a trailer with a 45-foot, 15-ton, 12-foot-wide boat on it into a spot I'd have a hard time putting a car into.

To say he was disheartened is putting it mildly. Each confirmation of his lack of ability to do things he used to take for granted made him feel more useless, as he put it.

I had scheduled an appointment to see an attorney Thursday after therapy to begin the process to make sure we were on the right track with legal matters pertaining to his business and our property. It would be another step into the reality that things needed to be taken care of properly and in a timely manner. It's not easy to see your whole life being stripped apart piece by piece. That was one reason I was trying to keep things as normal as possible.

The meeting was to look into making out a will and/or trust agreement, set up Power of Attorney for each of us, naming each other and then the kids in succession. I also had questions about some matters and, again, I felt it was imperative that Dave and Charlie join us. I had asked a friend for a referral, and he told me of an attorney he always recommended. I trusted his judgment and his referral. Doing this was long overdue, and because of what we were facing it was important that we begin to put it in place as soon as possible. I wasn't sure what the ramifications were if we didn't have this type of paperwork ready, and I didn't want to take any chances.

Thursday, December 20, 2012—Meeting with the Attorney

While waiting for the nurse to get Jack for his radiation session, we met a man we had seen before at the cancer clinic. Jack went over and shook his hand. He told the guy that he was an inspiration to him because the man was always so upbeat. The guy's face lit up. Jack told him he'd like to talk to him a little more some time. At this time we had two more sessions scheduled, one for the next day (Friday) and Christmas Eve (Monday), so I thought he'd have to connect quickly. However, we never did get to see him again. After our last session, Jack commented that he should have spoken to the man sooner and was disappointed that he didn't get a chance to see him again.

I called and set the schedule for the following Thursday to get the port put in his chest at Henry Ford West Bloomfield Hospital. I knew that would be a long day. Once that was in I could schedule chemo, and that would start after January 1. I was trying to get organized, but it was so hard. So many things kept changing, and so many things still had to be handled. There was so much paperwork I felt like I was getting buried under it. There were also so many things to think about. I was slowly plodding through receipts to make sure I didn't throw away something important. Then I color coded file folders. I was hoping it would make sense down the road when I needed something.

We had a good meeting with the attorney. Dave and Charlie met us there. I needed to make sure we did the right thing and asked the right questions. When we were done, there was a lot to think about and discuss with the kids. I was very glad they were all going to be home the next week. We decided for us it would be best to have a trust set up, with a will to capture anything not listed in the trust. Then for each of us there was a Power of Attorney to be drawn up—one for medical issues and one for financial decisions. Once again I was overwhelmed and not sure how much of the information I would retain.

Friday, December 21, 2012—New Schedules and Preparing for Christmas

After today we only had one more radiation therapy—Christmas Eve! We were looking forward to being done with it. It had been a long and grueling two weeks. We scheduled the chemo for January second, third, and fourth. Those sessions were to be at Henry Ford Macomb Hospital. I was so glad Dr. Doyle was okay with transferring the treatments from Novi to Macomb.

The chemo port was still scheduled to be put in at Henry Ford West Bloomfield on December 27, 2012. The first infusion was scheduled for 8:30–12:30 on January 2, 2013, and then 8:30–10:30 the next two days. So each morning we would be tied up but it was only three days a week this time and then a break for three weeks.

We were looking forward to Rob and his family to arrive on Saturday sometime in the afternoon. We were getting excited at the thought of all the kids being here for Christmas. Even though Jack was fatigued, he was looking forward to seeing everyone.

This day, though, was another busy, run-errands day after radiation. We finally got home about 11:00 A.M. I was so tired I had to lie down on the couch for a while. The kids were doing schoolwork. After resting for a very short time, I started working on paperwork—again. It never seemed to end.

I was finally able to get all of the gifts wrapped that I had bought or made. Saturday would be the only day I would have to finish shopping, but thankfully, by this time, I didn't have a lot to get. I had hoped to be done by now, but as usual I was not able to completely finish each time I went to the store.

Jack was extremely fatigued and had gotten sores in his mouth from the radiation or steroids or both. They gave him a prescription and said it should start clearing up right away. He didn't want to eat because of the pain, and eating was important. They said he had lost six pounds, and they did not want him to lose weight, so we needed to find a way to keep his appetite up. His tastes had changed though, and I had created a monster. He loved the lattes and cappuccino I was making for him, especially the caramel latte. Also he had been eating Greek yogurt. He said that was easier on his sore mouth and throat. What he was eating and drinking was not truck driver fare. We weren't sure what other drivers might think, but all we cared about was whether he was eating and drinking.

At this point, though, he was not eating and drinking very much. I knew it was important to get food and liquid into him, but the sores were so bad he didn't want to do either. He had not mentioned it to me, so I didn't know he was struggling. I was glad they found it at the clinic.

Saturday, December 22, 2012—Beginning of Some Issues

Today Jack was very fatigued and still had no appetite. I wasn't sure if it was the radiation or if the tumors were growing or if it was still from the sores in his mouth. There was really no way to know what was going on in either his lungs or his brain. None of the doctors indicated they would run any tests. They kept saying it was too soon for any results to show up. It was so hard to not know what was going on. Waiting was so hard because we couldn't make any decisions on how to go forward. He was so miserable he wanted to just give up. I fully understood that. It was his decision to make.

Fighting this disease is not easy any time of year, but it is particularly hard at Christmas. It's not that I didn't have the joy of the season; it was just hard to focus on it when so much else demanded my attention. Trying to keep things normal was hard, too. So much would go through my mind I could not even express it. Thoughts would swirl around, and it was hard to capture any one thought and focus on it. I would just zero in on what had to be taken care of as a priority and put the rest on the back burner. The trouble is that burner was on low but was never really turned off.

I knew then, and I still know, that God was and still is in control and, believe me, I would not have been able to function at all if people had not been praying for me—I truly felt the prayers.

Sunday, December 23, 2012—Things Were Not Going Well

The medication for the sores in his mouth took effect fairly quickly, and Jack was doing a little better on eating and drinking but not enough. He was only eating a few bites of food and less than sixteen ounces of fluid in a twenty-four-hour period. I was getting worried. He kept saying he had no appetite, and he didn't want anything to drink. I knew that drinking was crucial to keeping him going, but I could not force it on him. He was never much on drinking water, so I tried other things to hydrate him. The problem was that nothing was working because he just did not have any interest in eating or drinking.

Dave had been doing almost all of the cooking. He missed his calling—all his meals were gourmet, and we were not about to complain. In fact, he had made out menus for every day the whole time his siblings were due to be in town. He did a major shopping and had all the ingredients to feed everyone every day. What a load that was off my mind. I was so thankful that he was willing and able to take care of all the food and cooking for me. I told him I felt he was God's blessing to be able to be at home to help me at this time.

Monday, December 24, 2012—The Last Radiation Therapy

It's a good thing I know the real reason for the season because if I had been lost in all the materialism and trappings of the event, I would have been having a real hard time enjoying myself.

While I was not having the best time, it was not because I missed what the season is but rather that the stress and uncertainty had not allowed me to really focus on celebrating Christ. He knows my love is true, He loves me even when I fail; His love is greater than mine will ever be. I don't have to dwell on that to know it, but it would have been nice if I could have spent even a little time thanking Him for His unfailing love and His presence as we traveled this path. I know He knew my heartfelt thanks—I just needed, for me, to express it.

So . . . I did, in one of my journal postings, which I will put here.

I love you, Lord Jesus, and I truly thank you that I see Your hand on all that has happened and I thank you for holding on to me when I can't hold on to You. The peace You give is immeasurable—I don't know where it comes from, I just know it's here. Yes, we're already grieving and struggling but even in the midst of it I have peace. Does that make sense? I can't do this without You.

As we marked the end of the radiation therapy and were looking to a new chapter with the chemo, I was certain our path would once more be rocky, but in a new way. I knew I would not walk this road alone—I had so many prayer partners who would be there with me. I knew the Lord would be with me. My family would be with me. Yet in some things, I would still be alone. Decision-making in some cases would be mine alone. My thoughts would be mine alone. Yet I was never really alone. That may make no sense to some of you, but it made perfect sense to me.

By this time all of the kids were in town, and all had been at the farm to see Jack. Rob and his family were staying at Charlie's. Karen and Riley were staying with us. Rich, Michele, and Luke were also staying with us at the farm. The plan was for Michele and Luke to stay on until January 5, so Dave had initially said he would stay at a friend's house, and they could use his room. That didn't work out and he ended up sleeping on the couch, which wasn't good for his back, but we had no options at that point.

Rob and family came out to visit for the day and then left to go to visit Tracy's family. The plan was they would return and spend the night at the farm, so all except Charlie's family would be at the farm first thing Christmas Day. The weather report was not good, and I was glad all the family was in town but cautioned them that later it could get bad and to watch for bad road conditions as night fell.

Karen and Michele wanted to do last-minute shopping even though the stores would be packed. They left late in the afternoon and said they would meet me at church for the Christmas Eve service. I wasn't sure I should go because I felt Jack's condition was getting worse. Rich told me to go ahead and he would stay with his dad and would call me if anything happened. I took Luke with me and went to church. Karen and Michele made it at the last minute and said it looked like bad weather was moving in.

When we returned home, we saw that the roads were going to be very bad later in the evening. Rob called and said they were at Charlie's and the roads had gotten so bad they would stay there and come out in the morning when it was light and they could see better. I was much relieved. It was one less thing to be concerned about.

Tuesday, December 25, 2012—Christmas Day

Saying Happy Birthday to my Lord Jesus Christ seemed so trivial in comparison to what that really means. He was born for me because He was to die for me. I just could not comprehend it. How do you thank someone for so great a gift? For those reading this who have never asked Christ to be their Savior, my prayer is that this will be the beginning of a new life for you—one with Him as your Savior.

Even with the joy of knowing the Lord and what He had done, this was a difficult day. I wanted to celebrate Christmas as usual, but I knew early in the morning that things were not going well with Jack. This was not going to be a normal Christmas. He struggled from the bed to his chair, less than twenty-five feet apart. It was all he could do to walk that far and sit down.

He opened the quilt from Diane—it was beautiful and meaningful. The kids had gotten him a few things even though he said not to buy him anything. He only sipped the coffee we made for him and didn't respond much as the kids were opening their gifts. He was not himself; that was obvious, and it worried me greatly.

Breakfast had always been his big meal of the day, but he said he was not hungry and didn't want to eat. The medication for the sores had helped, but his eating and drinking had been minimal since Friday. This was the fourth day he was barely eating and drinking. I knew it was not good that he would not eat, but more important, he needed to drink and that was not happening, even with the lattes he had grown to love.

I did everything I could to try to get him to agree to go to the hospital, but he kept refusing, saying he did not want to disrupt Christmas.

He already had disrupted it—not that he wanted to—but his condition was so bad it was hard for me to concentrate or enjoy the day.

The plan was to have Christmas dinner at Charlie's later in the day. I knew Jack would not be going. He was so weak he could barely move and stayed in bed most of the day. In fact, as soon as gift opening was done he went back to bed.

The kids insisted I go to Charlie's for dinner. Rich offered to stay again so I could get away. Rob was staying at Charlie's, and he and his family joined us for the evening. I had planned to only be gone a short time, but it ended up being four hours, and it was a relief to get away and focus on something besides what was happening at home.

We ate dinner and then sat in the living room and played Apples to Apples. That game always generated a lot of laughs because we gave some outrageous answers, just for fun. We had a good time and laughed a lot, which I needed to do. It was a wonderful stress reliever.

When we returned home though, I was once again thrown into the stress-filled knowledge that things were not going well. I made up my mind that the next day if he didn't improve, we would take him to the hospital even if he fought against it.

Wednesday, December 26, 2012—Making a Decision for Jack

For several years on the day after Christmas we met my sister and brother-in-law for a family breakfast we dubbed, "The Beliveau After Christmas Breakfast Bash." Anyone who could make it was invited to come to a restaurant near where they lived and the entire tab was paid for by my brother-in-law. We always had a great time, and it was usually a sendoff to my kids who came in from out of town. This year I knew none of us were going to make it, so I offered to have it at the farm. That was before I knew how bad Jack was going to be that day.

It was too late to cancel the day, though, so I went ahead with plans for the breakfast and decided to make the best of it. As soon as I got up, I knew it wasn't going to work as planned. We still had family come out, but I was so distracted by Jack's worsening condition that I never really was a part of the festivities.

As the morning wore on, I knew that whatever it took, he would have to go to the hospital this day. There was no way he was going to survive if he didn't. I was pretty sure he was seriously dehydrated. His weakness was getting worse, and that was the hardest thing to see. He told me he didn't have enough strength to roll over in bed, much less get up.

I sat in a room in the back of the house that we use for an office, crying and trying to pull myself together. A couple of the grandkids came and offered comfort or tried to ask questions. I brushed them off and told them to go join the others. Later I felt so bad that I had done that, but at the time I could not answer their questions and just wanted to be left alone.

I finally told Rich and Charlie to do what they could to convince their dad to go to the hospital no matter what it took. They kept saying I should stay and spend time with family, and I insisted I needed to go along. For one thing, I would have to possibly sign papers and for another, I had to give them information as to what had been happening. The kids knew what was going on, but they hadn't been there for the past ten days to see his condition getting worse.

He did agree to go, and they got him into Charlie's van. I barely told the rest of the family what was happening and grabbed my coat and the paperwork and went out the door. It's a good thing I had planned to go along because as soon as they got Jack into the van he asked where I was and if I was going along.

We got to the hospital about 11:00 A.M. They saw him fairly quickly and ran some tests. Within an hour the doctor told us he would be admitted and that he was seriously dehydrated. Once I knew for sure they were admitting him, I called West Bloomfield and canceled the next day's scheduled medi-port surgery.

It took most of the rest of the day to get everything set up and get him into a room, but at least he was now where he needed to be and getting the treatment he needed. I was very relieved. By the time he got into his room, he had drained four IV bags. I took that as a sign that his body did not have much fluid in it.

One of the signs of dehydration is mental confusion and general weakness. I knew the weakness was mostly from the radiation, but he had been pretty much mentally alert, and his confusion and apathy were what had been bothering me. I was so glad I had pushed to get him to the hospital. Like before, he insisted I stay with him or he wanted to go home. I agreed to stay because there was no way he was leaving until he was better.

Thursday, December 27, 2012—Pre-planning a Funeral

I had asked Spencer if we could meet when the kids were in town because I wanted them in on what we discussed and also wanted them to have opportunity to ask questions. This was all new to them, and they had never been through anything like this in their lives. They had lost grandparents but no one close to them had this type of terminal illness, so they were dealing with a lot of unknowns.

We had been trying to set something up and had not been able to get it together. Finally I asked if he could meet us at the hospital while they were all there to visit Jack. Even though we were getting two inches of snow, he drove over and met with us. We all met in the hospital cafeteria and talked for over an hour. It looked like the kids pretty much understood everything we had already talked about. They only had a few questions for Spencer.

What a blessing that meeting was. I was so glad we were able to all get together. I had already discussed with the kids what their dad wanted as far as a funeral and burial were concerned and had told them that Spencer had given me some good advice regarding Jack's wishes in that regard. I wanted them to meet Spencer and have him explain what his role was and see if they had questions.

When I went back to Jack's room, he said he was hungry. That was the first time since the previous Saturday that he had wanted to eat. He had only been eating popsicles and ice cream. At first they had a hard time trying to find a vein for blood tests. By the fourth IV bag they finally found a vein that was easy to get to for blood tests.

The dehydration had also caused him to be weak and very unsteady. Because of that he had an alarm on his bed that rang every time he tried to get off the bed. He was not happy about being told he could not get up without help, but I told him that if he fell, I could not help him, so he had to do what they said. He tried to get up to use bathroom but was still a bit weak. He was better than yesterday but not by much. A little progress was better than none.

Friday, December 28, 2012 — Going Home

Jack did really well this day; he ate two meals, was drinking, and the IV had done its work. By the time we left my last count was eight IV bags. By then it was passing through his system, which meant his body was retaining some of it but did not need it all, which is what we wanted. He was so much stronger and more alert by afternoon it was good to see. I wasn't ready to lose him like that. I knew that time would come, but I didn't want it to be like it was on Christmas Day the last time the kids saw him.

Some of the kids had planned on leaving today but had opted to wait until Saturday since it looked like Jack would be released by evening. In fact, we had sent an invite to several people to join us for a roast dinner as a homecoming celebration. We had set it for 6:00 P.M. thinking we would be home in plenty of time. They didn't release him until after 4:00 P.M., so we barely made our own party.

I wasn't sure how he would react to a houseful of people since he was just getting home from the hospital. He was much stronger though and in a better frame of mind. He was so glad to get home I don't think he cared who was there. He did well with dinner and was able to sit and talk with everyone for a while. He was especially happy to see Pastor Garry and Martha there.

His next decision would be whether or not to do chemo. If he decided not to, I wasn't sure how long he would have. If he did decide to, I wasn't sure how long he had. Only the Lord knows our days, and He did not give me any indication. I never did ask Him for a date, just for time to do it right.

Saturday, December 29, 2012 — Saying Good-bye to the Kids

The past five weeks (yes, it was only five weeks ago Friday) had taken their toll. I couldn't get my mind to function for more than a few minutes at a time. I would get up, eat, do a little, and then have to lie down. I was utterly exhausted. I think it's normal. If not, I was in trouble.

Karen and Riley headed back to Toronto. Rob and his family headed back to Illinois. Destiny had decided to stay for the week since she was off school, but Ryan did not want to stay. Tracy told me he was afraid Papa would die while he was here and that would scare him. I told her to tell him to come back when they came to get Destiny so he could see Papa was still okay. Dave and Rich headed to Phoenix. Michele and Luke were to stay with me for another ten days. Michele undecorated for me, and late in the afternoon we went grocery shopping. It looked like we bought enough to keep us for a month. Rica, Reina, and Elisha would be out several times, though, so we were sure the food would get eaten. We were all set to stay in until we got cabin fever. I told Michele by the time she went back to Arizona we would either still love each other or she would be glad to escape the madhouse.

Jack had decided to at least start the first chemo treatments and see how it would go. I told him it was critical he eat and stay hydrated or he would be back in the hospital. A home care nurse was sent out to do an evaluation. Our insurance would cover her visits, and she would monitor his BP, heart, and other vitals.

Since it was the weekend, I would have to wait until Monday to call and reschedule the medi-port, which we canceled when he went into the hospital. Also on Monday the nurse would come back out for a home care visit. Tuesday nothing would happen as it was a holiday. Wednesday I planned to call the attorney and set up a time to sign the POAs, will, and trust. Rob had decided to buy Jack's pickup, so Wednesday I also planned to take the title to get it cleared and give a copy to his credit union. I was sure Thursday and Friday would have their own issues, and Saturday I would be taking Michele and Luke to the airport. I was looking at a full week again.

Sunday, December 30, 2012—Another Busy Day

This was a busy day but not hectic like the last week. Jack ate a good breakfast. He slept well the previous night and said he felt better than he had in a couple of weeks. He opted to at least try the chemo, so I would have to make those arrangements.

For this day, though, I *had* to get some of the paperwork in order. I could not put off some of the critical stuff that I needed to start addressing. Michele emptied, scrubbed, and refilled my fridge; then she did the dishes. The kitchen looked so much better. Now that we knew what we had food-wise we could go forward with meals. I was so glad she and Luke were staying a week. It was good to have someone here to help and talk to.

I took the opportunity to lie down again with a book. I was hoping I could keep my eyes open long enough to read some of it. Even though I was not doing the heavy work, I would get tired quickly. I never did note if I ever read the book or not, but I suspect I didn't. If I did, I remember absolutely none of it. I was so exhausted most of the time I could not stay awake once I sat down for more than two minutes.

Monday, December 31, 2012—The End of a Year

There were times when I was so exhausted my mind just refused to work. I could not think nor process anything. A couple of good nights' sleep had helped with that.

The first thing I did was call and reschedule the surgery for the medi-port. Jack had decided to try at least the first three-day session of chemo, and that had to be set up quickly. We were already behind on starting the chemo and had to begin as soon as possible.

I still had a ton of paperwork to do but was picking away at it, and each piece I completed was one less stress for me. There were still a few things I had to do because it was the year's end and company paperwork does not wait for anyone, even if you have a family crisis. What helped was having my daughter-in-law stay till January 5 to help me out.

Tomorrow (New Year's Day) a man who said he was interested in the Kenworth wanted to come and see it. I was praying it would sell for an amount Jack could live with. Rob was approved for a loan and was buying the pickup, so I needed to find the payoff book and contact the bank to set things up to clear the title since it would be retitled in Illinois. We would then be down to one vehicle, so another prayer was that my pick-up truck would hold up because it would then be all we would have. Dave had a car, but I needed my own transportation.

Jack had been complaining that his hair kept falling in his food and he was tired of eating it with everything. A good friend, Cindy F., came out and shaved off the rest of his hair that hadn't fallen onto his clothes and into his food. All that beautiful white hair—gone! Four-year-old Elisha wouldn't even look in his direction. He would go through the room and look away from his Papa as he walked. It took him a few days for him to realize that man was Papa; he just looked different.

January 1, 2013—New Year, New Beginnings

A new year had begun. What it would hold I had no idea, but at the moment the sun was shining. It looked so good and bright outside, which was deceiving because it was frigid! We started this year the way we ended the last one, making preparations to move ahead fighting this disease called cancer. Right now since everything was closed, we took the day off. The next day would be phone calls and things to do in preparation for having surgery Thursday to have a medi-port put in for the chemo infusions.

We were blessed to have Michele and Luke stay for the week. She cleaned my kitchen, baked banana bread, helped with the kids, and was great company when I needed to talk. Elisha and Luke had a great time playing together. I was so glad for the company and the help.

When Jack weighed himself this first day of the new year he said he weighed 150 on my scale and that it must be broken. It wasn't; he had lost eighteen pounds since November 23, which was not good. Most of it probably was the past week when he was so sick and did not eat or drink for three days. I started stuffing him with whatever I could when he was even a little hungry because he couldn't take the weight loss—he needed it to fight.

It takes a lot of energy to overcome the effects of the radiation and would take a lot to overcome the effects of the chemo. The nurse had told him it is very important that he eat and drink a lot because he would burn it off trying to heal.

I cleaned our room and put things away that were cluttering the dresser and table. Jack complained that he couldn't find anything. But then he admitted he didn't need much. For years his big complaint was that I either hid his stuff or threw it away. Well, sometimes that really was true, but right now I was only trying to keep things somewhat organized so I could find them quickly when needed. When the nurse or therapist came or when we might have to go to the hospital,

I had to be able to "grab it and run," so it needed to work for me. I simplified much and if we weren't using it, it was put elsewhere for now because the clutter was too much for me.

Well, the day ended with no call from the man who said he was so interested in the truck. I was disappointed but not surprised. Back to square one on this deal.

Wednesday, January 2, 2013 — Prepping for Surgery

I hoped Jack would eat a good meal because after midnight tonight he would not be able to eat till Thursday afternoon after the surgery for the medi-port. Charlie told me Josette "might" be able to get off and go with me if I wanted her too. My own favorite nurse — does it get any better than that? It would be nice to have company and even nicer to have someone who actually understood what they were saying. Yep, I was sure hoping she could get off.

Jack said he was feeling a little weak and that was because he still was not getting enough fluids in him, and the cumulative effects of the radiation were now taking its toll. I kept water by his chair, gave him coffee, decaf pop (he liked Vernors with Edy's vanilla ice cream floats). It was so hard to get him to drink a lot of fluid. He had never been one to drink much water or anything during the day except coffee. I kept telling him it was crucial to keep hydrated, and he kept telling me he was drinking all that he could.

I needed to find the payment book for Jack's pickup, and I had no idea where I had put it. I needed it to get an account number. It seems like a small thing, but the Lord was always helping me with those small things that overwhelmed me. There were a lot of small things too because I was forever misplacing something or not remembering what I did with things.

I went to the bank where Jack had the loan on the pickup. After days of hassling with the bank and them telling me I could not pay off the pickup loan and get clearance, Jack talked to the bank and they finally agreed to let me have the paperwork to get the payoff amount so we could clear the title for Rob. I did not need their aggravation and could not understand what the issue was when all I wanted was to pay off the loan. Such a hassle I did not need. I left the bank and said I would be back with the money and pay the loan in full. The next day was scheduled for surgery so I planned to go to the bank on Friday.

As I had done before with Rica, I encouraged Destiny to write a journal of her thoughts and feelings while she was still visiting. I am including hers below. I think it is important to know what kids are thinking when families go through something like this. Since she was fourteen, I felt she could express herself in a journal writing. Here is hers.

Written Jan 2, 2013 4:58 P.M. by Destiny Shelton

When I first found out about my Papa, I was devastated. I was crying and praying! Rica and I had talked on the phone for three hours that day (most of it was crying and tears). Papa is also one of my heroes. When I would get suspended (from school) my Papa would tell my dad not to yell at me because it was just a little thing, and that I'm my Papa's girl (but he was kidding) but we would make a joke out of it. Now when I look at my Papa and see how weak he is, it just kills me because just last summer me and Papa were outside doing yardwork! It's a lot different to see him with no hair, but I talk to him and joke with him while I'm here visiting, and every day I tell him how much I love him and I give him a hug and a kiss. I pray every morning and every night for him and my family, when I hug him I lose it and tear up! But I love the time I get to spend here with my grandparents and my family!!! Please pray for my family and my grandpa and grandma through this rough time and as all this is happening. Thank you!!!

Then I had Rica write another one. Hers is below.
Written Jan 2, 2013 5:11 P.M. by Rica Shelton

Papa already told me he wants me to sing at his funeral. It's really strange when he talks about how he wants his funeral and stuff. Tomorrow he gets the port for the chemotherapy. He also got his head shaved except for his beard and it seems so strange, although it was going to fall out anyways. I just hope his beard doesn't get shaved or fall out. I can't even imagine him without it. I hope the chemo does more good than harm. It's just so hard to prepare for everything that's happening. Thank you for prayers, it really helps. P.S. sorry this was kind of a jumble just kind of fell out of my brain.

I am glad the girls put their thoughts in writing. It helped them and it helped me. I am sure if they would have written out all of their thoughts we would be amazed. I am glad for the insights I gained reading what they wrote.

Thursday, January 3, 2013—Surgery Day

We had to leave the house by 10:00 A.M. at the latest for Henry Ford West Bloomfield Hospital. They told us to expect to be there at least till 4:00–5:00 P.M. I knew it would be another long day. I left Michele and the kids at the farm to clean house while we were gone. I had no problem asking for help or accepting it when offered. I had way too much on my plate to let pride get in the way of getting things done. The house was a disaster, and I simply could not do all of it on my own.

Jack and I met our favorite nurse at her house, and she drove us to the hospital. I was very glad to have some company, and especially someone who can explain what they would say. I was also glad to have someone else drive for a change. I was tired from all the driving I had been doing. This was a welcome respite. We got to the hospital about 11:00 A.M., and they prepped him. Then Josette and I sat with him till they took him in to surgery.

While they did the procedure, Josette and I went and got something to eat. I made a lot of calls while we waited, so the next week was already full of appointments. I felt I was going to meet myself coming and going. They kept asking if he was on blood thinner, and I kept saying no. They kept asking why. I kept telling them because he had tumors in his brain. I was getting tired of repeating myself. It was computerized, so they should have been able to see it. He told a nurse it didn't matter if his cholesterol was high since he was terminally ill, so why didn't they quit asking about it.

68

The procedure took about an hour, and then it was two hours in recovery to make sure the port stayed in place, to make sure he didn't start bleeding or having other problems, and to let the anesthetic get out of his system a little. He ate there before we left, but he said the pizza he had wasn't very good.

We drove home during rush hour but were still able to make good time. Traffic was at a standstill so instead of going the usual route, we took a couple of back roads and got away from the traffic before getting back onto one of the main roads across town. I'm not sure how we did it but it actually worked out pretty well, and we were home at a reasonable time. Jack had complained about the pizza he had not tasting good, so we fixed something else for him to have for dinner.

Even though we had the port put in and were scheduling the chemo to start, he would say this is all a waste of time and he should not be putting me through this. Then other times he would say he might as well try it and see if it does any good. I told him since I had scheduled the chemo, he had to make a decision and stay with it, at least for the first three sessions. I had scheduled it for him to start chemo on Tuesday, January 8, 2013 from 12:30 P.M. until 4:30 P.M. They would not give me times for the next two days until we completed the first appointment. They said that once we did the three days, we would have a break of twenty-one days.

They had told him after they put the port in not to lift anything more than ten pounds for ten days. That was easier said than done. I wasn't sure how I would keep him from doing something if he wanted to do it. He did not like being told what to do or not to do. I was just hoping he would not argue about it. I didn't want that port to move or start bleeding. I had enough on my mind without that, and I told him so. He didn't argue, and he did behave and not try to lift heavy things. I think he realized he should not cause me any more stress than I had. For this night, though, Michele and the kids had the house clean, dishes done, and laundry done, and then the kids were off to Charlie's for the night.

Friday, January 4, 2013—Getting Something Accomplished Finally

I took a break this morning and had breakfast with a friend. We had met on Saturdays for over a year and had a Bible study. She agreed to meet this day, though, as I would be heading to the airport the next day. It was a much-needed break.

I then went to the bank where no one seemed to know that I had gotten approval on Wednesday to get the payoff on the loan for the pickup. I went into the manager's office and had Jack call yet again, and she finally agreed I could get the needed letter. Then I went to Rob's credit union where there was no issue once they knew who I was. Zip, I was out.

Two errands later and I was home for the day. The next day would be hard as I would be taking Michele and Luke to the airport to fly back to Arizona. Oh, how I would miss them!

Saturday, January 5, 2013—Saying Goodbye—Again

I was glad for the weekend because it meant no appointments. It was, however, going to be a sad weekend. They say time flies when you are having fun. Well, I was not having fun, and time still flew by. Jack said he was feeling okay, so I felt comfortable leaving him home alone for a while. I had to get up early to take Michele and Luke to Detroit Metro Airport before 10:00 A.M. I fixed Jack some breakfast, and we left. We still had a little time, so we stopped at Tim Horton's on Middlebelt for coffee, and then I dropped them off. I knew I was going to miss them terribly. They had been such a blessing.

On the way back across town I met Rob, who had come back to get Destiny. He had picked up Jack and the kids and met me at Cracker Barrel for what I thought might be our last outing there. Whether we would be able to go out any more would depend on how well Jack did with the chemo. He would not be able to be in many public places because they said this chemo would wipe out his immune system. I would not be able to have anyone over that had even a slight cold, runny nose, etc. This "new normal" was really hard to work with because it kept changing.

As with the radiation, the effects of the chemo wouldn't take effect immediately, but I had to start getting prepared to keep him away from as many people as possible. I was sure he would get cabin fever if he was not too tired to care. I was thinking he could listen to some audio books on my IPhone, even if he fell asleep listening. At least it would be something to do.

I was afraid I might get sick. If I were to get sick, I didn't know what I would do. I decided to look into getting some surgical masks so I would be prepared!

We weren't sure how, but now Jack was constipated and in pain from it. This was another of those critical issues, like dehydration, that could devastate his system. We needed to get it under control as quickly as possible.

Sunday, January 6, 2013—On Our Own

On this day we officially were on our own. All the kids and grandkids had left. Dave would not be back from Arizona for a week. It seemed so quiet and empty. I spent the day going through the mountain of papers that never seemed to get any smaller. Today, it was old junk mail that had accumulated. The only redeeming feature to that mess was a stack of Christmas/birthday/misc. cards, some pens, note pads, and wrapping paper that some organizations send with their plea for money. I figured I was set for the year.

I also had to do another load of laundry (that pile was getting smaller) and started a pot of bean soup with a ham bone I found in the freezer. When Rob had moved to Illinois the previous summer, he left a huge, old TV behind the door in the room we used as an office for the company Charlie and I were working for and that Jack had hauled boats for. While he was home, I had him take it to the Salvation Army resale store. Then I rearranged the office and put my scrapbook stuff on a shelving unit that I put behind that same door. The door now opened further, and my things were more accessible. Scrapbooking journals for the grandkids was my stress reliever, and they made great birthday and Christmas gifts.

I also had papers to correct and was behind on getting the kids' schoolwork in order. They were way behind at this point, but I was getting caught up. Little by little I was working at getting organized. It seemed to be taking forever.

It was either the cold or because I had used my hands a lot, but the pain level was getting up over 5, so I had to quit and warm my hands up and stop using them for a while. The left one was worse than the right. The flare-ups were happening too often and causing me a lot of pain, keeping me from getting things done. There is nothing you can do though when a flare up happens except try to lessen the stress and quit doing so much with your hands. That was easier said than done.

Jack was still constipated. I had given him enough stuff to clean you out for a colonoscopy and still nothing. I told him it will be another trip to the ER if something didn't happen soon. He could not go on like this—it was too dangerous. Not only that, he said the pain was almost unbearable.

Monday, January 7, 2013—Canceling Appointments—Again

I had to cancel all appointments this week because of a setback. It wasn't the same issue we had just after Christmas but had the potential to be serious. He was eating only one meal a day and not all of that sometimes. He said he felt "full" or "bloated." We needed to get this taken care of before he had a rupture or some other problem.

They were not happy with me canceling the chemo again but I could not take him in for it. There was no way he could stand it, and he refused to go anywhere since he was in so much pain. We also canceled the meeting with the attorney that we had set up for the next day. We really needed to get that done because all that paperwork would be critical if he didn't survive these setbacks.

We couldn't move forward with the chemo, though, until he felt he could stand it. This cancer was aggressive and fast-growing, so the doctor was concerned (and so was I). I could not do anything, though, when he was too weak and in pain to go through with it.

He looked more gaunt to me every day, and I saw him every day. I could only imagine how someone would feel that hadn't seen him in a while. Watching someone suffer is hard, especially when you can do nothing to alleviate the problem or the pain.

Tuesday, January 8, 2013 — An Appointment We *Must* Keep

The nurse in the chemo center called when they told her I had called and canceled. She asked why and I told her what was happening. I said I didn't know when Jack would be able to continue because it's been one thing after another.

I told her I had canceled the doctor appointment on the 17th because he wanted to see Jack after the chemo and that wasn't happening. She called me back in less than an hour. She had emailed Dr. Doyle all that I had told her and he said he wanted to see Jack *this week*!

So, we now had an appointment on Thursday at 11:30 A.M. I had tried five different things to alleviate the constipation, and so far we saw only a little success. A little is better than none, but we were still in the danger zone. He ate one half of an English muffin with sausage and egg (I left it greasy hoping that would help), and he had a cup of coffee. After that, he had a glass of orange juice. He still was not drinking enough but, again, it was better than nothing.

We were caught between the proverbial rock and hard place. He could not eat because he felt full and bloated. I could not get him to drink anything for the same reason. He did not want to go back into the hospital and was determined to work out this problem on his own. He told me to go to the store and get something that would help him. The problem was, I didn't know what would help. Everything we tried did not seem to work.

Wednesday, January 9, 2013 — A Break-through — Finally

In desperation, Jack turned to an old remedy his mother used when he was a kid — castor oil. How he drank it I have no idea. Just the smell of it gagged me. But, it worked. He felt some better and said he had cabin fever and wanted out of the house for a while. Since he was feeling better and less "bloated," we went to breakfast. He ate more than half of his order, which was good since he had not been eating much at all lately.

I had a list of questions for the doctor for our visit on the 10th. I was hoping to get some answers about what to do in these cases and if we could learn how to hook an IV to a PIC line so we could hydrate him at home. Staying hydrated would be critical once we started chemo.

On Tuesday night I had asked the Lord to speak to me so I could hear Him. Then I had to keep stopping to apologize as my mind would wander, and I asked Him to quiet me so I could hear Him if He did speak. When I woke up in the morning I felt I had not heard from Him. I was a little disappointed. I don't know what I wanted to hear, I just know I wanted to know He was still with me. I knew it—I guess I just needed reassurance.

As I was checking out at Kroger, the man putting stuff in my bags (I was going to go to self-serve and changed my mind at the last minute), mentioned that it looked like someone was having some problems. I had gotten suppositories, castor oil, etc., etc. I told him my husband had cancer and the treatments were causing a lot of intestinal problems, among other things.

He then shared with me that a few years ago he was diagnosed with Stage 4 esophageal cancer. He was eighty percent blocked. He said he was now in remission, able to talk and work and considered himself a walking miracle who had been given a second chance to enjoy life. I walked away thanking the Lord for allowing me to see someone who knew what I was going through. He does answer in weird ways, but I'll take the answer no matter how it comes. I believe His message of hope was for me on that particular day.

During the day I was so busy I didn't have time to think about what was going on and how to react to it. Nights were a different matter. Last night as I felt the warmth of Jack's body, all I could do was cry. That was when I had called out to the Lord to speak to me. I believe He did that through the bagger at Kroger. We have been given a "second chance" so to speak in that God was giving us extra time to appreciate what we had.

There would be good days and there would be bad days—that I knew. I knew that when they would get bad the Lord would be there to lift me up; He had shown me that. For now, it was one day at a time, and I really didn't want to know what tomorrow would hold.

Thursday, Jan 10, 2013—Moving Forward—I Hope

Before we get into today's long day, I need to tell what happened yesterday because it is another thing that could have been very stressful but wasn't. I am sure it is because so many people were praying for us.

We paid a quarterly estimated income tax because Jack was self-employed. We had opened a new checking account with Charlie's and my name on it. Going forward we knew I would have to have someone on an account with me. The decision was to go ahead and set that up now. I had put money in the new checking account, updated the IRS site with all the new information, and made the payment. In monitoring the bank accounts, I saw that they took it out of the old account, which we had not closed entirely and did not have enough to cover the check. Yep, I bounced an IRS payment. I called the bank as soon as I saw it and asked the Assistant Manager how I could take care of it. She immediately transferred the money for me and told me they would submit it again, and this time it would be covered.

Then I got a statement of billing for NSF (non-sufficient funds) on the old account. I called same woman and explained what happened. She remembered me asking her to help with this issue and said our account had never been overdrawn before, so she would have the fee waived. Praise the Lord! One stress gone!

The IRS did NOT automatically resubmit the paperwork to get paid. I had to call them and explain the situation, then go online and formally request a change in accounts for withdrawal. Lesson learned.

So, now onto the day's events. We had an appointment with Dr. Doyle because of Jack's intestinal issues and our canceling of the chemo treatments. Well, two hours before we were to leave he was able to get some "movement." So of course he didn't want to see the doctor for nothing. However, I had some questions for the doctor, so we went even though Jack was resisting.

The half hour visit ended up being three hours. Dave had returned from Arizona by this time, so again, we took him and Charlie with us. We spent one hour with the doctor going over our questions and then two hours getting him hydrated with two liters of fluid. What a difference that made. When we left there to go eat, he ate everything on his plate—that was a first in over two weeks. Staying hydrated, I think, was the key, but he was drinking less than a quart of fluid a day and needed at least two quarts, according to the doctor.

While we were at the doctor's office getting him hydrated, I called Henry Ford Macomb and told them we had the doctor's orders to start chemo the following week. While we were sitting there, a nurse came up and said the nurse coordinator from Macomb had called her and first chemo was set for 9:30 A.M., Tuesday, January 15, 2013. That one would be a four-hour session, then two hours after that on Wednesday and Thursday. I was praying that there would be no more setbacks. The doctor insisted we begin this no matter what because it was so critical.

From Novi we raced across town to meet with the attorney at 4:00 P.M. Even with our stop to eat lunch, we made it with thirty seconds to spare. An hour later, our wills, powers of attorney, and trust agreements were signed.

Getting these things done was a huge relief to me. Now, I would be back to the mountain of paperwork, but it was somewhat smaller. Everything I could check off was one thing I could get off my mind. Eventually, I wanted to get enough off my mind to be able to sleep through the night. This night we brought three of Charlie's kids home with us for ten days because they (Charlie and Josette) were leaving in the morning for a vacation in Belize.

Friday, January 11, 2013—A Day at Home

Today was uneventful in that we were home all day. Nothing was scheduled until next Tuesday so I was again working on paperwork, paying bills, and working on schoolwork (with my niece assisting). Having the three kids was not really a stress for me because they were good, and they did help with the housework. The only stress was getting them to do schoolwork.

I had two vacuums in the house, and neither one was working properly. My niece brought hers out so we could use it. I had to get some vacuuming done because I had to send the vacuum home with my niece when she left for the day.

The nurse came out, and for the first time the sound in his lungs was mentioned. What she said was, "I can tell the difference in your lungs—your right has a lot less air flow." That was an eye opener. Of course we knew that was where the tumor was, but no one to this point had ever mentioned hearing something substantially different in the sound. It made the chemo treatments that much more important, knowing they could potentially shrink that tumor. It also made the issue more real, if that makes sense. Not that it wasn't real— but no one had put it in words before.

Saturday, January 12, 2013—Cleaning Up

A friend came over and helped me gather up the trash in the yard and in the out buildings and take it to the local dump. We could pay for trash pickup or, since we lived in the township, take it to a "transfer station" where they loaded it into garbage trucks and hauled it to a landfill. We had been doing that for years because it was cheaper than paying for trash pickup, and we weren't restricted by how much we could take or how it was bagged or boxed. Large items were only allowed on certain dates, but mostly what we had right now was just regular garbage. Again, it was another item I could check off my list of things that needed to be done.

When the nurse had come out, she suggested I get a thermometer and a blood pressure monitor so I could track those two things every day or at least every other day. After doing the trash run, I went to the store and picked them up and also got some small cans of juice and ice cream for Jack. He still would not eat much but he liked Vernors ginger ale with ice cream, and he would eat mandarin oranges. It wasn't much, but it was something, and fluids were critical.

Dave had returned from Arizona earlier in the week and had been out running errands also. As usual, it was a long day, and we were all tired. No one wanted to cook, so he picked up some pre-cooked ribs and chicken for dinner. After dinner I told the kids to take a shower. I hoped to get to church tomorrow for the first time since Christmas Eve.

Sunday, January 13, 2013—Good Messages

Today was an awesome day at church. Our Sunday school study was on Heaven—a book by Randy Alcorn. John Robertson did a good job leading the study about the book. The study was good, and I needed it at that time. It gave me such peace to hear about Heaven even though we can't really know what it will be like. The message from Pastor Mick was great—what is *your* passion? Both messages were ones I needed to hear and process.

After church I had errands to run, so I took the kids to lunch. I had to pick up some paperwork for Josiah's caregivers at Charlie's house. While waiting for some of the paperwork to be done, I cleaned their kitchen. As I was doing dishes, I said, "I wish I had someone cleaning my kitchen—Rica!" Well, guess what? Rica didn't have to clean my kitchen—son Dave had it done when we got home.

I had asked my niece Suzanne to come out to help with school-work on Monday as I would be gone almost all day. Dave said he would be fixing grilled chicken to go on a chicken salad he was putting together.

Monday would be my turn—my turn at the doctor, that is. I had two appointments—one at the chiropractor and one at the rheumatologist. I needed both. I knew I had to keep myself healthy so I could keep going.

Monday, January 14, 2013—My Turn

My chiropractor was sick on this day, so I only had one appointment and then an errand to run. It was good to hear from the rheumatologist that there was no further joint damage and I only needed a blood test every two months. She said I didn't have to come back for six months as long as nothing showed on the blood work or I didn't have a serious issue. Her office is a forty-five-minute drive from home, so I knew I would be gone for several hours on this day.

From there I met with Spencer and the funeral director, who was a friend of his. That funeral home was not far from my doctor's office. We went over all the items we had discussed with Spencer and I prepaid for the funeral. Sounds weird to say that doesn't it? However, reality is that we knew it would happen; we just didn't know how soon. Spencer and I had discussed that doing it like this would keep it from being done as an emotional decision. It was one more thing I could check off as being done. I had the option of changing things and that, of course, would entail extra cost; but the initial arrangements were made.

Tuesday, January 15, 2013—Starting Chemo, Finally

After two cancelations, we finally started chemo treatments. I left the kids at the house with schoolwork to do and told them to see Uncle Dave if they had any problems. We left the house at 8:30 A.M. and returned at 3:30 P.M. I felt like I'd lost hours, days, weeks, lately. Things got to be a blur after a while.

Jack did very well during the treatment. The guy next to him almost passed out, and they were working on him, giving him oxygen, checking his vitals, etc. Jack said if that happened to him—he would be done. I didn't blame him—it was quite nerve wracking. We found out later the man had a reaction to some of the medicine, but that didn't change Jack's mind about quitting treatment if it happened to him.

While he was getting the treatment, I had gotten a baked potato with broccoli, cheese, sour cream, and salsa in the cafeteria for my lunch. I told him about it. He said it sounded good. By the time we were done though, the cafeteria was about to close, so we went to a nearby Wendy's, and he had a baked potato with bacon and cheese. He ate the whole thing. When we returned home he went right to bed for a nap, which I would have liked to be doing, but I had three kids to care for, and one needed to leave for youth group. My night was not over yet.

I took Rica to her meeting and took the other two with me to visit some friends in the area. It was too far and too expensive to run back home and then back to pick her up. Since Dave was at the house I didn't have to worry about Jack being alone.

Wednesday, January 16, 2013—Today's Events

I finally got to see the chiropractor. He said I was in decent shape for not having seen him for two months, but he could tell the stress had knotted me up. I felt much better when I left his office.

After two weeks of more hassle, I finally had the necessary paper-work so I could get the pickup loan taken care of. There had been a "late fee" since I had not paid it off before the payment was due earlier in the month. I was so tired of this. I went to the bank and paid it off but was told I would still have to wait until their corporate office sent out the lien release. I was tired of the runaround but had no choice but to wait for them to complete the process.

After I finished at the bank, it was back to the hospital for the next chemo treatment. This one was only two hours. Then we were back home, and when we walked in, we could smell a delicious dinner cooking, compliments of Dave. I honestly don't know what I would have done without him being there to take care of meals. After we ate, I made the girls do dishes so he would have a break from that chore. If you cook, you should *not* have to clean.

When we got home, Jack insisted on getting in the semi to see if it would start. That part was okay, but when getting out, he fell to the ground. That was not good. I had gone inside, so I didn't see him, but Rica was out feeding the dogs. She saw him on the ground and had to help him up because he could not push himself off the driveway. I didn't say anything, but in my mind I was thinking, "There will be no next time to try that if I can help it."

I did some paperwork and looked over some schoolwork. It was a good thing my niece had been coming out to help with that. There was no way I could have handled all the appointments, issues, and schoolwork by myself while their parents were gone.

So far the chemo was not having an impact, but they did warn us it could take up to a week to feel the effects, so I was thinking the next week would not be fun. Jack and I had talked about the fact that thirty-nine years ago on this day we were awaiting the arrival of Mr. Charles Dean Shelton. That time had surely flown.

Thursday, January 17, 2013—Some Thoughts

I decided on this day to write about something that had been on my mind. I wanted to let people know I had a lot of faith, but that didn't mean I expected Jack would be healed or in remission. I knew God could heal him if it was His will, but I had no confirmation that it was His will. I was trying to be realistic and face what was to come. My faith had nothing to do with what I was facing—it had a lot to do with *how* I was facing it.

What I had received was confirmation that He would help me take care of all the legal and financial issues we were facing. He had also confirmed that He would walk with me, so the spiritual issues were handled also. That's not to say I didn't fall apart some days—it was to say I knew I would never be alone.

So why would I write something that sounded like I was giving up? It depends on what you think I was giving up on. I was being realistic—the doctor had repeatedly said there was no cure. He had repeatedly said the treatments were to make him more comfortable and give him some time to get his affairs in order. Did that mean we wouldn't try the treatments or try to stall the inevitable? No. But the decision was Jack's. Whenever he was ready to stop the treatments because they caused him too many side effects, I would be okay with that. I wouldn't like it, but I was okay with it. This was not about me—it was about him and what he wanted.

I had done some research online on this "SCLC with mets to the brain." It was a bit discouraging. Without treatment the prognosis was two to four months. Even with radiation the prognosis was only six to twelve months, and that's if you didn't have other problems, which he had. Also, he had two tumors in the brain, which added more to the issues.

Bottom line—only God knew how much time he had. All I knew was He showed me He would help me take care of things. When we were trying to get the will, trust and POA's done, we had one setback after another. I almost doubted the Lord. Those were now completed. We had one matter taken care of relating to the business and at this time still had one more to go. I knew the Lord would help me take care of that—I was trying to be patient, but I have to admit it did get worrisome.

What I wanted from my family and friends was support to face the inevitable. I asked them to not be afraid to ask what it was like to watch someone die (it was horrible). I didn't want them to be afraid to ask if I had bad days facing this (I did). I didn't want them to be afraid to ask if I got angry at the situation (I did).

One day one of Jack's friends called and asked Jack how he was doing. I heard Jack tell him "Well, you know I'm dying a little more each day." I'm not sure what his friend said to that because they were on the phone but they still continued to talk so apparently it didn't scare him away. I hoped his other friends would also continue to talk to him even when they saw the changes and knew his time was limited.

The most important thing was that I knew where he would be when this was all over—he had made a commitment to have Christ be his Savior, and that was and is the most important thing. It made the rest at least bearable.

Friday, January 18, 2013—More Thoughts and a Break for The Kids

I was concerned about the grandchildren and how they were dealing with all this. Three of Charlie's were at my house three to four days a week. They saw and heard what was going on. I doubt the four-year-old was aware of how sick Papa was, but the other two knew and sometimes I thought they needed to talk to someone outside the family about their fears and questions. I wasn't sure if they would open up to a family member. I was so distracted with what was going on, I didn't think I would be a good source of comfort.

The others that were out of town had the same need but in a different way. They did not see what was happening on a daily basis, and sometimes that is harder. They only got information second hand and were, I'm sure, shocked at the difference in how Papa looked when it was days or weeks or even months between visits.

Reality says kids need to know death is real. The problem lies in how they see it happen, their age, how it's presented, how others react. It can't be hidden, but we in America try to hide it because it's not a pleasant subject. I think we do our kids a great disservice because when they do have to face it, they are not equipped.

How we react is crucial. I was trying to let the kids know that while this is not something that is easy to go through, neither is it evil. They knew Papa would be with Jesus. That helped. The part that we needed to let them know was that it's okay to grieve because we will miss that person—not that he's going to a bad place.

My prayer was that God would lead all of us (parents/grandparents/aunts/uncles) in the proper way to handle this situation.

For now, though, we were still trying to live as normal a life as possible. After we took Papa for some blood-work and a shot, we stopped at Barnes and Noble so they could "cruise the books." I told Reina there may be a birthday gift in there somewhere if she found something she liked.

Jack went in to look for some magazines that he might want to read. He didn't find any and decided to wait in the van because he was tired and there weren't any comfortable chairs to sit on.

Reina found a book she liked and was happy to get an early birthday gift. Then we were off to the house for the day.

It was getting obvious the chemo was beginning to have its effect on Jack, and it was not a good one. He was getting tired quickly and was uncomfortable sitting for any length of time. Lying down was uncomfortable also. In fact, he said he was not comfortable in any position for any length of time. I felt so bad for him.

Saturday, January 19, 2013—Party Day

Reina's birthday. Mom and Dad were out of town. I felt she should still have her special day, so we invited a friend over for the night. The plan was to have pizza and maybe a movie marathon. It needed to be somewhat quiet for Papa but still fun for the kids. I was hoping I could pull this off. We picked up some decorations for the party and decorated the bedroom they would be in. She had invited a friend over and so did Rica.

Jack was not feeling well, nor was he eating or drinking again, so to keep the house quiet I took the kids with me when I ran some errands. First stop was the store to get some cupcakes and treats for later. Then on to McDonald's so they could burn off some energy. After they played for a while, we picked up the pizza and headed back home.

They had pizza and the cupcakes, and then Reina opened her gifts. I told them it was time then to settle down with a movie. They did really well being quiet and not disturbing Jack. He was not doing well at all. The last chemo session seemed to have taken everything out of him. I knew by the next day if he still wasn't eating or drinking, I would have to ask him what he wanted to do because he could not go on like that, and the next option was back to the hospital, which I knew he did not want to do. I was running out of options though, and with Charlie gone, it was so hard to juggle everything.

Juggling all this was getting tiring. I knew Charlie and Josette were having a good time and were probably torn between wanting to get back and not wanting to face what was going on when they did get back. I just wanted someone else to take over everything, and I knew that just was not realistic. I wanted to break down and cry, but that was not an option with the kids in the house—I didn't want to upset them, especially with their mom and dad out of town.

In the meantime, Reina deserved to have a good day, so I focused on that. They had a good time, and it actually was a good diversion for me because I knew something was not right with Jack, and if I kept focusing on that, I would go crazy. I did know, however, that something needed to be done, and fairly quickly. For this day, though, I worked at having Reina's birthday be something special for her since it was completely different than any she had so far.

Sunday, January 20, 2013—More Decisions

Jack had not eaten since Friday morning. After the last chemo treatment he had no appetite and was again not eating or drinking much. We fixed his favorite meal—roast. I knew if he didn't even try a nibble, we were in big trouble. He finally did drink some fluid. Since midnight on Friday he had had about four ounces Coke and maybe about sixteen ounces of water. He was supposed to have sixty-four ounces (or two quarts a day), so we were far short of that again. They said a lot of water was critical to get the toxins out of his body. I couldn't force him, though, so again we were beginning to deal with the effects of dehydration. This was beginning to wear on me. Watching him sink so low and then stabilize was like living on an emotional roller coaster. Was I doing the right thing? Were we doing him any good trying to keep him going when we knew the end result would be the same—zero survival rate? It was just so hard to know the right decision to make.

By this time I wasn't even sure he would make it till Charlie got home (Monday night at midnight). But since he at least had some fluids, I felt he could make it that far. I wasn't so sure after that. I was pretty sure he was waiting for Charlie so he could tell him he didn't want to do any more treatment. Either that or he was waiting for him to get home so he could just let go. Either way, I didn't blame him.

Going into this he didn't have a lot to give, and the radiation and then the chemo took a lot out of him. He had no appetite, and nothing tasted good. He said he was nauseated, and the nausea pills didn't help. It was just one thing after another.

I could not wait for this day to be over. We did not make any major decisions, but in the back of my mind I knew we would not continue chemo. What we would do was still up in the air.

Monday, January 21, 2013—A Scare Today

First thing in the morning Jack said he wanted to get out of the house and maybe try to eat breakfast. That sounded encouraging since he hadn't eaten since Friday. He did nibble on the roast we had Sunday night and a piece of bread and one small bite of potato.

Things changed when he went into the bathroom. I thought he was going in to take a shower. He came out shaking like a leaf though. I asked if he was cold, and he said no. I had him sit down and took his blood pressure. It was 150/96. Since his runs low, that really threw me. I warmed a couple of blankets and wrapped him up. I wasn't sure if he was having a seizure or what.

Two hours later, after rotating warm blankets on him, I checked his blood pressure and it was 105/62, so I was relieved. He also had stopped shaking. I wasn't sure what was going on. But this up and down, yo-yo kind of stuff was tearing me apart. Obviously with that, and the weather being only 14 degrees, I told him he was not leaving the house.

Once I had him settled and felt it was okay to leave for a while, I told Dave I was leaving and would meet him at Charlie's later. I left Jack wrapped in blankets and took the kids with me while I went to my doctor to get a renewal for my handicapped tag. I had gotten a six-month tag for the past three years because of a knee injury, then an ankle problem. Now with the rheumatoid arthritis, they classified my condition as "permanent" instead of "temporary." This tag would be good for five years.

From there we went to get gas in Charlie's van, and then stopped at his house and met Dave. He drove my pickup there so Charlie would have a vehicle for the next day. I kept the van "just in case." It was easier for Jack to get in and out of the van if I had to take him anywhere.

I was so glad Charlie would be back tonight. I had several things I wanted to discuss with him. I wanted him to have time to settle back in, but I had too many urgent things to attend to, and we needed to talk a few of them over. The plan was that he and Josette would be out in the morning to get the kids, see Jack, and talk things over. What an end to a vacation!

Tuesday, January 22, 2013 — Getting Stabilized Again

When they came out in the morning, I told them what the past ten days had been like. I explained that the three days of chemo had just about wiped him out. I also told them he had little to eat and drink since the previous Friday. We had to decide what to do.

The decision was to hydrate him, so Josette set up an IV and hydrated Jack with two units of fluid. He was then doing somewhat better. In fact, I made breakfast for them, and Charlie sat with his dad in the living room and ate with him. Jack ate a small amount of egg, two pieces of bacon, one piece of toast and some hash browns. Not much, but way more than he had been eating. Being hydrated made all the difference.

His blood was dark, almost black, and Josette could barely find a vein. His urine was dark brown — both are signs of dehydration, which in his case would be fatal if it went on another few days. We were almost back to where we had been the day after Christmas. He just was not drinking enough fluid. It is a common problem with chemo. I was so glad we had a nurse in the family because he did not want to be in the hospital any more. Four hours and two IV bags later, he was more comfortable.

I knew the hydration was not going to give him more time, but it would give him more comfort for the time he had left. His mind was even clearer. I knew that because he was crabby, which is a good sign—unless you are the one he is crabby at.

The kids were *not* a problem while they were here, but the added responsibility does take its toll. I was glad their mom and dad were back, but I had to admit it would be quiet and lonely without them here. I still had a lot of work to do before the end of the month though and needed time to focus on it.

Pastor Garry stopped by and talked with Jack for a few minutes and prayed for him. Jack told Pastor Garry he always felt better after he stopped by and prayed. Jack also told him he was welcome to stop any time and didn't need an invitation.

Jack asked me why I had been sleeping in my chair in the living room the past few nights. I told him I had a runny nose and sniffles and did not want to take a chance on making him sick. He said tonight I would be in the bed because he needed to feel me there with him so he could sleep better, and he would take the chance on getting sick.

After ten days with three kids, the house was empty. As we prepared for bed my thought was that we would either sleep well or not sleep at all, depending on whether the quiet was too loud. With the hydration Jack was more stable, more alert, and more comfortable. That made me more comfortable, and I am sure it is why we were able to get a good night's sleep, which we both needed desperately.

Wednesday, January 23, 2013—One Positive Thing

Today there was only one positive thing to post—well, no make that two—and neither had to do with Jack.

I was finally able to get some information corrected that would allow me to go forward with doing the company income tax and filing the 1099s. The downside was I found two small errors I needed to tell the owner about so he could have the accountant revise the return if he had already filed it. They were small, but they changed two account totals. I needed to finalize all the paperwork for the company so I could concentrate on other things. Having it hanging over my head was causing a lot of stress.

The second is that I was able to pick up a five-year handicap tag instead of one every six months. This was going to make it much easier than having to remember to get a doctor slip every six months.

That was all the good news. The rest wasn't good.

Again, Jack was not eating or drinking. Then his temperature spiked to 101.5. I was not sure what was going on. I called the doctor's office but did not get a return call before the end of the day. The nurse may not have been able to get an answer from the doctor before she left, but that didn't help me. I needed to get some answers, so I would have to try again in the morning.

When the visiting nurse came she said she didn't feel there was much more she could do, and she suggested calling in hospice. That was one of the things I wanted to discuss with the doctor's office. They would have to give the referral. I was hoping I could get some answers from his office on how to move forward.

I was so not looking forward to this. It was heart-wrenching to watch and not only have no control over it but be at a total loss as to what to do to make him more comfortable. Maybe that was why the tears were flowing—because there was just nothing else I could do, and that made me feel bad.

Thursday, January 24, 2013—The Decision

I called the doctor's office and put the wheels in motion for hospice. I explained to the doctor's office that Jack was not strong enough to endure any more treatment of any kind. His two nose dives had taken their toll on him and on me. I knew he could not go on like that, and neither could I. He had been shaking and freezing again with a blood pressure of 138/114 and pulse of 140. I finally got him warmed up by rotating warm blankets so he was not shaking. It took a couple of hours to get him settled down and comfortable. I also fixed him a cup of tea to warm him inside. He drank maybe two ounces.

The doctor gave the referral because if we were not going to continue treatment, there was nothing else they could do for him.

I understood that. I also understood this meant we were totally on our own. There would be no more treatment, no surgeries, no medications, no office visits, no hospital stays. He would be home from now on.

The hospice nurse called me and we set up a meeting for 10:00 A.M. on Friday. I asked Charlie and Dave to be here if they could. I notified all the kids so they knew what was going on—or at least as much as I could tell them, which wasn't much. If it was hard being here, it had to be harder in some ways to be so far away.

I paced the house most of the day, unable to concentrate on any one thing. I was second-guessing myself. Was I doing the right thing? Was I making a hasty decision? Could I handle all this? What should I do next? I really needed some answers. That whole day was a blur because I was so unsure of what I had done. I knew it needed to be done, but doing it was another matter. These decisions were not getting easier.

Friday, January 25, 2013—Getting Ready

I can't express the immense relief I felt having talked to hospice. The nurse was wonderful. I knew Jack's time was short, and he was ready to go. Calling them in was to find ways to make him comfortable and to let me know where to turn. They brought in so much equipment that day I felt like the house had turned into a hospital ward; in some ways it had. I was sure we had more equipment and supplies than we would ever use, but it helped to know they were available.

The nurse, whose name was Joette, was here for four hours. She was amazing and thorough. Suzanne was here also and told me later that she had worked at Henry Ford Hospice for a while, and while she was there, she had heard that Joette was the best nurse they had. She was thorough, compassionate, helpful, and friendly. They all were really, but she was considered the top one.

By the time she left, I was on information overload again, but I had a peace now knowing there were things I could do to make him comfortable and help with the pain. Charlie had not been able to come because of a new work assignment, but Dave was available while she was at the house. He didn't have any questions but just listened to what she had to say.

She asked Jack if he wanted an aide to assist with bathing. He told her he didn't want anyone coming out or helping him. He would do it himself, thank you. She said, "Well, Prince Charming, if you change your mind, let me know and we'll schedule someone." When I told her later what she said, she was mortified. She didn't remember saying that and said she had never said that to a patient. I thought it was funny and told her so. I explained to her that Jack was a very private and very independent person. For him to even consider having someone help him was unthinkable. She had picked up on that, but also must have sensed that he had a good sense of humor because her statement about Prince Charming was, as they say, "right on." Every time it came up after that, we would both laugh about it.

A few hours later Jack said maybe he did need an aide because he could not stand long enough to take a shower by himself. I gave him "the look" and then called Joette and told her of his change of mind about the aide. She said she would schedule it for Monday.

Before bedtime a hospital bed was brought in and assembled in the living room. We moved an end table into a bedroom, shifted the couch down, moved another end table, and set the bed on an angle so he could look out the front window and also be able to look at the TV. This was going to be his bedroom from now on, so it had to work for him. There was no privacy, but then, again, we didn't know how long he had or who would be coming over. It was the only place I could put him where he could be involved in things and not be confined to a small bedroom.

Oxygen, breathing treatment machine, and medications were delivered. I had one set of twin sheets so I took those off the bed the kids used and put them on the hospital bed. I would need to buy two more sets of sheets before long. I would need one to change for him and one to put on the bed for the kids. I would be rotating sheets quite a bit unless I got yet another set. I wasn't sure how long I would need them, so I decided to go slow and see what we would need before spending a lot of money. Jack was much more comfortable there than in our bed. It was much easier for me to help him get warm and work with him on the hospital bed rather than on his chair or in the bedroom.

It also helped to have him close to our pellet stove because it gave off a fair amount of heat, and that kept him comfortable.

I was exhausted and could not think straight by the end of the day, but I also had a peace about this, and even if it was over the next day, I could rest knowing I had done all I knew to do.

Charlie had called all his siblings and told them what was going on and that quite possibly their dad would not survive the weekend. I didn't know he was doing that until he told me later and said that Rob had decided to make the trip and would be in the next day, Saturday.

Saturday, January 26, 2013—Family

Jack had a lot of visitors this day. His stepson Jerry and Jerry's wife Lori were out. It was good to visit with them. Pastor Garry stopped by, talked for a few minutes, and prayed for him. Then my sister and brother-in-law stopped in and brought food, and Rob and family arrived. They were quietly talking in another room. Because Jack was now in a hospital bed in the living room, I told Rob and Tracy to use my room, and I would sleep on the couch. Two of the kids were going to stay at Charlie's and the other two were in the smaller bedroom.

Even as we were here facing sorrow and grief, our family was preparing to celebrate birthdays for Reina and Elisha. God never ceases to amaze me—in the midst of sorrow there is life and joy and hope. Celebrating the birthdays of two really unique individuals took some of the sting out of what we were going through, and it was a reminder that life goes on—and it does—for us here and for those who go before us.

As I sat there with family in the other room I was reminded that at the end, it's all about family. I feel for those who die alone, are neglected, or are forgotten, or who have destroyed relationships and have no one. It is a lonely place to be. This process was easier to bear because I was reminded again and again I was not alone. I not only had the Lord, I had family and friends.

Even as I was thinking of the process of dying, I was thinking of the process of living. Do we really understand the value of relationships? I had never set out to make memories; I just raised my kids like most people did—day to day. But they bring things up, and to them those are the important memories, because they were special. Sometimes those are some of the silliest moments. Who else would remember your goofiest or silliest stuff except your kids—and then remind you of it?

Someone had recently said to me—it is not "goodbye"; it is "until later." Heaven is rejoicing—not because Jack was dying but because he had made the commitment, and he will live with Him who is preparing a place!

Sunday, Jan 27, 2013—One Day at a Time

That's what it's been right along, one day at a time. Sometimes it was one hour at a time. The one thing I was thankful for was that Jack had not yet had the pain that so many with cancer experience. That could change, but in the early days he only had a headache and some pain in his left side. We were not sure what that the pain in the left side meant, and with hospice they would not do more tests—what would be the point? We did have liquid morphine, which I thought was much better than the Vicodin. It was easier on his stomach and worked quicker. The problem was that he didn't want the morphine, at least not at first.

He had always said he didn't want to be a vegetable and not know who he was and who everyone else was. So far God had honored that prayer. He was alert and pretty much knew what was going on around him most of the time. He did lose track of time, though, because he was sleeping so much and didn't always know what day it was. But then, neither did I. Every morning I would ask myself what day it was and what I had to do that day.

Sometimes things were actually funny. One night I was reclining in the chair next to the bed, and he was holding my hand. Rob walked by, and Jack said "Where is your mom?" Rob looked at him surprised and before I could say anything, he said, "She is right next to you and you are holding her hand." I was tempted to ask him just whose hand he thought he was holding—but realized he probably didn't know he was even holding my hand. Sometimes his cognitive skills weren't up to par.

He kept talking about his next session of chemo. That wasn't going to happen. For one thing, he was in hospice, so all treatment had ended. Also, physically there was no way he could handle it. He could barely make it to the bathroom and back—leaving the house was out of the question. Handling three days of chemo—I wouldn't even consider it.

We were in the middle of winter and kept hearing about storms and possible power outages. I was praying each time one was forecast that we wouldn't get the storm they were predicting. Losing power would be disastrous—I wasn't sure where we'd take him or how we'd get there. I knew there were others in other areas of the country with similar predicaments, and I felt for them, but I still didn't want it to happen to us.

Our first foster child, who became our sister-in-law when she married my baby brother, drove up from North Carolina to spend a few days with us. Depending on weather, we were expecting her the next day. I told her to stop somewhere if the weather got real bad. I didn't want to worry about her being on the road in a storm.

Rob had decided to stay over because of the weather and would head home the next day when the roads cleared up. While they were here, some of Charlie's high school buddies stopped in to say hi. They'd known Jack for a long time. These guys used to hang out at our house when the kids were growing up. It was so weird to see what used to be little boys now all over six feet tall. That's what happens when you don't see them for a while.

The guys stayed and talked and reminisced for a while. It was good to see them, and Jack did a pretty good job of staying alert and talking while they visited. I knew he needed visitors to keep his mind active and also because people wanted to see him and see how he was doing, but I needed to monitor the visits so he would not get worn out.

The nurse had suggested I put a sign on the back door with a note to call my cell when someone wanted to visit Jack. That way we would have notice, and I would have the opportunity to say "no" if he wasn't having a good day. I taped the note on the door the day after she visited. In addition to the note, I told his friends at the local restaurant if they wanted to visit to please give us some advance notice because there were days when he didn't feel up to company. Everyone I talked to was very understanding of this and always called ahead.

Monday, January 28, 2013—Busy Day and a Special Time

Today was supposed to have been a very quiet day with nothing going on. That changed when the hospice social worker called and then the aide.

First, the social worker came out and we went over information— again. She showed me some information on how to get veteran's assistance. We talked for over an hour. They also have some age-appropriate books for kids going through this kind of thing. I thought that would be helpful and was looking forward to seeing the books. She told me to remember that all the hospice services are available, and all I had to do was call. It was such a relief.

Then the aide came and gave him a nice warm sponge bath and changed him into clean, warm clothes. I know that helped. I was glad he agreed to that because with the rheumatoid arthritis I knew I could not move him around or do a good job of washing him. He was capable of moving himself at this point, but I didn't know how long that would last, and knew I could not handle it in the future, so better to get used to it right away. We set it up so when the aide came, everyone would leave the front of the house, and when I knew she was coming I could always give his friends a time that didn't interfere with the aide.

While all that was going on, Rob and his family and Charlie and his family were here, as well as my sister-in-law, so at times it was a little overwhelming for him. A long-time friend, Carol, stopped by. Since I had a houseful, she went to the store for a few things for me.

I had asked Pastor Garry to come out and give communion if that was okay with the church. He had said no problem, and so in the evening he stopped by and Jack and the rest of us were able to take communion together. There were fourteen of us in a circle around the bed in the living room. The kids were quiet during the whole time that we were listening to Pastor Garry read the Scripture about communion and during the taking of communion. What a special time! I was so glad Jack was able to do that at least once.

The previous Friday I would have said he only had a few days. The IV that Josette gave him on Tuesday actually improved and stabilized his condition. For how long, I did not know, but for now he was more responsive and alert. Also changing the meds seemed to have helped him to be more comfortable. He actually ate some ice cream Sunday night and had a piece of bacon in the morning. He complained that I hadn't offered him any chicken for dinner on Sunday. I wasn't sure he would even have eaten it, but he at least mentioned it.

Rob packed up and got ready to leave but found out the fog was so dense on the west side of the state that it was dangerous to drive, especially at night, so they decided to spend yet another night and leave in the morning.

Charlie left, but the kids stayed to spend the night. I had a doctor appointment scheduled for Tuesday and felt more comfortable leaving because Rica and my sister-in-law Bonnie would be at the house to keep an eye on Jack while I was gone.

Jack was coughing so much I could not sleep through the night. There were so many machines to learn how to use I got them confused and could not figure out how to run the machine that would help his breathing. I called the after-hours number, and the nurse walked me through the machine I was trying to use. I was so glad she helped me get it going.

Tuesday, January 29, 2013—Taking Care of Me

I gave Jack another breathing treatment and cleared his throat out so he would be comfortable while I was gone. I never thought something like this would consume your every waking moment. There was so much I had to do and learning all the machines was overwhelming.

While I was on the way to the doctor, the hospice nurse called. Since I had called in the previous night to ask about one of the machines and explained Jack's coughing problems, they called our assigned nurse, who wanted to come out and see what was going on.

I told her I was on the way to see my doctor, and she said she'd be out later in the day.

My appointment went well. I told the doctor about the stress, my RA, that I had been coughing up stuff and although I didn't feel sick, I felt I needed to keep on top of it. I was always at risk for anything that came along. Because the stuff I was coughing up wasn't clear, he prescribed an antibiotic to ward off anything that might be coming at me. He also said I was in great shape for someone with RA and the stress I've had. He ran a chest x-ray just to be sure, and there was no pneumonia or any other problem. That was all good news to me, and I needed to hear some good news about then.

On the way home I made a quick stop and had coffee with a friend and then stopped at the grocery store to get a few things. I forgot to get my prescription on my way home, so that would entail another trip the next day.

The nurse came and checked Jack over. She calmed his fears about one of the meds and told me to call anytime. It was such a relief to know I could call someone and either get answers or have someone come out to check on things. It took such a burden off my shoulders. The decision to call in hospice was the best decision I had made for all of us.

Bonnie said her sister was coming over with her five kids and asked if we could handle that. I told her as long as they were quiet. Two of Fran's kids gave Jack and me a massage. Mine was longer as my left side was knotted up, so they worked on that. Jack's was lighter and shorter because he was almost asleep. I felt so relaxed when they were done. We all went to bed early.

Wednesday, January 30, 2013—Things Go Bump in the Night

I would always try to go to sleep early because I never knew how much sleep I would get. Between Jack's coughing, restlessness, and other problems, it wasn't much on Tuesday night. I talked him into some pain and nausea medication and a breathing treatment and he finally slept for a while.

At midnight when I got up to get his meds, I stepped in water by the kitchen sink. I knew immediately that something happened under the sink because it had happened before. A year before Charlie fixed the pipes under the sink, so I wasn't sure exactly what it was, but I knew something had leaked. At midnight, I didn't care. I looked under the sink and no water was pouring out, so I knew it had to be a drain pipe, and that could wait. I went back to bed.

Our friend, Don Brundage, (bless him, Lord) came out and checked everything over. The connections had worked loose and allowed water to leak out, and since it was leaking and not pouring, it wasn't noticeable until the water ran out of the cupboard onto the floor. It's on cement, so we were okay there. The cupboard bottom was pretty well rotted though, and I knew it would have to be replaced at some point. Right at that moment, though, it was not a priority.

For this day I had errands to run, and I decided to get gas while it was somewhat warm. I decided it was better to fill the tank at 50 degrees than at 24 degrees. I always felt better if I had a full tank or at least a half just in case there was an emergency at night. I did not want to be caught on empty during this time.

I knew the aide was coming out to give him a bath, so I had to go find clothes and supplies. I decided I would set out three changes on the top of the dresser so I would only have to find clothes once a week. That action saved me much time and stress. All I had to do was go pick up the pile and set it out at bath time.

My sister-in-law Bonnie cleaned both my bathrooms. That was such a time saver for me. I just did not have time for normal cleaning, and it was helpful to have things like this taken care of so I didn't even have to put it on my to-do list. I did have some paperwork in the office to do though, and that was something I could not pass on to someone else.

It was another busy day, and I was exhausted again when I fell into bed that night.

Thursday, January 31, 2013—Two Patients

Bonnie had told me Wednesday night that she wanted to get an early start driving home because we heard a snowstorm was moving in, but she overslept in the morning and left later than she planned.

I was watching the weather and had heard of a serious accident on I-75 where she would be driving. I called her, and she had not left the area yet. I told her to wait a little while for things to get better and then heard it would be hours before the freeway was open. I called her back and gave her a different route around the accident site. Several hours later she called and told me she was past the area and into Ohio. I was relieved. Then she called later and said she was stopping in Kentucky. I was glad to hear she was doing okay, so I could then relax.

I had two patients this day. Rica fell on the ice while playing outside and split her knee open. When she came in the house her jeans were bloody, and she was shaky. I made her sit down and did some first aid on the knee. It looked like it needed at least one stitch, but I could not get her to the doctor, so I told Charlie about it and asked if he wanted to take her in. He was going to come out and get the kids and see how bad it was, but Josiah was throwing up, so he had to go straight home. Obviously, he could not bring Josiah to the house.

We then decided it made sense to keep them with me for the night. He could not handle Josiah and Rica's injury at the same time. I knew Josette would be off the next day, so she could take Rica to the doctor if she thought it was necessary. The cut was right on the knee and split open—only about an inch long but deep enough I thought for a stitch to close it. I had first aid supplies, so I cleaned it and bandaged it and wrapped her knee in an ace bandage to keep it still. I propped her and her knee on the couch. My two patients were next to each other.

It was a good thing Jack had a decent day. I don't know what I would have done if he had had a bad day. He was not coughing as much as he had been.

While I was in the back of the house in the office, Elisha came in and said he could not find Papa and that he wasn't in his "doctor bed," or in his bedroom or in the bathroom. Elisha was upset that he could not find his Papa. I knew Jack was in the house somewhere, so I looked around. I knew he was in the back bathroom because the door was closed, and I could see light under the door.

I showed Elisha where he was and told him to knock on the door and call Papa. He wouldn't, so I did, and when Jack answered,

I told him Elisha had been looking for him. I told Elisha that Papa would be out in a minute, and he could go wait for him in the living room, but he would not go away from the bathroom. He stayed in the doorway of the room across from the bathroom until Jack came out and then followed him back into the living room until he got back in his "doctor bed." He then curled up in the chair next to Papa and stayed there for a half hour just looking at Jack. I have no idea what was going on in his mind, but it was clear he was not going to let Papa out of his sight for a while.

We had several visitors off and on during the day. Pastor Garry stopped by with one of the men from church also named Gary. He told Jack he got two Garys for the price of one. Stan Czaplicka, another man from church, stopped by, and they talked for a while. Stan had an alternative cancer treatment called Cantron that Jack said he was interested in. He never did follow through with it though. Mark, a friend who also was a truck driver, stopped by for a few minutes. Jack asked him if he would take his van trailer to get it weighed so we could title it in Michigan and try to sell it.

Friday, February 1, 2013—A Quiet Day

Today was a relatively quiet day. Yesterday we had four visitors—today we had one.

My niece, Suzanne, came out again to help. She brought some food and helped Reina with schoolwork then played trains with the kids (Elisha mostly).

Jack's cough was better today. He was able to sleep much of the day without constantly waking up coughing and choking. I hoped he could do the same at night. It woke me up whenever he did that because it was scary. Since I slept in the chair next to the bed I could feel him getting restless, and his coughing would startle me awake.

Jack wanted some cookies, so I went to the store and got him some chocolate chip ones and slushies for the kids. He fell asleep while I was gone. When I came back with the cookies, I gave the kids each one with a slushie. Elisha sat in the chair next to Papa, waiting for him to wake up so he could have a snack with him. He just sat there staring at Jack until he finally opened his eyes. Then they had their snack together. Jack ate one of the cookies and drank some coffee. That was the first food he had eaten since Tuesday. He would say he was hungry, but nothing tasted good, and no matter what I suggested, he didn't want it.

When I weighed him on January 26th, he was 138 lbs. I was almost afraid to weigh him again. I was sure he was under 135 by this time as he was so thin his bones stuck out.

My other patient—Rica's knee was stiff and sore. It still looked like it should have a stitch in it. She was on the couch most of the day with her leg propped up, doing her schoolwork.

Charlie came out after work. He checked Rica's knee then worked in the office. After they left, we settled in for the night.

Saturday, February 2, 2013—Getting Things Done

Since the weather was bad today I opted to stay home. I didn't have anywhere to go anyway but plenty to do at home. I did most of the laundry and cleaned out one room. I finally finished the 2012 filing and started folders for 2013. I usually had the new year's folders done early in January, but that had not happened this year. I was so far behind on everything I thought I would never get caught up. I was not looking forward to my next project—the tedious job of gathering income tax information.

Jack complained all day of nausea. He would not take any pain meds but Vicodin, and I was sure that was what was making him sick. He argued the point, but that med on an empty stomach was horrible, and he only had one cookie yesterday and some coffee. That was all he had eaten for the past seven days. He did not like the morphine, but it was easier on his stomach, and he did at least eat something when on it.

Friday night, or rather early Saturday morning, I was up from 2:30 A.M. till about 4:00 A.M. when I finally moved from the chair to the couch so I could stretch out. Jack didn't know I moved and panicked when he got up and I wasn't in the chair. He thought I had left the house and left him alone. I told him I would not leave unless I told him I was going somewhere and wouldn't leave unless Dave or someone was going to be here with him. I was beginning to realize how dependent he was becoming on me and my presence, even when I wasn't helping him with something.

In the afternoon I found a leak under the back bathroom sink. I was not sure how bad it was. I saw water in the clothes basket under the sink but could not find where it was coming from. Since nothing was pouring out I decided it could wait until someone could check it out. Some things just weren't worth getting upset about. This would entail another call to Don. I hoped I would not ruin a good friendship with all our problems. Neither Dave nor Charlie had the time or the expertise to handle plumbing problems like this. I knew both toilets would need replacing too because we had issues with both of them, but now was not the time—unless they too sprung a leak, and I was praying that would not happen.

Sunday, February 3, 2013—Worship, Lunch, Rest

The theme at church for February was worship. What does it mean to you? We all worship something—my prayer is that you worship the right thing—the only true God. Our pastor Mick did an awesome job, as usual. With all that was going on in my life, it was good to put things in perspective, and this series helped with that. I felt such peace when I was able to connect with people and hear the messages at church. I told a friend I came for the hugs, not the message, but I really did go for both.

Just as church was starting, Jerry called to see if he could visit. I told him to go ahead, that I wasn't home but he was welcome to visit. I told him could not guarantee Jack would stay awake, but he was okay with that. Just as church was ending, Dave sent me a text and told me Jerry and Jack were visiting, Jack was drinking coffee and all was fine. He said if I wanted a break, now was the time to take it. Since I had just received an offer to lunch, I agreed to the much-needed break.

After lunch with Charlie's family and his in-laws I decided to do some shopping. I found a much-delayed birthday gift for Elisha. I was sure Papa would be his favorite person the next day when he would give Elisha the Thomas the Train set.

I also picked up a couple of bird feeders and some seed. Since Jack faced the front window and there is a huge evergreen in the middle of the yard, I thought the kids and I would hang a couple of feeders and he could watch the birds eat or watch the squirrels chase the birds away and try to eat their food.

When I got home Jack said he had a craving for Chinese fried shrimp. We used to get it years ago in Romeo, but that restaurant had been closed for years. He said there was one in Richmond and did I mind going out again, especially since he might not eat it. I told him I'd go anywhere to get something if he would try to eat. I left at the same time Jerry was leaving. As I started out, he put money in my hand and said he wanted to buy the food for Jack because whenever he came out, Jack would not eat, so he was happy to see him wanting something.

Jack ate two pieces of shrimp and two tablespoons of rice and drank most of a cup of tea. That was the most he had eaten in ten days. I hoped it would not make him sick after not eating for so long.

He was trying to watch the Super Bowl but kept drifting off. It was not my favorite thing to watch, so I finished some laundry and read for a while. Weekends were usually quiet, and I needed the break, so when I could, I would read or write or try to get to sleep early. It was good to have the down times because the weeks were usually pretty hectic.

Monday, February 4, 2013 — Trying To Eat Again

The nurse and the aide came today. When the aide helped with his bath, Jack had her shave most of his beard off because it was getting thinner and falling in his food like his hair had done. I was surprised it took so long to start to fall out. It had been three weeks since he had done the chemo, and I had thought it would fall out sooner.

Today he had another taste for something different. This time it was fried chicken livers and fried potatoes. I had not made that dish in years. But, if he was willing to eat, I was willing to fix it. I fried some up and gave him that with fried potatoes and a piece of French bread. He ate some of the potatoes, about half a slice of bread, and a piece or two of the chicken livers. He said he was just nauseated enough to not be able to eat even though he was hungry.

His coughing had been getting better. It didn't keep me up all night any more. I knew that could change, but I would take what I could get sleep-wise.

He asked if we were going to the hospital tomorrow to start the second round of chemo. I told him it had been postponed indefinitely because he was too weak to do it right now. He did not argue. I did not tell him that I had canceled it and we would not be doing it any more. There was just no point in upsetting him, and I knew if he tried another round, he would not make it through.

Tonight, for the first time in at least two weeks, he turned on the news. Last night he watched part of the game and kept drifting off. He could not concentrate long enough to watch anything. Watching the news didn't last long either, and again we went to bed early.

Tuesday, February 5, 2013—Don't Get Excited

When I emailed everyone I told them not to get excited when I let them know Jack was sitting in his chair today. He got out of bed and sat in the chair next to the bed. He sat down because he was too tired to make it to the bathroom. He was not coming *from* the bathroom but going *to* the bathroom! He was getting weaker by the day. He had been eating some, but his meals were not much more than a few bites.

Today he was only doing slightly better than he had been. At this point we were three weeks from the chemo he already had, so probably some of the toxins were out of his system. The problem was that since he was too weak to do any more chemo, the cancer would now be able to grow and spread more rapidly. Some things were good, but ultimately it meant things would begin to deteriorate—we just were not sure how quickly it would happen.

I would have liked to have been more positive, but I couldn't live in a fantasy world—I knew what we were facing, and I had to prepare myself for it—whether it was one week or one month. I just knew he would never survive any more chemo treatments—he was just too weak. I felt bad telling friends and family all that, but I had to be honest with what was going on as many were out of state and did not see him on a daily basis. I did not want to give them false hope.

I took a photo of him sitting in his chair and sent it by text to the kids and emailed it to his sister. I knew it would be a shock to them, but I felt that way they could see how frail he had become and better prepare themselves. In that photo he had no hair and his beard was very thin. He had it shaved but not completely off. He looked the same, but different. I'm not sure how much sense that made, but it was hard to explain the difference in him.

Wednesday, February 6, 2013 — Chicken Drumsticks

Jack said he did not have a good night on Tuesday. In the morning he said he felt awful — like he smoked a pack of cigarettes all at once. I'm not sure what that meant because he had smoked for years and never complained. He did not feel good all day.

He did, however, eat part of a chicken drumstick (his favorite part), some corn, potatoes, and bread. He seemed to be eating better the further we got from the chemo. He still did not have much appetite, and things didn't taste right, but at least he was trying to eat something. I was always trying to find things he liked.

I bought him a paper every day because he liked to read it. It took him a long time to go through it, and there wasn't much there. He said his eyes got tired quickly, and he could not read much at a time.

We were expecting yet another storm, and I was praying again that we would not lose electricity. I was not sure what I would do if we did because I didn't know how I would move him in the middle of a snow storm. It was hard enough to move just me.

We had gotten in sort of a routine by this time, but as always, some days he felt okay and some days he felt horrible. It was a routine, yet I was always prepared for things to change at a moment's notice. It's hard to relax when life is like that. You never quite know what might happen, so you could never let your guard down.

Thursday, February 7, 2013 — Storm Prep

Suzanne was out again to help with the kids' schoolwork, which gave me an opportunity to visit Lori, who was having surgery today.

We were relieved when we heard that the surgery went well. I then had lunch with Jerry and his son Jake at the hospital.

While I was out, I was able to get another set of sheets for the "doctor bed." I also got a few things from the store and filled the gas tank. I always felt better when the gas tank was full.

I fixed chicken livers again, and this time made it with hash browns. Jack had eaten some peaches earlier and ate some of the food I fixed. He was still only eating a few bites, but a few bites was better than the ten days he had gone without food.

I was watching the dark gray clouds move in and praying any storm would go around us. I was sure when I looked out in the morning I would see all white! I was praying it would just be snow and not a big storm.

Friday, February 8, 2013—A Picnic in February

We did not lose electricity in the storm, and I was very thankful. We do have a generator, but it is in the barn, and we had not thought to bring it up to the porch. I wasn't even sure if it was working this year. We had never checked it out, and that was usually done in the fall because many times we would lose electricity in winter storms. Talk about not thinking straight.

Since it was too windy and cold to be outside, we decided to have a picnic inside. How do you do that? I fixed hot dogs, and Dave had gotten some red-skinned potato salad. We didn't have chips, but I did have some tater tots to go with it for the kids. Jack ate most of a hot dog and some of the potato salad. The amount he was eating was improving each day. At this point I was considering a successful day one in which he ate even a small amount.

In the evening Charlie and I took the kids to McDonalds since we had some coupons. They enjoyed an hour in the play area. It was a good break for them. On the way home I picked up a baked potato with bacon and cheese from Wendy's for Jack. He ate about half of it. The two partial meals today were a big step forward in the food department.

I also did some more of the tedious work getting ready for filing our taxes. It was one of my least favorite duties, so I always put it off, but it needed to get done, so I kept picking away at it. I knew once I got done, I would be glad it was finished, so I needed to push myself to do it. It was harder this year because it was hard for me to concentrate on anything, and I would get so many interruptions.

I told Charlie tonight that sometimes his dad had to speak so I would know it was him. He had changed so much I wouldn't know it was him if he didn't talk. That is so sad—but it's what cancer does to a person. He was so thin, and without his hair and beard he looked different—plus his face was so sunken.

Saturday, February 9, 2013—Chicken Soup and Apple Pie

Today was a busy day for me. I spent the morning putting the information together to get our taxes done. I always dreaded this time of year, but I knew I had to keep plugging away at it. Jack slept most of the morning, so I worked in the office getting the information together. I would go check on him every so often to see if he was awake or if he needed anything.

Early in the afternoon my sister and her husband came out. Bernice folded clothes and also made chicken soup—which was nice of her since she is a vegetarian. Pierre straightened up the pantry and put some things in the attic for me. It was so good to get some of the clutter cleared up.

My sister-in-law Connie and her husband Dave came out and brought an apple pie. We had an all-American dinner. Jack ate some of the soup and a small piece of pie with a cup of coffee. After all that, Luz and George stopped by with tomorrow's lunch, so we had enough food to get us through the weekend.

It was beginning to feel like our lives revolved around food. In a way, it did. Since there was nothing else Jack could do, eating was a big part of our day. I needed to get him to eat as much as possible even if it was small meals several times a day. I was praying for a break in the weather because getting him outside was also important. He needed a change of scenery and needed to do something to help with the boredom and cabin fever.

Sunday, February 10, 2013—Trading Places

Today I traded places with Jack's stepson Jerry. Jack was married to Jerry's mom when Jerry was in his very early teens. They stayed connected through the years, and when Jack and I got married, we stayed connected with them. We didn't always get together, but we did at least exchange Christmas cards. You know how it goes; you get busy

Well, anyway, Jerry's wife Lori had some serious surgery the previous week and was still in the hospital. Today Jerry called and said he would come visit Jack if I wanted to go visit Lori. That seemed like a good idea, so after church I went to the hospital to see her. Their daughter, Brittany, who is a year older than our Brittany, was there too, so we had a good visit for a couple of hours.

I was getting ready to leave when Brittany said Jerry called her and said he would come see Lori when I got home. He didn't want to leave Jack alone, and Dave had gone out to run errands. I was pleased that he was so thoughtful in not wanting to leave Jack alone.

When I got home, Jack said he was going to tie a string on me because every time I left the house, I didn't come back for hours. That was so true, but it was because I always had so many errands to take care of. I didn't realize he missed me when I was gone. I always made it a point to let him know when I would be gone and, if possible, how long it might be. I thought it would make him feel more comfortable in my absence if he knew where I was and approximately when I would return.

Jerry had tried to get Jack to eat, but he said he wasn't hungry. He kept saying maybe he'd eat if we could go to Cracker Barrel. When I got home and they told me what he said, I told him we could make a Cracker Barrel run in the morning if he wanted to. He perked up and asked how we would do that. I said we'd figure it out. If he wanted to go, I'd find a way to get him there.

He said it was a long way to go if he could only eat a few bites. I told him it was no problem because for one thing, his sister had sent some money, and I was sure she would be pleased if we used it for something special like this; also, whatever he didn't eat, there would be five vultures that could finish it off (that was counting Charlie, three kids and me).

I did talk him into some more chicken soup and one bite of some of the ham George had brought over the day before. I ate the turkey, potatoes, and veggies that he had also brought.

Monday, February 11, 2013—Journey through the Valley of the Shadow

We were disappointed when Jack said he was just too weak and didn't feel good enough to go to Cracker Barrel. You know if he turned that down, he was not feeling well at all. I said I would keep the gift certificate I had bought on hand, and if he indicated he was up to a trip—off we would go! The thing about those days was there were good days and there were bad days, and there was never any indication as to which it was going to be until that morning.

I learned to accept what the day brought and would not get stressed about it. The goal was to keep him comfortable and try to find things that would lift his spirits.

Early this morning about 4:30 A.M. he looked over at me as I was sitting in the chair and said, "You don't sleep much, do you?" I said, "No, not a lot." I had actually been up about an hour at that time and was just getting ready to put the foot rest up and curl up again and try to sleep. Sometimes I would just watch him sleep and could not believe it had only been two and a half months since our lives had changed; it was hard to see how much he had changed. I had to quit thinking about it because going down that road would only make me sad. I knew I could not change what happened and what was going to happen. Thinking about it only depressed me. It was better to focus on what we *could* do.

Tuesday, February 12, 2013—Ice Cream Is the Answer and a Chaplain's Visit

I was two weeks overdue to get a blood test my doctor had ordered. I decided to do it today because I also wanted to stop by a funeral home to see a dear saint who had gone home to be with the

Lord and to hug her daughters. When I got ready to go, I asked Jack if he wanted anything. He said, "How about that Cold Stone Ice Cream we got that one day while we were out." I knew just what he was talking about. He liked the salty caramel flavor.

He asked if I'd feel bad if he didn't eat it after I took the time to go get it. I told him not to worry; what he didn't eat, I would. I got the small size and never even got a bite. I was so glad he ate it all. It was good to see his appetite improving.

The chaplain from hospice had called four times and tried to visit, and each time something came up, so when he called again today, I asked him to come later so I could run errands. He came about 3:00 P.M. He told me he was a Catholic priest with hospice; his name was Chaplain Luke.

We had a great conversation. I had an opportunity to share my faith with him and told him I knew God was going to be with me every step of our journey. At the end of our conversation Jack actually woke up, and he told Jack, "Your wife could be a preacher! She taught me some things today and helped me with my own faith." I was shocked. Me? Help a priest with his faith? Only God!

I doubt it was anything spectacular I said. I only shared how I felt about the Lord and how I felt He had given me comfort right from the start by letting me know He would be with me every step of this journey. I also told him I had two great pastors who had come alongside us. And I told him about all the family and friends who were continually praying for us and what a great support team we had. I also told him Jack had made a commitment to let Christ be his Lord and that he was ready for heaven. He prayed for us and left. I felt such comfort when people prayed for us.

Wednesday, February 13, 2013—Decisions and a Great Outing

The nurse and an aide were both out today. Before they came, Jack said he wanted to try Cracker Barrel. I told him the nurse and the aide should be here by noon and we could go soon after.

The aide was here first to help with his bath. This was a new one as the other gal was out ill. She was from Kentucky, so guess what they talked about? She knew Tennessee, and he knew Kentucky, so it was like old home week for them.

Then the nurse came, and we had a long and productive talk. I told her I suspected either the brain tumors were growing or there was edema (swelling) again. His left eye had seemed to droop, his balance was off, and his left hand was curling up again. She agreed with me that might be the issue. Jack had said no steroids. However, she convinced him to at least try them again to see if they helped with the symptoms and also the headaches.

They also talked about the chemo, and he made the decision (which I thought he would) to not try any more. He was now down to 132, for a total weight loss of 36 pounds since November. We were hoping the steroids would help get his appetite back. He felt, and so did we, that he would not survive another session of chemo. It took too much out of him, and he didn't have anything left to give.

He told her the doctor had told him there was no cure and he would only be buying some time. If what he had to go through to get the extra time was so bad it wasn't worth it, he could stop at any time. That was his decision today.

She talked about things to make him comfortable, the steroids being one of them. It would not shrink the tumors; it would only take the swelling down, which would relieve some symptoms. At this stage, it was all about making him comfortable. He said if he could eat enough to get strength enough to go outside he would be happy. That became our new goal.

Before she even left, he had his shirt on and was looking for his jeans. By the time he brushed his teeth though, he wasn't sure he had the energy to go. I told him to make it to the truck and we would do a carry out at Cracker Barrel.

That is just what we did. We sat in the pickup in the parking lot at Cracker Barrel and ate a late breakfast. He enjoyed the Sunrise Sampler—or at least half of it. I was so glad he was able to go. I called Charlie to let him know what we were doing. He drove over and met us there and ate and talked for nearly an hour. Josette was off and had the kids for the day. They were tied up with a project, so they did not make it to Cracker Barrel. The kids were very disappointed as they love it there too.

Mentally, it was good for him to get out, and the weather was perfect. We had both the sun and the Son. Can it get any better than that? On the way home, we had to make a side trip to pick up the prescription for him so we could start it in the morning. It had been a long day for him, and as soon as we got home, he fell asleep. It was all I could do to get him undressed before he fell (almost literally) onto the bed.

Thursday, February 14, 2013 — Happy Valentine's Day

I had picked up the new medication the previous night but it was too late to start with it so I waited till this morning. I mixed one pill with 1 ml water and using a syringe, he put it in his mouth along his cheek. Within two hours he was wanting to eat. Before noon he ate two bowls of corn flakes and a banana. I'd say the steroids worked for appetite! Also, his eye seemed less droopy, and he walked to the back room where the office is without using his cane. He felt so much better being able to do things for himself. The downside to the steroids is that he said they gave him such a craving for nicotine. He had been down to one cigarette a day and was now looking for the ones I had put away.

A friend came over, and they talked for quite a while. He told Harvey that he would not do more chemo. He knows the steroids will help with the swelling but not the tumor, so he isn't expecting to get more time but just better time for however long he has.

I had asked him earlier if he had had any headaches today, and he said that he had not. I was sure it was helping with that too. I was hoping he could sleep better at night if he didn't have so much pain. For tonight I made beef stew, and he kept asking when it would be ready. While he didn't eat like he would have at one time, he did do better than he had been doing for the past couple of weeks.

I was sure he would want to make another Cracker Barrel run, and that was okay with me. I didn't know how long this would last even with the steroids, but I would take what days I could get.

He had to stay in hospice because he was still terminal and had decided not to take any more treatment. There would not be any more tests run, which probably weren't necessary anyway since we weren't doing any more chemo. It left us not knowing how far the tumors had grown or if they had spread, but as he said, what did it matter? We knew he didn't have a long time, and we were just going to make the best of it.

Friday, February 15, 2013 — Visitors

Today Jack felt good enough to make a trip to the restaurant in town. We were going to wait until Saturday but he decided he felt okay today. Since we didn't know how he would feel on Saturday, we decided it was better to go when he felt up to it. Several people there stopped him and said they were glad to see him out and about. A friend who was there bought our breakfast.

Our friend Don stopped by after we got home because I had asked him to. There was a project Jack had started and had not been able to continue when he got sick. He had been assembling some truck accessories and needed to take them across the state to a dealer. I felt Don would be able to help him take care of it. Now that Jack was clearer mentally from the steroids, he wanted to take care of this project.

If we could work it out, they would make the short trip the next week to handle it. I knew it would do him good to be able to do something and feel he was productive.

We were a day late, but I had gotten some things for the kids to have their Valentine's Day party. We tried to celebrate the same holidays that public schools did so they would not feel left out. We had cards, candy, cupcakes, plates, and cups all decorated for Valentine's Day. I got them small metal buckets with tattoos and pencils. As I said before, we were trying to keep things as normal as possible.

Saturday, February 16, 2013 — Quiet Day and Visitors

Today was a quiet day, and I needed it. Jack wanted to go out again. He said whenever he feels up to it he would like to go out— either to breakfast or to run errands with me. It was good that he wanted to go somewhere. I knew he was bored and depressed—I would be, too.

When we got back, I vacuumed the living room and part of the kitchen. My house had taken a beating for the past two months, and I could not get caught up on the cleaning. I would use opportunities like this to quickly do something in the room he was in and then work in another room when he fell asleep. While he slept, I worked in two rooms in the back of the house. Little by little I was getting things cleaned and organized. Once the rooms were cleaned, I got the filing caught up. For once, I was up to date.

When Jack woke up, I finished vacuuming and swept out the back hall. The house needed dusting, but at least the vacuuming was done, and the laundry was caught up. Getting that accomplished made me feel better. I even had time to sit down and read a book for a little while. It had been a long time since I had been able to do that.

In the morning while I was cleaning, I had prayed that we would have someone visit that would encourage us spiritually. A few minutes later I got a text from Pastor Garry asking if they could stop by this evening. It was always good to have them come over. I told him that his message was an answer to prayer!

He and Martha were later than they had planned, and because it had been a full day, Jack had fallen asleep, and he slept the whole time they were at the house. I had a chance to talk with them though, and, as always, they lifted me up spiritually. Martha prayed for Jack, me, and the family. I tried not to keep them too late, but it was so good to sit and talk.

Sunday, February 17, 2013 — Visitors and Errands

Jack had two visitors today, so I took advantage of the company and ran some errands after church. I shopped for groceries and was set for the week. Sundays had become my shopping and fill the vehicle with gas day. It was the one day I could get away and run errands because usually someone would come out to visit with Jack.

On this day, one of his visitors took him out to breakfast. I was glad he was able to get out again because he had been homebound for so long. I didn't know how long it would, last but I had already decided I would always take advantage of it.

While I was away from the house, I had a call from a man who said he was interested in buying the semi. The man who had contacted us at Christmas had never called back and never came over to see it. This man said he would come out on Monday and talk to Jack about it. That was two people who had expressed an interest in the past week. I was praying that one of them would get serious and make an offer he would accept. I really wanted to have that burden lifted.

After I returned and everyone had left, I worked on more stuff that needed to be categorized and put away today. It helped to get the clutter in the house taken care of. That really drove me crazy, and it had been accumulating for quite a while. I needed to have things where I could get to them quickly, and I needed to not have things lying around that I wasn't using. Simplifying things at this point was critical because I needed to have little to no extra stress. As much as I cleaned and organized and straightened, it seemed there was always more. I really have no idea where it all came from. I only knew it was there, and at least once a month I felt overwhelmed by what had accumulated.

I was also behind on some curriculum that Rica needed to get started on. I had to get it typed and set up so she could continue her work. It was another thing I could check off, and I needed to keep getting things checked off so I could take care of urgent stuff whenever it came up again. I had to remind myself it was one step at a time.

Monday, February 18, 2013—Selling Stuff—We Hope and Pray

Today brought some news that I hoped was good. The man that had called me on Sunday came out with his brother-in-law to see Jack and make an offer on the KW and Jack's van trailer as a package. I was praying that they would meet on a price that they were all comfortable with. They talked for a while and then said they'd talk it over and get back with him. We really needed these two things taken care of, and sooner was better than later.

We had set it up for Wednesday for Don, Charlie, and Jack to take some accessories across the state to a dealer Jack had sold some through before. He was looking forward to the trip and said he would like to be doing something constructive. I didn't know if it was the steroids, which he only took twice and again said no more, the idea of being able to accomplish something, or a last hurrah, but he seemed to be eating better and mentally processing stuff better. He was always exhausted by late afternoon though from any activity during the day.

The steroids made him jittery, and he wanted to quit them. The problem was still that he had the craving to smoke. I was hoping that when he quit the steroids he would quit smoking also, but he never did.

Tuesday, February 19, 2013—The Weather Is the Only News Today

Today was windy and cold. That was about all I had to write about. Things had settled into a sort of routine; not that life was routine at this time, but as close as it could get. Jack ate two pieces of bacon and a biscuit this morning. It seems his appetite was up and down, like everything else that was going on.

The cold, the snow, and the clouds all worked to make him tired and a little depressed. He was looking forward to the trip across the state the next day but was a little apprehensive about it. He hoped he didn't get too worn out making the trip.

I told him we would bundle him up, send his meds, and pray for a smooth trip. So far his energy level seemed to be up from what it was a few weeks ago, but that wasn't saying much. I could never figure out why things either went really well or really fell apart. He had only taken the steroids on Saturday and Sunday, and I wasn't sure how long they would be effective. I didn't think it would be long before we'd see some deterioration again.

Since I didn't have to totally focus on what was going on with him right at the moment, I had been able to get some things done around the house that really helped me to feel better. I know I've said that before, but it was important for me to keep on top of so many things, and when they got out of control, it was extra stress. I gave the tax information to Dave, who does our taxes, and was hoping I had everything in order this year. I really did not want to have to do any more digging for information.

For tonight, I was taking Rica to youth group and maybe shopping with the other two somewhere near there. They were all coming back with me for the night so the guys could get an early start in the morning. It was too costly to drive back and forth, so staying in the area made more sense. By the time we got back home it was after 9:00 P.M. and time for bed. Since they were already at the house, Charlie could come out early and not have to take time to get anyone ready except for himself.

Wednesday, February 20, 2013—Road Trip

I didn't go on the trip with them, but I heard it was a good trip. Jack didn't feel well when he got up, but he was determined to go. He said when he got home, he was wiped out from going but was glad he had the chance to get out and do something. That something was to recline in Don's van on the trip across the state. Don's back seat folded out into a bed, which was what Jack needed for that long of a trip.

They went over by Grand Rapids to take care of some truck accessories Jack had been trying to sell. It was one thing he was worried about getting completed. Now he felt better about it and said mentally it was good to get out and do something constructive.

They ate well, from what I heard. They stopped at Cracker Barrel for breakfast and again for dinner. I had them bring back a meat loaf dinner when they came home. It was good, and the best part was I didn't have to cook it.

I didn't know if Jack realized it, or if he was just trying not to face it, but his left side was still a problem, and since he would not take the steroids, I could see it was deteriorating again. He would stumble with his left foot, and by late in the day his left eye was drooping again. Without the steroids to take the edema out of his brain, I knew the symptoms would return. I didn't know how quickly or how severely they would return, but I could see it beginning.

While they were gone, the kids and I got a lot of cleaning and straightening done. It was good to have things caught up. I knew I would not have the kids until Monday so the next four days I would probably rest, catch up on paperwork, maybe read some, work on some more paperwork, clean, and maybe get the paperwork finished and in order. It just never seemed to end, and I had to stay on top of it, or it got out of control in a hurry.

I made a phone call today and found out the last piece of something I had started in December finally got cleared up. I was so glad! One more thing to check off and be done with. For now, it was time to relax, something I didn't get to do too often.

Thursday, February 21, 2013 — More Snow?

I was ready for this winter to be over. It was hard to get Jack out of the house when it was so cold. With no hair, even with a hat he would get cold pretty fast. We were hearing about yet another snow storm for the weekend. I was getting so tired of winter. I just wanted a nice day so I would not have to deal with the snow, cold, and dreariness.

He wanted to get out, and since we never knew when we could go because of the weather and his energy level, we took advantage of no kids and went uptown this morning to eat. His friend Mark came in, and since they were going to be talking for a while, I went home. He stayed a while talking to Mark, so he had the morning away from the house, which was good. Between that and yesterday, he was ready to sleep when he got home. Just about that time the nurse came to check on him — just like in the hospital, eh? She did call ahead, though, so I knew she was coming.

I was able to get away today, too. I met Luz and Suzanne for a late lunch. It was late because the nurse had come later than expected, but we still had a good time. Both of them had evening appointments, so we didn't have much time to sit around and talk. I was hoping for another time to do that as I did need the breaks. Luz sent bean soup for dinner, so I didn't have to worry about cooking today either.

Another friend called and wanted to pick Jack up Saturday morning and get him out of the house. I was all for that. He needed the time away, and mentally it was good for him to be doing something.

Friday, February 22, 2013—Snow Day

Well, they didn't close the schools because of the weather, but we had a snow day. Most of the morning we watched the snowflakes fall and decided it was a good day to stay in.

Just about the time I thought I could say all was going well, we would have a dip in the road. Today Jack said maybe the trip caught up with him as he was not feeling well. He ate two pieces of bacon and half a biscuit for breakfast and cornflakes with a banana for dinner. While he was at least eating, it was a drop from what he had been doing for the past week or so. It was a reminder to me that with cancer, you can never be certain of what a new day would hold.

Mentally, he was still alert. I noticed, though, that sometimes I would answer a question he had asked only to have him ask it again later in the day. They did say short-term memory would be a problem from the radiation, or it could have been caused by the tumors in the brain; I never knew for sure.

I was looking over some early journal pages and realized it was ninety days ago today (Thanksgiving Day) that Charlie first had an indication that something was wrong with his dad. So much had changed in our lives in those ninety days! But through it all, God had been so faithful and had, as Scripture says, been a light to my path.

I was not looking forward to the next ninety days because I was sure there would be even more changes in my life, and these particular changes that I had already been through had not been easy. But just knowing I had a support system, even though I could not physically see everyone, was comforting.

Saturday, February 23, 2013—Team Penning—What's That?

Jack said today he felt horrible. I was not sure what that entailed. I knew he was not eating much again. He said he was weak, but again that was from not eating much. It was a vicious circle. Even though he felt bad, he was determined to get out of the house. Harvey picked him up to go to breakfast. He struggled to get ready and almost didn't go, but his desire to get out of the house outweighed how miserable he felt. I knew he really wasn't feeling well when he brought more than half of his breakfast home because he could not eat it all.

I asked if he was okay with my going out with Carol in the evening to see her brother Greg ride his horse in an event called "team penning." Dave would be home, and he was okay with my going out because I would not be far away.

Team penning is where two people on horses work to get a calf penned into an area that is boxed in three sides by fences or gates. It was quite a treat. Carol had been telling me about it because her brother Greg rode in the event. I had been trying to go see it but never had a chance to get away.

Greg did very well in the competition. There were several teams, and sometimes the team members switched so you were not always with the same person. That made things interesting. It was cold in the arena, and Carol had warned me to dress warm. I was glad I did. After the program, we stopped and got something warm to drink and a snack. It was late when I got back, but Jack was still awake. Either he had been awake, or I woke him up coming in the house. He asked how the program went and how Greg did. We talked for a while, and then I went to bed.

Sunday, February 24, 2013 — Celebrating With a Friend

Today I left church early to celebrate the seventy-fourth birthday of friend and former co-worker, Shirley Shiels. We met another former co-worker for a sushi lunch. Shirley was seventy when I introduced her to sushi, and she loved it. She thought this was a great way to celebrate. I didn't feel bad about being gone because Jerry and Lori said they'd be out to see Jack. It was good to get away and spend some time with friends. I never knew when those days might end, so I would always take advantage of them. I keep saying that, but it is so true. When you are dealing with someone who is terminally ill, you never know from day to day how things will be. Taking advantage of the good days is critical. All involved need a mental and physical break.

When I got back, Jack said Jerry and Lori left when he had fallen asleep, but then Mark came over and woke him up and took him uptown for soup and coffee. He also ate some chili and crackers that I had made, so he still had somewhat of an appetite, and that helped.

I had noticed, though, that his left side was starting to show symptoms of what might have been swelling in his brain again. We had gone through this before, so I knew what to look for. The problem was the only thing that helped with the swelling was steroids, and he said he would not take them anymore. I knew if he would not take them, he would continue to have issues as the swelling would worsen, and then the other symptoms would return also.

I could not force him to take the medication, but I also knew what happened when he didn't. I knew he would have more and more problems on his left side. Eventually, he would either get to where he was in November when this started, or he would get like he was in January when he was dehydrated, not eating, and barely able to get around. And I knew at that point that the end would be close.

I didn't know what to do. I couldn't make him take the steroids. I knew that when he got worse, I would only be able to watch it happen unless he decided to take something that would help. I didn't like this. It was so hard. I knew God was in control, and I knew He would walk with me through all of this, or I could not have faced each day. Even with that knowledge, it was so hard!

I called his sister to let her know what was going on. She was getting a daily email update, but I was not putting everything in there, and I wanted to give her some background so she would be prepared when it got worse again, and I knew it would. Besides, I just needed to hear her voice. She is such a great and gracious lady.

Monday, February 25, 2013—Lovin' the Sun and the Son

The sun today looked so good. I knew we were looking at a storm moving in, but I was glad for the sunny day and decided to enjoy it. We saw six deer playing around by the trees across the road. They were way across a field, so they were hard to see, but we all enjoyed watching them through the binoculars

For some reason watching the deer reminded me that the Book of Psalms was always a comfort. I remembered reading so many psalms whenever I was in a tough place. It was good to go back and read them again. If you are struggling, it's a great place to look.

Rica asked why Papa's eye looked funny. The nurse noticed it too, and we talked about it. His eye looked a little swollen, and it was droopy on the left side again. It was one of the first signs of the edema (swelling). I told the nurse it would have to get bad before he would agree to the steroids, which was the only thing that helped the edema. She said to keep her informed and if there was a big change to let her know. The problem could be that he might start having seizures and would not even know it because they would be minor at first. Just what I needed—another issue to worry about.

And again, he was eating a lot less. For breakfast he was down to a couple pieces of bacon and half a biscuit. Supper was just a few bites of whatever I made. He was eating though, which, once it got worse, he would eventually stop doing.

Feeling helpless was probably the worst part of this. I knew I could not make it better; I could only make him comfortable, and that had its limits also. Trying to make someone comfortable when nothing makes them comfortable is difficult, if not impossible. It is not their fault, and they are not trying to be hard to please; it's just that they really can't get comfortable. Nothing feels right. Food doesn't taste good. They are tired all the time. It's a horrible time.

Tuesday, Feb 26, 2013—F.R.O.G.

F.R.O.G. (I Forever Rely On God; or I Fully Rely On God) I read that on another site. There was a two-and-one-half-year-old girl with kidney cancer, and the tumor ruptured while they did emergency surgery. Her grandfather is a Wesleyan pastor in North Carolina. This had been a nerve-wracking and traumatic couple of weeks for them. They were told that all tests showed no cancer anywhere else. She still had to have radiation and twenty-eight weeks of chemo. Her site had frogs all over it. I wondered why so I read up on it. Now I know.

That became my new motto. Whenever I struggled I would just say FROG to myself and remember who is in control.

Today we were looking at a trip to Flint on Wednesday. Don had offered to drive us, which relieved me because we would be stuck if anything happened. The problem was that Jack said if he felt as bad on Wednesday as he had all day today, he wouldn't be able to make the trip. This trip was to try to get a partial refund on the truck license plate. They told us in a letter that if we missed the evaluation on that day, they would revoke his driver's license and reschedule in up to ninety days. The longer this dragged on, the less likely we were to get any refund at all. That plate was expensive, so it would be nice to get some type of refund on the cost. It was another test in my decision to Fully Rely On God. I hoped I was up to the test.

Wednesday, February 27, 2013—No Go

Well, we did not make the trip. It wasn't the weather; Jack did not feel up to it. I called the office number on the letterhead and talked to a supervisor. When I explained what was going on and why we filed in the first place, she suggested we not come at all as it would be a wasted trip. They were going to suspend his license anyway. She said they would do it for sure since we didn't show up. Her advice was that once we got the official suspension, we go to Secretary of State, get a "refund application," fill it in, and send with his driver's license, the Kenworth license plate, copies of doctor statements, and a letter explaining that we did not come because he was physically not able to. Would they refund? Who knows? It's the government, remember!

Anyway, that was done and behind us. I planned to type up the letter, and when we received the suspension I would get all of it in the mail and see what happened. It was one more thing I didn't have hanging over my head.

He did not eat this morning and only had one-third bag of popcorn with some Coke this afternoon, so his appetite was dwindling which was not good, but expected.

Thursday, February 28, 2013—More Paperwork

I typed up the letter today. I wanted to get it out of the way, and if I could have all the paperwork ready when the suspension came in, I thought it would save me time, and I could also check to make sure the letter said what I wanted it to. I would be sending at least eight documents or up to fifteen pieces of paper. So much for saving trees and being "paper savers." The government wants documentation for everything.

Things were not changing with Jack except to steadily get worse. He was eating less each day. It was not a big difference day to day, but over a seven-day period it was quite noticeable. On this day it was two small pieces of bacon, half a biscuit in the morning, and about half of a chicken thigh and half a piece of bread for dinner. He had been sleeping a lot also, but that was because he was weak again from not eating. It was the same vicious cycle. I knew it would not get better, but that didn't ever make it easier to handle.

Suzanne had come out again to help with schoolwork with the kids, and Dave made dinner, so I had a little bit of a break. I used the time to work a crossword puzzle in the newspaper. Wow! How exciting is that? At least it was a mental break from all the other stuff going on.

Friday, March 1, 2013—It's Sold!

This was a hard day for Jack. We received a deposit on the Kenworth and the trailer. If all goes as planned they will take possession on Monday. I knew he would be depressed over this as that truck was his baby and it was the last piece that said, "You are done." As I said when this all first began back in November, hearing he had cancer was not as bad as hearing he would never drive again. That was official when his license was suspended Wednesday for not showing up for the assessment.

I knew this had to be hard on him mentally and emotionally. I had a little idea because for the past year I had been dealing with rheumatoid arthritis and, little by little, had to ask for assistance with things that should have been a no-brainer physically. Before that, it was a knee injury that kept me from driving for three months. Giving up those pieces of independence had been hard for me because I have always been so independent. It had to be the same way for Jack, only worse. He had driven in the forty-eight continental states and was now relegated to a bed in the living room with a view out an eight-foot-by-eight-foot window. I could not even imagine.

Saturday, March, 2, 2013—Reflections

I borrowed the following quote from the blog of a woman whose granddaughter was diagnosed with cancer in February. I thought it summed up so beautifully how I felt about those who had come alongside us in prayer.

Your prayers have been woven into our daily lives. Many times during a day and many times in the middle of the night I would stop and realize—I know there are people praying—it's just a weird kind of thought that I don't have usually—I know people are praying—right now. There are no words created that could express how that makes me feel, the hope it gives, and the appreciation I have in the knowledge of those prayers. I want to be that faithful for you some day!

I wanted our friends and family who had been on this journey with us to know how important it was to me to know they were praying for us and thinking of us. What a comfort that was. If you have never been down a road like this, you can't understand it, and if you have been there, then you know how much it is needed and appreciated.

Today was another emotional day for Jack, and I knew tomorrow would be even more so as the final paperwork and deal were finished on the sale of the truck. He told me the day it would go out the drive I would see a grown man cry.

Unless you have had to give up something you love or have had it taken away, you won't understand the emotion. It may sound childish or even selfish; but understand, it was his life! It's who he was. As I said before, it was the last piece that said, "This part of your life is over." And at this point, he could not even try to learn a hobby because we didn't know how long he had, and since he was getting weaker, he didn't have the energy to try.

Because of what was about to happen with the truck and because it was a quiet day with no one around, we started talking about the past. What brought it up was that we were sitting in the living room looking at the evergreen in the front yard and discussing how I put

Christmas lights on it when we first moved in and the ladder reached the top of the tree. That same ladder would not even go half way up now. From there we began to discuss many things that had happened over the past almost forty years.

We also talked about the fact that he had worked for a boat hauling company located at the end of a street that was about three blocks from the street I lived on when I was in high school. We were that close and as far as we know, our paths never crossed. We remember a lot of the same things from that area though. It's a small world after all.

At this point many of our family and friends had been our prayer partners and were with us on this journey about ninety days. I had started posting prayer requests about the first of December of 2012 and I told them that I hoped they were not bored and ready to drop out because we needed their prayers and support now as much as we had in the beginning of this journey.

As I told my prayer team, it was a roller coaster ride—sometimes up and sometimes down and the down times were sometimes fast and scary, just like on a real roller coaster. I was sure that sometimes I did not make much sense because I could not put my thoughts together. I was glad though and appreciated it so much that they stuck with us and by us.

It was always hard to tell them how much comfort and peace it gave me emotionally to know they were praying and to get emails or calls from some of them. Every time I read a comment or an email, I felt such a comfort knowing so many people cared about us and took time out of their busy lives to pray for us and to reach out in a call, email or comment.

Sunday, March 3, 2013—A Bittersweet Day

On this day, the semi had a new owner. I knew Jack was struggling with that. He seemed to be doing okay, but I am sure it was preying on his mind. Giving up driving in November was difficult. Having the state suspend his license in February was another blow. Signing off on the titles for the truck and trailer was the final step in closing that chapter of his life.

I know it was hard. I didn't know how to ease the pain. In fact, I knew I couldn't, and that made it hard also. I know how I felt having to give up doing things I used to be able to do. It's tough to do. Only when or if you lose your independence or even just a part of it will anyone really understand. If I didn't know the Lord was walking with me through this, I knew I could not make it. I certainly was not doing it in my own strength.

One of the songs in our service on this day was from Psalm 23. Oh, how I was clinging to that Psalm. He truly was with me in the valley. Someone had told me that you don't have a shadow without light, so even though I was walking through the shadow of the valley, it meant there was light somewhere casting that shadow. Not only was it not all darkness, the light was His light. That was such a comfort to me.

The positive part of the sale of the truck was that it would not be a legal issue later on. There would not be a need to probate anything because all the business assets were now sold. The other thing was I could pay the medical bills that were now starting to come through the door.

As odd as it may sound, while it was sad to see something that meant so much to someone leave our possession, I was greatly relieved that it had happened. With that sale, God had made provision to take care of some other needs. I was reminded again and again that when you pray, you'd better be willing to accept the answer God's way—not yours!

Tomorrow? Well tomorrow will have its own issues, so I won't dwell on tomorrow tonight. I will enjoy tonight for what we have and rest in Him.

Monday, March 4, 2013—Getting Out of the House

Today was a beautiful, sunny day. I'm thinking that may be why Jack struggled into his clothes and ran some errands with Charlie. He had planned an oil change on the truck and had bought all the supplies before he knew he was sick so he took all those supplies out to a man who had changed the oil for him before. Mike said he would change the oil for the new owner and only charge a little for labor.

Many people won't do that if you bring your own supplies, but Mike understood the situation. He also told Jack if he wanted to get out of the house he would come and get him, take him out to the shop for a while just to gab, and bring him home when he got tired or needed to lie down. Jack said he probably would never feel up to it, but he was pleased that the offer was made.

From there they went to see a friend who does body work and talked to him about replacing the rusted panels on my pickup. I was surprised because I had talked about doing that a year ago but never had the money. Jack said he wanted to do that so I would have a decent looking vehicle to drive, and it is in good shape other than that.

They were gone about three hours, and he was totally wiped out when they got back and could not wait to lie down on the bed. He said it hurt to sit because he does not have enough meat on his bones to cushion him when he sits. I'm sure he is less than the 132 that he was last time I weighed him a couple of weeks ago. He ate part of his breakfast this morning, and that was all he had all day. He said nothing sounded good.

We also reactivated his phone under Charlie's plan so it cost a third of what it was before. This way he had some independence and control and could reach me when I was away from the house. He said he didn't feel so cut off from everything and everyone since he could now make and receive calls. I hadn't realized how much he felt abandoned and alone without his phone. It made sense to let him use one to keep in touch with people.

I baked four loaves of pumpkin bread today while they were gone. I have no idea why I did that as tired as I had been. It made a mess in the kitchen that I had to clean up. What was I thinking? We were both worn out so after I ate we called it a night.

Tuesday, March 5, 2013—A Visitor and a Phone Call

A good friend and fellow Stephen's Minister, Roxanne, stopped by with a roasting pan full of goodies. There was cheese, venison sausage, grapes, fruit, cookies, hummus, little pita breads, bagel chips, and a magazine for me. What a treat! Jack was so appreciative of her visit and the goodies. I also appreciated her visit. We talked for a bit until she had errands to run, but it was good to touch base.

A phone call brought some great news. Rich had made arrangements to fly in for the weekend on March 15. I wished Michele and Luke could have come too, but we would take the visit from Rich and enjoy him. It was a year ago this month they came to Michigan and we celebrated Jack's seventy-fifth birthday (which is in April). It was hard to believe that it had been a year already.

I picked up some new pain medication for Jack today. Well, it was the same med, but it was a patch because he was taking so much the nurse said this would be easier on him. I put the patch on at 11:00 A.M. He ate at about 1:00 P.M. Within minutes he lost it. I don't know if the patch was too much—because he had said he was nauseated already—or maybe it was a combination. I didn't want to stop the patch because once he got used to it, I thought it would be better. I'm telling you, these decisions were just never easy, and, it doesn't help that you never really know what causes a reaction.

Part of it could have been yesterday's outing too. He had been sleeping most of the day because he was worn out from being out yesterday for three hours. Put it all together, and it was—*not fun*! I could think of so many things I would rather have been doing than going through all this.

While I was out getting the medication, I had breakfast with Luz, which was a nice break. Then I picked up the form from the Secretary of State's office to apply for a refund on the license plate for the semi. We had received the official driver's license suspension in the mail. I put all that paperwork in the mail, and we would then have to wait to see what would happen. Maybe nothing.

Anyway, even on a day when the sun is shining, a friend brings a pan full of goodies and I get to have breakfast with a friend, there are always bumps. I shouldn't have been surprised after all this time at how much mental energy it takes to go through this, but I was. It was 4:15 P.M., and I could have gone right to sleep. The problem was I would then be up at 2:00 A.M. I was *already* up at 2:00 A.M.—last night. No wonder I was tired.

Yesterday I said I would not worry about today because today would have its own issues. And it had. All of the issues weren't with

Jack. As I said, I was so exhausted I could have gone to bed as soon as I got back from running errands, but I could not, so while I was in a slump physically and mentally, I still had to take care of Jack.

I had to remind myself that I said I was not going to worry about what tomorrow might bring. I had enough to deal with all that went on today — the good and the not so good. I was still hanging on to the One who was in control (and it wasn't me!)

Wednesday, March 6, 2013 — Some Days Are Different

I would say I didn't get anything done today, but I actually did accomplish some things, just not all I planned. When I went to get the kids, I decided to get some water and groceries. I was low on water, and it was important to keep Jack hydrated, so I liked to stay stocked up. I spent more than I planned, but that is always the way when I don't go with a list.

By the time I got back, put the groceries away, and the kids ate, the aide was here, so we didn't start schoolwork until after 2:00 P.M. Needless to say, they didn't get much done today.

Jack didn't eat breakfast, which is usually his big meal of the day. He did try a couple of crackers and cheese after I got back. He never asked for a cup of coffee either. If you knew him, you'd know this was abnormal. In the evening he had a couple of small bites of some turkey leg that Charlie brought.

I didn't know if the patch was working because I didn't have anything to measure it by. He thought it was what made him nauseated, but he had been that way for a long time. I was hoping it would help his stomach since it goes directly into the blood stream and not the stomach and taking meds on an empty stomach can't be any good.

Because he was not sleeping well, the nurse ordered some sleep meds and said to start them on Thursday night. It seemed like we were always trying something, and sometimes it didn't work, but since the goal was to make him comfortable, we had to keep trying.

Charlie said he could stay and spend time with his dad so I went to a Stephen's Ministry meeting. I hadn't attended since December 12, and it was good to be with the group. When I read in the email what they would be doing, I knew I should be there. Yes, I was meant to hear what two people had to share. It always works that way.

One of the men shared how he and his wife had lost a baby through a miscarriage and another just before the adoption was to go through. He shared how God had walked with them through these two trials and how it strengthened their faith. One of the women shared how she and her husband felt about her diagnosis of cancer and how they felt led to praise God through it so the rocks would not cry out. She was referring to Luke 19:40 and it was a good reminder to me to praise God even in the hard places.

Thursday, March 7, 2013—Trying Another New Med

I fixed breakfast today since Charlie and the kids were out early. Jack ate very little, and as I said, breakfast was always the biggest meal of the day for him. For him to barely touch it told me his appetite was on the downturn or he was nauseated or both. I fixed fish, summer and zucchini squash stir fried with yellow, red, and orange peppers, and waffle fries for dinner. There wasn't much left in the leftover dish, which was good. Again, Jack ate very little.

During the day, I got some paperwork done in the office and caught up my filing. I also cleaned out an area in the laundry that was overdue. Every little bit helped. Suzanne was out and worked with Reina on schoolwork, which gave me a chance to work with Elisha on his work. He knew his numbers to ten pretty well. He was still having a problem with the alphabet, but he could pick out the letters in his name—even though he didn't know what they were. He was learning them though. Rica was learning about Michigan in her civics book, which was part of her history class.

In the afternoon I got a text from Karen—she and Riley would be coming the same time as Rich if the weather stayed good. Even in March there could be bad weather between us and where she lived near Toronto. There is a snow belt that sometimes is dangerous and can be a problem until sometime in April, so we had to monitor the weather for her trip. We were waiting to hear if Rob could make it. I said I would put together a list of projects to keep them busy. Well, they did ask, so I was doing as they asked.

In the evening I took Reina and Elisha to get a movie and to McDonalds to play for a while. When I walked in, I saw some old friends—Rick and Chris Bindig and Adrienne (Bindig) Hayes. It was good to catch up on news with them. Chris and I had done Laborer's Network together several years before, and we had gotten to know each other better.

That evening I gave Jack the new sleep med about 8:00 P.M. I was hoping it would work and that he would get a good night's sleep for a change. Like I said, every new med was a challenge.

Friday, March 8, 2013—Special Visitors

During the night I had checked on Jack three times and he hadn't changed positions, so I know he slept for quite a while—I think about six hours, which was a lot for him. He was still a bit groggy in the morning, but after eating a very small amount he felt much better. I hoped being out in the sun would pick him up some.

Charlie took him out to run errands again. Jack didn't feel up to it yesterday, and besides, the weather was too bad. Today he was determined to get out for a while since the sun was shining. I was sure when he got back he would be wiped out because he usually was after being outside and going for a ride. He was, but since we had special visitors, he made the effort to stay awake.

Pastor Garry and Martha came over for a visit. We had a great time. Jack told them they have been away far too long. I'm not sure if he meant from him or from Michigan (they were in Florida for a week in February). At any rate, he let them know how much he appreciated their visits and looked forward to them.

He and Martha talked about their growing-up years. It sounded like Jack's dad and Martha's dad were quite a bit alike. Both were outdoorsmen and both knew how to handle themselves in dangerous situations involving wildlife. They reminisced together, and Pastor Garry and I just sat and listened.

Charlie and I had planned to go to a history of Stoney Creek Park at the Van Houssen Farm in Rochester. Jack was okay with our going as Dave was there if he needed anything. Charlie was going for work, and I was going for fun. That might not interest some people, but I like the history of the area, and it was good to get out and do something besides run errands or shop for groceries. It was a good evening, and I learned a lot about local history. Rochester and Stoney Creek Park are linked in a lot of ways historically.

Rich and Karen had asked for a list of projects for when they are home next weekend. I emailed them both a list—they'll be sorry they asked. Depending on weather, they will either do a lot inside or a lot outside.

Saturday, March 9, 2013—Something Different

Today Jack said he could not get comfortable on either the bed or the chair. I suggested he try our bed and see if he felt better when he could stretch out and move around easier. When he lay down and put his head on the pillow he said, "Ah, I feel like I'm home." Then he took a two-hour nap. I think we'll try sleeping in there tonight.

Then he wanted to get out of the house, so we went for a ride. We were going to go to the Cracker Barrel in Port Huron but got only as far as Richmond when he said he could not do it. Well, we tried. Maybe another day. He had been out yesterday with Charlie, so two days in a row might have been too much.

He had eaten only one small meal today. Yesterday he did fairly well with a piece of roast and some potatoes and a little bit of salad.

He had bought an electric razor when he went for a ride with Charlie yesterday afternoon, but told me he didn't know if he could stand long enough in front of a mirror to shave. He doesn't want to shave the whole beard off (there's not much there yet), just enough to make a goatee. I told him I had a hand mirror.

I got the hand mirror and duct taped it to a canning jar. Then I set the jar with the mirror on the adjustable table that came with the hospital bed from hospice. I raised the table up to a comfortable level and he can now shave, and then I can vacuum. Maybe I can get a patent on this invention.

I filled four boxes and two bags with old files from the office, so I feel like I accomplished something today. Then I washed some blankets he had in the truck and hung them outside. They smelled so good!

I turned the clocks ahead early for daylight savings time so when I was ready to go to bed, it wouldn't be an issue, and I was hoping I would not keep telling myself it's really an hour later. This time change drives me crazy. As far as I know there are still only twenty-four hours in a day. The deer in the field across the road don't care if it's 5:00 P.M. or 6:00 P.M.—all they know is it's time to graze the cornfield. I think they are smarter than we are!

Sunday, March 10, 2013—It Worked!

What worked? Sleeping in the big bed worked. Jack only got up once and looked at his watch at 5:30 A.M., but since he hadn't turned it ahead, it was 6:30 A.M. EDT. Looks like sleeping in his own bed was better. We decided to try another night.

At 6:00 P.M. he was eating for the first time for the day. He had three Zesta crackers (three small squares that is) and three small slices of cheese. Actually I was in the office when he called from his cell phone to ask where the cheese was. That would be funny, but it isn't actually because he didn't have the energy to walk as far as the back room where the office was.

He said he'd love to go for a ride but just couldn't get enough energy to get dressed. Since he slept off and on all day, after church I went into the office again and was still purging files. There would either be a huge bonfire or I would fill the truck at the landfill.

Other than that it was a quiet day, and I'd take all the quiet I could get.

Monday, March 11, 2013—A Good Night's Sleep

Our friends would say this is "too much information", or TMI, but we snuggled together and slept well in our bed during the past night. He may have gotten up once, but we both didn't get up until after 7:00 in the morning. I asked how he slept, and he said, "Real well since we could snuggle!" I guess that says it all. So for now it was going to be "a real bed" as he said. Down the road he would have to go back to the "doctor's bed" so we could take better take care of him, but for now comfort ruled.

He ate a little bit of cracker and cheese again and two bites of soup. I asked if he'd like some Cold Stone ice cream that I would pick up while out running errands. His face lit up, so I took that as a "yes." He liked the salty caramel. He might not eat much, but I planned to get it and see.

As I've said many times, I never knew when he would feel good, when he would eat, when he would sleep well, or when he would want to try to get out of the house. We would do whatever worked for that day.

Tuesday, March 12, 2013—A Full Day

Today started out slow and quiet but didn't stay that way. I got a call that the social worker wanted to come out about the same time as the nurse. The nurse was bringing an intern and did I mind? Well, it was kind of hard to say no.

I was late getting back last night, so Jack didn't have the ice cream. This morning he said he wanted some, so he ate a few bites for breakfast. Not exactly the breakfast of champions but whatever works. He tried a cup of coffee for the first time since Saturday and only drank about half. For some reason his taste for coffee had changed. I put what he didn't eat of the ice cream in the freezer for later.

The social worker arrived a little after 11:00 A.M. The nurse was running a little late because she had to get some meds for us. Jack had a good visit with social worker and then the nurse and intern came in. All three were here together for a little while. My niece came to help the kids with schoolwork, which was good because I ended up being tied up for almost two hours with the hospice workers.

By the time they left, Jack was pretty worn out. He hadn't done much except answer questions, but that seemed to wear him out. His blood pressure was pretty low—lower than it had been. That may be why he was so tired. He had been sleeping most of the day since they left. That might mean he wouldn't sleep well at night.

He did not eat much again this day. The lack of eating was getting to be a problem. He had lost even more weight—I could tell by his weight loss even though I hadn't been weighing him regularly.

One good thing was that the signs of spring were beginning to show up. I saw a red-capped woodpecker by the feeder in the tree. I had never seen one at a feeder, but it definitely was a woodpecker. I saw a flock of geese flying north also, and several hawks have been in the area lately. I was looking for the first robin.

Other than that, we were in kind of a holding pattern. Nothing changed significantly from day to day. That didn't mean we didn't need prayer—we still did.

Wednesday, March 13, 2013—Passing the Buck, so to Speak

I let Charlie be the doorkeeper today so I could concentrate on schoolwork for the kids, especially since he didn't arrive until late morning. Being the doorkeeper meant he had to monitor who came in and how long they stayed even if Jack was up to a visit.

I took time out to see the chiropractor today. I was a month overdue to see him, so I really needed to go in. He told me to come back on Monday to get another treatment and then hopefully come back to once a month. That's what I got for putting it off.

In the late morning, Chaplin Paul came over, and Charlie talked to him for about a half hour. Yesterday I was tied up for two hours, and today I did not want to lose more time with the kids and their schoolwork, so I made Charlie visit with whoever stopped over.

Jack had slept for the most part of the day, and we both had gotten a good night's sleep on Tuesday night. I don't think he got up even once.

Other than that, there was not much change on this day.

Thursday, March, 14, 2013—Out and About

It was a nice, sunny day so Charlie offered to take Jack for a ride when he got to the house. It was too early, and Jack didn't want to go anywhere just yet. He said he had to wake up first, then work at feeling up to getting off the bed. Then he had to try to get dressed to go out. All of that took a lot of mental energy, which wore him out. A little after noon he said he'd like to try, so he got dressed, and we packed him in the van and headed out.

We decided to go to Port Huron by the scenic route. It was scenic too because we didn't know where we were part of the time, but finally we found our road and ended up there about 2:00 P.M.

Of course we had to stop at Cracker Barrel. We were hoping that would perk up his appetite, but he still ate only a very little. We brought some home in a box to see if he would try it the next day.

Once back home he was exhausted and fell asleep pretty quickly. I was pretty sure he would because a trip usually wore him out, and this had been a long one, almost four hours. It was good for him mentally, though, to get out even if he didn't do any more than try to eat.

Friday, March 15, 2013—Sleepless in Armada

I think last night we could have topped *Sleepless in Seattle*. I don't know why Jack was up so often. He said he was nauseated but didn't want anything for it. I may have kept him awake because I was in pain until 3:00 A.M. I have no idea why I wait so long to take something for pain. It was either hip arthritis or sciatica nerve on left side—either way I finally took something and fell asleep sometime around 4:00 A.M., after tossing and turning half the night.

Today I had an appointment with the eye doctor. It was a follow up from cataract surgery that I had back in the fall of 2012. Since Charlie was at the house, I ran errands before the appointment because I knew they would dilate my eyes, and I didn't want to be running errands after. Good thing because it took them a while to get back to normal, and the report was good.

Karen was due in sometime in the evening, which could be late depending on traffic at the border. Rob would be driving in later. We were hoping the snow was not too bad in Chicago. A big early spring storm could cause some major problems for the drive. Rich was to arrive at midnight, and Dave would be picking him up. I was looking at it being a busy weekend as they were coming to help with some spring cleanup in the yard.

Jack could not deal with big crowds or a lot of noise, so I would have to keep the noise down and keep them busy somewhere other than near the living room. I was hoping the snow would not be too bad because I really did need to get some major stuff done outside.

I was looking forward to all the hands being able to get some things in place before mowing season.

Charlie was to do a maple sap at a maple syrup program at Wolcott Mill on Sunday, and I wanted Rich to be able to see how it is done. We would then get to keep the syrup since the sap was ours.

I found a note from one of last year's Stephen's Ministry meetings where we were to write a short note on the following:

I need to trust God for His. . . . .
wisdom
joy
courage
I had chosen "joy" and wrote the following.

"Timing is perfect [meaning last summer] because someone just asked me about having joy in stressful circumstances. It's not the joy *in* the situation; it's the joy of knowing He is in it with me. So, over the summer I need to trust Him that, yes, I can see joy even in stressful things. See James!"

I have no idea what the stress was, but it was now so appropriate for what I was going through. I should never be amazed at God's timing, but I always am.

Saturday, March 16, 2013—The Checklist

Jack fell in the middle of the night when he got up to use the bathroom. We had been sleeping in the bedroom, and when he got out of bed, he had no support to hold on to and fell on the floor by the dresser. I checked him in the morning for bruises or scrapes when he told me about it but didn't find anything. He seemed really out of sorts but did better as the day went on. He did eat a little bit and talked with Rich for a while, so I was sure he was okay.

He was crabby because all the kids were here at once and there was a lot of commotion, but I told him they would be outside working and not bothering him. With all of them here we got quite a bit done that just Charlie and I couldn't do by ourselves. It was just too much for two people. There still was more to do, but I said we could pick away at it over time. We were outside quite a bit and came in to warm up once in a while. Someone was always with him as I didn't want to leave him alone. I knew I would have to monitor him the next few days to make sure he didn't fall again or have any issues from the fall he did have.

Rich had asked for a list so I made one. My list was detailed and we followed most of it. I felt better about getting some big projects done. Checking them off as we completed them made me feel so good.

Dig out burn pit—check
Burn papers/wood—check
Cut up limbs with chain saw—check
Stack cut up wood—check
Stack cages—check
Sort metal—check
Clean out coops—mostly check

Those were the outside jobs. There were inside jobs, but we didn't get as many done because even though we froze our toes, the guys wanted to get the outside stuff done.

Clean and organize laundry room—check
Clean bathrooms—check
Fix dinner—check (delicious, Dave)
Time to call it a night—check

Sunday, March 17, 2013—Family Time

First thing in the morning, Rob called to see if his dad was able to go uptown for breakfast (Rob was staying at Charlie's). He was, so we all got dressed and headed to the restaurant. We were just sitting down when my sister and brother-in-law came in. Rob had told them where we were going, and they decided to join us—from 15 Mile Road and Harper, which was about a forty-minute drive. They must love family to drive that far to join the group.

Jack did pretty good with his meal, better than he had done of late. When we got back, he was pretty much wiped out as usual. Everyone sat around and talked for a while before heading home— all except Rich, who would be heading home the next day.

I didn't work them enough yesterday; Karen was still finishing up—dishes, boxing some stuff, straightening the bedroom. Rich and I had to run an errand. When we got back, he burned some more trash and helped me put some things in the attic. We were getting there. Wow! We sure had a lot of junk. I was glad to be getting it cleaned up. Ran one more errand and then it was time to fix hot dogs and tater tots for dinner.

Monday, March, 18, 2013—Let There Be Light

On one of our errands on Sunday Rich and I had bought a floor lamp for Jack. Rich set it up over the bed so Jack could read the paper. The lamp on the small end table by the couch was not giving off enough light. He said his eyes were getting worse, so we hoped this lamp would help him to be able to see to read the paper more than he had been. We also got an extension cord with an off/on switch and zip-tied it to the bed rail so he could turn the light off and on himself.

When Jack put his shirt on during the day, he had trouble buttoning it, so I helped him. He said buttoning was getting to be a problem. I suspected it was because it was hard for him to see and hard to manipulate the small buttons.

Later that day Dave took Rich to the airport. The last of the chicks that were in for the weekend had flown the coop. It was too quiet—at least for me. The quiet was probably better for Jack though. I needed people, especially the kids, around, and he wanted no one around and mostly quiet. It was hard to balance both.

After everyone left, Charlie and I finished up the maple sap/syrup that he had done as part of a program at Wolcott Mill. I was so thankful that it worked out so we could get our sap boiled down in one day except for the finishing touches. We even made some fudge, which was completely gone in one day, with the small remainder of sap. So our approximately thirty-two gallons of sap equaled four pints and five half pints. At a forty-to-one ratio, we didn't do too bad.

It was time for a cup of tea and a quiet evening.

Tuesday, March 19, 2013—Do I Make the Right Decisions?

Do I make the right decisions? I asked myself that all the time. This one was in regard to doubling the pain med on the patch. On Monday night we added a patch to up the amount of pain med as he was still taking too many pills (I thought) with the patch. I asked the nurse if we could do two at the lower amount so if it didn't work, I could go back to one patch. If it was only the one patch at the higher dose and it was too much, we would have to take it off and then have none. That was my rationale.

He slept through the night and until 10:00 A.M. on Tuesday, so I knew the pain did not wake him up, which was one of the goals. But then I wondered if that was too much. He was sleepy all day. The nurse did warn us that the first forty-eight hours he would be more tired and sleepy until his body adjusted to the higher amount. During the day he only took two pain pills for the first time since Monday night, so it was helping. I just always worried if I was doing the right thing.

The plus was that he was not taking as many pills, and I think that was helping with the stomach issues. He also had not asked for as much nausea medication, so I think that was helping there. He was still mostly only eating cheese and crackers, which didn't make him sick to his stomach, so that helped. He just had no appetite.

Getting him out to breakfast on Sunday was good because he ate more than he had been although that wasn't saying much. I kept going back to the statement that breakfast had always been a huge meal for him, so this tiny bit was quite a dramatic step down.

I looked at the calendar and realized that Friday would be seventeen weeks since this started. It was incredible to think it had been that long. That was four months and one week. Where did the time go? What would the future hold? How would we handle this going forward? What's next? You can go crazy trying to figure all that out. Mostly I didn't try to dwell on it. It was enough to get through each day without trying to figure out tomorrow. As I said before, and would probably say again, I did not know what tomorrow would hold, but I knew who held tomorrow, and that was enough for me.

Wednesday, March 20, 2013 — Ask and Ye Shall Receive

Tuesday night I stopped and asked a friend, Don B., if he could help finish putting some paneling on our north living room wall. By way of explanation, I took out a water baseboard heater three years before, leaving an area either five inches or nine inches high and the length of the wall, approximately twenty-five feet, without paneling.

He said, "I'll be there in the morning." And he was. He had to cut each piece off of three small sections I found that I had kept. It just made it. Not only that, he had some baseboard molding and shoe molding given to him, already stained. It looked like a room now — well, a finished room, that is. It was a room before obviously, but molding makes all the difference. It cut the drafty cold air and was warmer by five degrees at least. Jack commented on how much of a difference it made as soon as it was done. We gave a huge thanks to Don.

Our next issue was that the auger bearings on our pellet stove were screeching, which was keeping me awake at night. It was horrible. I had the stuff to use to oil the bearings but wasn't sure exactly where to spray. I told Don the issue and asked him if he could spray the bearings for me. Don found them quickly, sprayed them for me, and viola — quiet. Ah, yes, wonderful quiet. Double thanks, Don!

Before bed I would be putting two new patches on Jack. It would be the first time I put both on new at the same time. He'd been nauseated, so I thought he might argue against it. I hoped he would not resist because it had been helping him sleep better, and he was taking fewer pills. I was convinced taking the Vicodin on an empty stomach was causing his nausea and other problems. He did not argue about the new patch, which I was thankful for. I was able to put the new ones on and relax for the evening. He was again sleeping on the hospital bed because he was afraid he'd fall again if he tried to get up from our bed without support.

Thursday, March 21, 2013 — Down Memory Lane

When the kids were home the past weekend, we went through closets, cupboards, file cabinets, and boxes. I had been getting rid of a lot of stuff that had accumulated far too long. I had not thrown away anything important even though Jack thought I had. He always said I threw away his treasures. Any of you wives have the same issue? What was junk to me was a treasure to him. I think, though, that he would have agreed that files going back to 1998 really did need to go.

I was in the office going through boxes that Rich had brought down from the attic, and one held some of their more important" stories from school. Now that they have kids, I thought it would be great to pass these things on. Hopefully they got good grades on them, but I had not read all of them yet, so I wasn't sure. I did know it was fun to sit and read through them, but, oh no, I didn't get the office work done. I really needed to spend some time back there in the morning earning my pay, even if it was only part-time work and part-time pay.

Jack slept most of the day because he was not feeling well at all. The only thing he had to eat that I know of was a shamrock shake from McDonald's that Suzanne brought out—actually she brought one for all of us. The kids loved the treat.

Suzanne worked with Reina on schoolwork while I ran to the post office to mail a package. Then after we ate dinner, she did my dishes. I really appreciated her willingness to come all the way out to the house to help with schoolwork and give me a hand taking care of some things.

After they all left, I tried to get Jack interested in any kind of food, and then I fixed a cup of tea and worked the crossword puzzle in the newspaper. After he ate and I did the puzzle for a while, I dug out the stories and took another trip down memory lane. That was my evening's entertainment since there was nothing worthwhile on TV.

Friday, March 22, 2013—Cleaning House and a Night Out

Last night Jack asked me to take the pain med patches off, so I did. I didn't think it was a good idea because they did help with the pain, but he said they made him too sick. He wasn't much better in the morning though, so I was not sure the patches were the problem. He did not eat again and did not take any pain meds by pill, either, so I was not sure what was going on. Again, he slept most of the day.

Since I didn't have the kids, I cleaned the pantry and another cupboard in the kitchen. I rearranged some things because I had thrown out several bags of things I had not used in at least five years. That freed up a lot of space. I put some things in the attic also. The attic now needed cleaning out, but it would have to wait. One thing at a time was my new motto. Saturday was dump day, and I knew I would have a pickup load for sure.

I told Jack I wanted to go to a Stephen's Ministry Commissioning Service and Banquet tonight and would be a little late getting home. Since no one was going to be with him, I wanted to make sure he would be okay by himself. Dave was out of town for few days, so he would be alone till I got back. I told him I would try to not be too late and I would leave his phone right next to him in case he needed me. He told me to go and have a good time and not worry about him. He did not want me to miss out on things just because he was sick.

Saturday, March 23, 2013—More Cleaning

I filled the pickup with trash and took it to the dump. I could not believe how much junk we had accumulated. I had some papers I needed to burn in our fire pit that had account numbers on them. That was sure to be a roaring fire. And I was not done yet, but I was getting close. Getting rid of a lot of useless stuff allowed me to rearrange some things and make it easier for me to keep up with stuff I really needed. I was trying to get the big stuff done while Jack was feeling somewhat decent. He wasn't feeling good, but he was not so bad that I had to stay in the room with him. This had allowed me to do some major cleaning in several rooms. I would just check on him every so often.

I was also taking breaks and typing or copying some recipes I had found and was putting in a notebook. I hoped that would make it easier when I wanted to cook something—or talk Dave into it.

When I got ready to take the trash to the dump, Jack said he wanted to try to eat. He didn't feel up to going out, so I got an omelet from the restaurant in town because I didn't have any eggs. He ate about four bites of half of the omelet that I got, and I ate the rest. He had a few bites of American fries. I think he ate about one quarter of one piece of toast.

Later in the day I asked him if he wanted to try to eat something, and he said he was not hungry. He did say, though, that he was not nauseated. I had put some pills out earlier, and he had not taken them. He said his headache was "tolerable." I put a couple pieces of chocolate candy on the table, and he ate them. Maybe chocolate is the answer.

Some days just before dark we would watch the deer play in the field across the road. They were not close—they were across a field near a tree line. Tonight, though, they were only out a few minutes, and we almost missed them. There was still nothing that interested me on TV, so it was time for a cup of tea and continue with the recipes.

Sunday, March 24, 2013—No Appetite

Jack asked me to get him an omelet again today, but I was at church, so I had Jerry and Lori pick it up for me. They had called and said they would be out while I was gone, and they were more than glad to get the food for him. He cut the omelet in half and gave me half when I got home. He ate maybe two bites of the other half, a one-quarter slice of bread, and a couple of bites of American fries and was full. I know his stomach has shrunk, but he was not eating enough to stay alive.

Jerry and Lori were leaving when Luz and George stopped by, so for Jack it was a full day, and he was exhausted. And since he was barely eating, it didn't take much to wear him out.

I was wishing Jack had an appetite because we were given a complete gluten-free meatloaf dinner today, including mashed potatoes and corn. I put a few small bites on a dessert plate that I hoped he would eat. He didn't.

He had stopped all meds on Saturday until late at night. He took some for pain at bedtime and again about 1:30 A.M. This morning he said he had a "drug hangover" and had not taken any meds all day. I asked if he had a headache, and he said he was starting to get one. That is when he should have been taking something, but he fell asleep instead.

I picked up a newspaper for him, and he had not even tried to read it. That is one thing he tried to do every day, so not reading it was another indication that he was getting pretty weak. I didn't know if he ever read the paper on Saturday either. The TV was rarely on, and he used to watch the news at 5:00 A.M. (which woke me up it was so loud) and again in the evening. He had less and less interest in what was going on. I think it took too much energy to think about all the issues.

There was no progress at this point, just setbacks. It was pretty sad to see someone who was so full of life and interested in current events lose interest in almost everything. I didn't think we were that close to the end, but the hospice paperwork did say the patient would lose interest in things as the time got closer. I wasn't sure what to think. He seemed to be failing rather quickly. There were getting to be fewer "good" days in the week. We decided we would still try to take advantage of those and do something. I felt if the weather would just warm up, it would be a lot easier to try to get him out.

Monday, March 25, 2013—A Combo of Issues

The hospice nurse was out today. She said Jack's problems were probably a combination of things. The patches made him sick he said, so I took them off last Thursday evening. The problem was that he went cold turkey off of them rather than let me take one off, then the other and come down slowly. On top of that he quit all meds until Friday night, which further complicated the problem.

In addition to that, he had not eaten much since last Sunday morning, and that wasn't good, either. He was drinking less than a quart of fluid a day—add it all up.

If that wasn't enough, we knew the brain tumors could cause nausea and were probably growing again; there was no way to tell except by symptoms since we would not be doing any more testing.

We had pretty much gone back to square one and were trying to regulate the nausea med, which he only wanted to take it when he was nauseated, and she wanted him to take it on a regular basis because the nausea was chronic. He only wanted to take the pain med at night because that was when he had the headaches. That was okay except he waited until he got the headache and then it took a while to be effective.

Today he had a few crackers, and I fixed him a Vernors and ice cream float. He drank it all, so he got at least twelve ounces of fluids today. I was hoping his system would calm down by morning so maybe I could get him to eat something. Dave was fixing ribs for Tuesday dinner, and he liked ribs, so I was hoping he would try them.

It was time to wind down with a book, if I could concentrate enough to read it.

Tuesday, March 26, 2013- Another Day, Another Inch of Progress

Starting over with the meds looked like it was the right thing to do—at least for now. His system appeared to have calmed down a bit. At least he was not in the tail spin he had been in. It wasn't that he was climbing up or anything, but at least he had leveled off.

This morning he asked for biscuits and honey. He ate one half of a biscuit and drank some coffee. In the afternoon he had three sections of a Zesta cracker and a Vernors and ice cream float. Dave made some delicious ribs, which he loves, but when I asked him if he wanted some he said, "Maybe later." Turning those down was just not like him.

He actually watched the news for about fifteen minutes for the first time in days, so he was showing some interest in the world around him again. He didn't stay interested for very long, though, not that the news is interesting on your best day anyway.

I was still cleaning and sorting and made some headway today: four more bags to burn or take to dump. You'd think the house would be empty by now, but we had a lot of stuff to get rid of. You couldn't tell I had done anything because a lot of it was behind the scenes in file cabinets and closets. Now I had a place to put some things that I really did need to keep that had been cluttering up the place, and since I was labeling things, I could actually find something when I needed it.

It was finally time to relax. This roller coaster ride was taking a lot out of me.

Wednesday, March 27, 2013—Paperwork Again

I had used the title about paperwork before, but this time I was using it for a different reason. Yes, it *was* paperwork again, and it could mean a return of almost half of the $2100 Jack had paid for his commercial license plate last September. I had mentioned it before so there was no point in repeating the whole thing again, but it was an "apportioned" plate, which meant each state he drove in or through was given a part of that $2100.

Well, last week we got a check for half of the Michigan portion. We thought at first they were just being super cheap but in looking into it, we realized that we had gotten back half of their portion. Today we got a packet in the mail from the State of Michigan. They sent a letter addressed to the "IRP" office in each state telling them that Michigan had refunded a portion of his plate because of a medical situation. They told us to forward that letter and the paperwork they sent with it to each state that had been paid.

There were thirty-nine states I would be forwarding this to. There were several where the amount we would get back was less than $10.00, and I had already read that the states would not give a refund if it was under $10.00, so why waste the stamp? I figured it out and we could possibly recoup over $800 I addition to the $214 from Michigan. If we did get half back from each state that would be almost half of what was paid. Even making copies and mailing costs was worth it to recoup part of the money.

We were working on reregulating the meds to try to get him on a more regular schedule, which didn't always work because he was sleeping a lot. He still was not eating much either. Today's food consisted of one half of a cookie, an apple pie from McDonald's and a Vernors float. He also had half a cup of coffee and about four ounces of water. He told the aide today he feels awful. He felt that way before and blamed it on the patches. At this point he had been off them for almost a week, so it was not the patches causing the problems. The main problems were heartburn, nausea, and headaches. I was still of the opinion that the Vicodin on an empty stomach was the problem.

I had hoped to be in bed by 9:00 P.M. The problem there was that I would be up pacing the floor at 3:00 A.M. I was planning to go somewhere with Charlie Thursday night, so I needed a good night's sleep tonight

I decided to kick back and fall asleep watching a boring movie if I could find one on Netflix, which Charlie had set up on my laptop.

Thursday, March 28, 2013—Paperwork Done, Going Out Tonight

The paperwork was copied and mailed—I sent it to 45 states. Hopefully it would generate some income. It cost $30.00 for postage as each package was 66 cents. Since we had already gotten some money back from Michigan, we had recouped our $30.00 postage. There was another $10.00 for copying and envelopes. We had already broken even and then some.

Tonight Charlie and I were going to a program where he would learn (I would watch) how to make his own Native American shirt and pants or whatever. Anyway, he was making something. I was tagging along because it sounded interesting, and I could always use a night out.

Before we left, Jack ate some crackers and cheese and a couple of bites of Suzanne's cheeseburger casserole—and he does not like casseroles so it had to be good. He was not up much. He kept saying he was too tired to try to do anything or go anywhere. We were hoping for about 50 degrees tomorrow and sun, so if he was up to it at all, we planned to stuff him in the van and take him for a ride—somewhere—anywhere—just to get him out and mentally stimulated.

Charlie and I left for the program and left Jack's phone on the table by his bed. At the meeting they also talked about Native American culture. It was very interesting. We are Native American through marriage of a native woman to a French fur trader back in the early 1700s. So, now I knew why I liked the things I did—the outdoors, certain types of clothing, and so on—must be genetic.

Friday, March 29, 2013—Lots of Questions, No Answers

Going back to last night—about half an hour after we got to the meeting, Jack called. I knew it was his ring because I had a ringtone set so I would know when it was him calling. I went out into the hall to take the call.

He said the electricity was out and asked where Charlie was. I told him we were at a meeting, which I had told him before we left. I asked if it looked like anyone else's was out. He said he didn't know because he could not see anyone else's house. But he didn't look outside either because if he had, he would have seen our light on the barn was on. At any rate, I told him I would have Dave check it out and see what was going on.

I called Dave, and he said he had lights in the back of the house, so I knew it was a circuit breaker problem. I asked him to go to the front of the house and check everything and see what his dad was talking about. While I was on the phone, he went into the living room and told me there were no lights and the pellet stove was off. I told him to check the circuit breaker box. He did and fixed it, and everything was okay.

When I got home about 11:00 P.M., Jack told me he was afraid when the stove went off that the house would get cold and he didn't know what to do. So, here was my question. What was going on in his brain? He would talk to you and make perfect sense. Why, then was he worried about the heat and electricity when all he had to do was get up and look around? He would have or should have known it was a circuit breaker as soon as he saw lights elsewhere in the house. That incident was pretty scary to me because it indicated he was not thinking clearly. For this man to not think to get up and check other lights or the circuit breaker—well, let's just say this was absolutely not even a little bit like him.

During the day he told me that the previous night had been awful. He had had a headache and a "pain in his heart." I asked what kind of a pain. He could not really identify what it was like—sharp pain, dull ache, heavy weight on his chest. Was he sure it was his heart? Not his lungs? He wasn't sure. All he said was it hurt. So, another question—was it heartburn or were we looking at the beginning of heart issues? Heart attacks are not uncommon with this type of cancer.

When I got him settled for bed he said, "It's the beginning of a long, hard night." When I asked him what he meant, he said he didn't sleep well and had a lot of pain at night. Why at night? I'm not sure what night had to do with the pain being worse. Or maybe he just felt it more because there were fewer distractions to take his mind off the pain. Lots of questions, no answers. And this was the first I was hearing of these types of problems.

We had hoped during the day to get him to go for a ride. Charlie even offered to help him into the van. He said he just didn't feel well enough to make the effort. It would have been nice to get him out because it turned out to be a beautiful day.

The kids and I did some yard work and burned a pile of limbs and old dead plants from the garden. Then the girls went with Charlie to get the last of the sap from our woods; he and I planned to boil it down at Wolcott Mill the next day. While they were gone, Elisha and I had popcorn for a snack.

I needed to call it a night early because I had not slept well the night before either. When Jack was restless, I could not sleep. I tried not to disturb him, but sometimes I just had to get up and go do something. I tried to quietly go back to the office and work where I would not be making any noise. Sometimes it worked, and sometimes he knew I was moving around and wanted to know why I was awake.

Saturday, March 30, 2013—Maple Syrupin'

It was a beautiful sunny day. I left the house at 7:30 A.M. after making sure Jack had something to eat. As usual it was very little. He just ate half a biscuit and two pieces bacon. I think all he had yesterday was three crackers. I told him where I was going and that Dave would be there if he needed anything. I also told him I'd be back at noon to check on him and give him his meds.

I headed to Wolcott Mill, which was only about four miles away, to help Charlie finish the sap/syrup program and then do our own. There was so much sap from both the Mill and our woods that I knew it would be a late night. The Mill had about fifty-five gallons, and we had about forty, so it was almost one hundred gallons—we should get about two-and-a-half gallons of syrup. Was it worth it? Yes!

Using a commercial evaporator made boiling down the sap so much easier than the way we had been doing it. Even with that we knew it would be an all-day event. For some reason, the evaporator was not boiling like it had been, and by noon we knew we would be way behind. It was really going to be a late night.

I left Charlie at noon and went home to get Jack's meds out and see what else he needed. He still wasn't hungry, so I just fixed my lunch, checked the mail, and straightened a few things, and when Jack fell asleep I headed back to the Mill.

Sunday, March 31, 2013—Easter

Well, this was a quite different Easter for us. Christmas was chaotic with all the kids and grandkids here. Today it was just Jack, Dave, and me. From total noise to total quiet: what a change.

This morning I went to church service, which was awesome. Mick does an incredible job of making the Bible come alive, and he apologizes for none of it. Nor should he. From start to finish the whole thing was a blessing.

I didn't go anywhere for dinner, even though I was invited to Clarke's (thank you). Jack had not been feeling well, and I didn't want to be away from home for too long.

When I got back, I fixed him a Vernors float, which he drank. He then took a nap, so I worked out in our mini barn sorting through the stuff that had come out of his semi. I'm telling you, he had more stuff in that truck than I had in the house. Okay, that's a slight exaggeration, but I had filled five bags of stuff for the dump, one small trailer full to be burned, and still had at least six more bags to go through. I'm not talking grocery bags—I'm talking thirty-gallon garbage bags.

I had a lot of sorting to do, but as a first pass it wasn't too bad. I knew that once I got through the things that were truly trash, I would need to take my time to sort through tools, hardware, and personal stuff (toothpaste, aftershave, Ziploc® bags, etc.). That was going to

Journey Through the Valley of the Shadow

take some time. I had a small TV out there for the kids, and I decided the next time I worked out there I would take a movie with me and watch and listen as I sorted.

Dave fixed us a steak, asparagus, and potatoes for dinner. Jack ate some of the steak, a few bites of potato, and a few crackers. I weighed him, and he was 125. I had been pretty sure he was under 130 for a while now, and I had guessed correctly. He was 132 on March 19, so that is seven pounds in twelve days. Not good, but no surprise since he was hardly eating anything.

Mentally he was doing fairly well. He could hold a conversation and knew who everyone was. He did struggle, though, with some thought processes. He did not know it was the end of March and was surprised when I told him his birthday was Thursday. I told him he had to make it till then because he would be seventy-six, and that was a milestone.

I had to keep fixing his sheets and blankets because he was restless, and they kept getting tangled up. Everything I have read says this was normal because it was hard for him to get comfortable for more than a few minutes in any one position. When there's not much muscle and fat left in the body, there's not much protection against anything, even something like a soft mattress.

As I have said before, we did not know where we were in the progression of this disease. With his weight down to 125, I knew we were in a downward progression, but we still had no idea how long he had. When this all started in late November, they had given him two months if he did no treatment. He did do the radiation and one round of chemo, but I didn't know how that changed things. I had read extensively online and those without other issues—he wasn't in the best of health before this—usually only live four to six months even with treatment. Rarely did anyone with SCLC live a year. We were just past the four-month time frame.

As I said before, his time was in God's hands. He had said he didn't want to be here if he was not mentally stable. God had been gracious to allow him to be mentally alert all this time. I prayed that would continue, for his sake as well as mine. I wasn't sure how well I could handle it if he slipped drastically mentally. It was bad enough to watch him slip physically.

Monday, April 1, 2013—But It's Still Winter

Spring had come on March 21st, but you'd never have known it from the weather. I was so tired of the cold. The sun did help though. I kept hoping it would warm up so maybe we could talk Jack into going out.

Charlie asked him tonight if he wanted to do Cracker Barrel for his birthday on Thursday, and he said it was too much effort to get ready. He still had two days to think about it but was already saying it was too much. I bought him some new pajama bottoms for an early present. They didn't really look like pajamas; they looked like men's shorts because I had gotten some with designs on the legs. Do you think we could get away with him wearing them to Cracker Barrel? I heard people wore weirder stuff to Walmart. But I didn't think he'd even consider it, so we never did ask him.

He didn't want any kind of celebration—just some chicken and dumplings. The question was, would he even eat them if I fixed them? And again, the answer was, if he would even consider a few bites, I was willing to make him whatever he wanted.

I had been tired all day, so I decided to make it an early night. I could have fallen asleep about 4:00 P.M., but I knew if I did, I'd be up half the night. I decided to try to go to bed and hopefully fall asleep about 9:00 P.M. and hoped I would not wake up at 4:00 A.M. again.

Tuesday, April 2, 2013—Downturn

We went into a downward cycle again today. Every time we took a dip, we did not come back to where we were before, which was disheartening but expected. Today his blood pressure was 88/50. It had been consistently low, and sometimes it would drop like this. When it did, he was miserable, uncomfortable, and mentally sluggish and had no appetite.

His only food today was part of a biscuit and syrup and a few crackers. For liquid, he had not quite a cup of coffee. He had not taken any meds either. He wanted to see if that was what made him feel so bad in the morning. I was sure that was part of it, but I was sure it was also the tumors. We were far enough from the radiation and the chemo that I was pretty sure the tumors were growing fast again. All my research said they would grow quickly as this was an aggressive cancer.

He slept a lot during the day, which meant he did not sleep well at night. If he didn't take the meds at night, neither of us would sleep well. While Vicodin was not a sleep aide, it did have the benefit of helping him sleep because it relieved the headaches he had at night.

I had been falling asleep in the chair earlier in the day when Charlie stopped by. I usually don't do that, but I had been tired lately and would drift off easily. Since I was not sleeping well at night, catching some sleep during the day was helping.

I had been sleeping in our bed after he had the fall and went back to sleeping in the hospital bed. But tonight I decided to grab a blanket and stretch out on the chair. If I was not going to sleep well, I might as well be nearby if he woke up. I hoped it would help him sleep better if he saw me there. Maybe that was wishful thinking, but I decided to try it anyway.

Wednesday, April 3, 2013—Yogurt?

Who would have thought? I had a new Greek yogurt that I was trying. Jack saw it when I was eating it and asked for one. He ate it and said it was the only thing he had recently that hadn't given him heartburn. Was it the yogurt or the fact that he hadn't taken any meds in twelve hours? Who knows? Whatever it was, he decided to have a cup of coffee and that stayed down without heartburn too.

In the afternoon he had another yogurt—blueberry this time—and another coffee. Two "meals" in one day—amazing. Did I not tell you this is a roller coaster ride? One day up, one day down. If this yogurt thing would actually work for a while, maybe he would get comfortable and we could both get some sleep.

For dinner he actually had a small amount of a beef stew I made in the crockpot. The meat was super tender, and all he complained about was not enough salt.

In the afternoon I called our family handyman, Don B. because I blew out a circuit breaker four times. It was the same one that went out the night Charlie and I were out, and it had gone out two weeks before that. Yes, there was a lot of stuff on it but we've run a lot of stuff before. Charlie had ordered a new breaker online a while ago, so we actually had a new one available. It was a good thing too because Don said he didn't think you could get this kind anywhere, except maybe special order online. That circuit breaker box was at least fifty years old. Don had the old one out and the new one in in about five minutes. Thanks, Don!

Tonight I decided to give Jack some melatonin. I had read that melatonin is a natural product that helps with sleep, and I was hoping that would help him sleep better without having to take the meds. He was really resisting the meds because they made him feel so bad. I was sure it was because he had been taking them on an empty stomach but I wanted to try whatever would make him feel better. I was about ready to call it a night also. We would see what tomorrow had in store for us.

Thursday, April 4, 2013 — Celebrate!

Celebrate! That's what we did today — celebrated his seventy-sixth birthday! We weren't sure he would feel up to going out, but we stuffed him in the van and out we went.

First, though, in the morning, Pastor Garry and Gary B. stopped by and wished him happy birthday and prayed with him.

Then we rested a bit and left about 1:00 P.M. We took him to Cracker Barrel in Port Huron. He got catfish and dumplings and actually ate a fair amount of it. (Yippee! I didn't have to cook).

When we got back he fell asleep immediately. A little later his friends, Mark and Harvey stopped by for a few minutes. Then George and Luz stopped by. George had some truck magazines for him. Then Carol stopped by. He didn't expect all that attention and accused me of telling the world. Funny thing is, I didn't tell anyone except Pastor Garry. Jack had told Mark and Harvey earlier in the week; George and Luz already knew, as did Carol.

I don't think he was upset though even if he did pretend it was too much. I asked him later if he enjoyed the day, and he said yes.

So, today for a change, instead of requesting prayer I was requesting praise. I wanted to praise so the rocks would not have to cry out (look *that* one up in your Bible). Praise that he made it to seventy-six years of age (in November, December, and January we did not think he'd make it this far). Praise that it was a sunny, if cool, day. Praise that he was able to get out and enjoy the day. Praise that so many stopped or called to wish him a happy birthday. Praise that he was still pretty much mentally alert. Praise that the yogurt seemed to be helping with some of the stomach issues he'd had for the past two months.

Praise because we knew who walked with us through this valley, and we were not alone.

Friday, April 5, 2013—The Truck Is Gone

We had sold the semi-truck and trailer two months ago. The new owner finally came today to pick both up. Jack knew it was sold and would be gone eventually. But he still had a rough time watching it go down the drive. It was the finality of it. It was done. It was over. He was more than a little bit depressed about it.

He had been feeling a little better though with the stomach issue not hurting as bad. The yogurt seemed to be doing a good job in that regard. Of course two yogurts a day wasn't enough to keep him going either, but if it kept calming his stomach, I hoped he might try other things also.

Saturday, April 6, 2013—The Struggle Continues

It was not the struggle against cancer; it was the struggle against feeling worthless, which was what he said tonight. It was still on his mind that the truck was actually gone. He would no longer see it when he walked into the kitchen or went outside. Mentally, that was really wearing on him.

He could not fall asleep even after taking a sleeping pill and a pain pill. I told him to quit thinking and let his mind relax. He said he couldn't quit thinking because all he could think about was how worthless he was and how much he'd like to be able to do and couldn't. I, unfortunately, had no answer to that.

No one had ever been in the driver's seat of his truck (while it was moving) since he had bought it. To see someone else drive it away was pretty emotional for him. As I said, I think a part of that in the back of his mind was that now it really was final. Not that it wasn't before, but each thing that happened, or left, or changed, was one more final event.

For the most part I could handle what was going on. I was trusting the Lord to walk with me and guide me. I knew many were praying for us. That helped more than people knew. It was still hard, though, with all the ups and downs. One day he would feel good and eat, so I would think maybe we'll do a little better, and he will get up and around. Then he would take a downturn, and I was never sure if I should warn the family so they could be ready for whatever happened. Then he would come out of it and be okay for a few days again. It was sooo hard!

I absolutely could not predict or make plans for anything more than one day at a time because I never knew what the next day would bring.

Sometimes I would journal things that happened that were a normal part of the day because sometimes I needed to focus on normal stuff so I could keep on keeping on. Besides, the more normal I could keep things, the more I could handle mentally. It wasn't that I was trying to avoid facing what was going on—I just sometimes needed a break from it. So sometimes I would just journal about our daily routine.

Like today—I finished the maple syrup. Charlie had boiled down forty-five gallons of sap to about five or six gallons. Of that we further boiled to about a gallon of syrup, and I put some aside and made fudge. I added walnuts because it would get so sweet. It didn't harden up like it usually does because I didn't cook it long enough. My back was on fire as it was. Anyway, even eating it with a spoon it was delicious. The thing is, it was so sweet, one tablespoon and you could go into a sugar coma. Good thing I put the nuts in there to balance the sugar content. I decided try some over oatmeal in the morning.

For tonight, I need to get my feet up. I was done for the day.

Sunday, April 7, 2013—What a Day!

Today was an awesome day at church. There were two baptisms, and my niece was commissioned for a mission trip and for finishing an intense program called "Boot Camp." But let me back up a minute. Before I even got to church I called one of my brothers to run a few things by him. He's my mentor and always had some good insights for me. Good thing I drove back roads because we talked the whole time I drove to church. Thanks, Allen. I needed that and I needed to just hear your voice.

Then at the first service, Pastor Mick interviewed his brother, who was in remission from leukemia. Wow! What a powerful testimony. Then he baptized his brother. I can only imagine the emotion and feeling that comes with being able to baptize your sibling. What a day for Pastor Mick and his family

Then Suzanne was commissioned for both events—Boot Camp and her upcoming mission trip. And the worship songs! Well, I could go on and on. It was an awesome morning. In the second service, my nephew, John, was baptized. Just him. They were planning a baptismal service for the next Sunday, but Suzanne would be on the mission trip, so they decided to baptize John today so she could be a part of his special day. I took them out to lunch to celebrate. We met their daughter and her friend there and had a good time.

What can I say—it was all good.

I knew Jerry and Lori were at the house with Jack so I wasn't too worried about being a bit late. However, while at the restaurant, Jack called. I asked if everything was ok and he said yes but asked when I would be home. I told him I would not be long. He told Jerry it made him nervous when I was gone for a long time even when someone was with him. Jerry told him sometimes I needed to get away and be with people for a little bit and not to worry—I'd be home soon. Thanks, Jerry. It helped when others told him that because I did need to get away

He had also told Jerry he felt worthless, and Jerry told him he was *not* worthless and to not feel that way. Thank you, Jerry. He needed to hear that from someone besides me.

Later Jack told me he didn't like it when he fell asleep and then woke up and I was not there with him. I hadn't realized how much he had come to depend on my presence. It's not that I did so much for him, it's just that I was there.

He had told me once he was afraid I'd leave because he was so much trouble to take care of. I told him he was stuck with me for the duration because when I said, "in sickness and in health; for richer, for poorer," I meant it. It had not always been easy or fun, but I had made a commitment, and at times when I did want to say, "I'm done with this," the Lord made it plain I was to "stay with it." So, here I was, and he was stuck with me, like it or not!

It had been such a great day I knew it would be hard to wind down and go to sleep, but I had to get some rest. The past couple of nights had not been good sleep-wise for a couple of reasons. He could not take the sleep med anymore because of a problem it was causing. It was too bad, because he was getting about five to six hours of sleep after taking it

Monday, April 8, 2013 — Emotional Swirls

You know all emotion is not negative. Usually when we say someone is emotional, we think something is wrong. Not always. Take yesterday, for instance. It was an emotional high: seeing two guys get baptized, taking one out for lunch to celebrate, hearing a great message. Even good emotions take energy though, so today I was really tired. I didn't get anything accomplished. Oh, wait, I take that back. I got the taxes mailed. Now *that* takes some emotional energy. I hate tax time.

The other part of emotional energy is that it sometimes is very erratic. You can be on the mountain one minute and racing toward the valley at breakneck speed the next. Why does that happen?

We had so many ups and downs that I kept saying it was like a roller coaster. Right now we were ticking our way back up to what I hoped was a level plateau. How long it would last I did not know. The hard part was knowing we would head back down at some point. The good part was enjoying the leveling off while we could.

So, just what was I talking about? Well, for the past several days Jack had eaten some yogurt and not complained of heartburn or stomach problems. That was a good thing. When every bite you eat causes pain, you just avoid eating. He had lost seven pounds in twelve days and was saying he was starving to death. He was. Today he said he needed more calories or he could not go on. I had been telling him that, but he needed to come to grips with it himself. He had been getting so weak he could barely make it to the bathroom—twenty feet away.

We discussed what he might like, and he agreed to try a McDonald's shake and apple pie. (Some friends had suggested Ensure, but he refused to drink it.) I went to McDonald's and got a shamrock shake and two apple pies and decided to get a strawberry pie to see if he would eat it. Today was a red letter day! He had a yogurt, coffee, an apple pie, and then later another coffee, another apple pie, and a cup of potato soup (a friend had gotten the soup at the restaurant uptown and brought it over). He didn't eat all this food all at once obviously. But, for today, we were close to 1,000 calories. That was quite a step up from the 340 he had been getting with only two yogurts a day. He was full so I put the shake in the freezer for later.

Because of all the issues with the different meds, he was only taking pain meds when he needed them. He said eating the yogurt helped his stomach, so he could now eat a little more, which I think helped because he was then not taking the meds on an empty stomach.

So, yes, the emotions swirled all around and sometimes up and down. It was hard to relax and hard to focus some days. Then, because it was so up and down, I didn't take time to eat properly either, which didn't help. Last night's dinner was a bag of popcorn. I just did not feel like putting something together, and Dave had been too busy to cook. At least I had a good lunch.

In the evening friends Stan and Emilia stopped by and dropped off a belated birthday card for Jack. We had a good conversation with them, and they prayed for Jack before they left. It was been a pretty good day after all. The next thing was to get Mr. Restless to settle down so we could both go to bed.

Tuesday, April 9, 2013 — Rainy, Lazy Day

There was so much I need to do, and I just could not get the energy to do it. Well, it was not only energy; I just did not have the ambition. Maybe it was the weather. Rain always made me want to curl up and read a book. But that took too much effort, so I would just close my eyes. I could have dozed off, but the thunder sounded like it was right next to me.

I did stain some molding today, even with the humidity. I had bought it for the kitchen and back hall. It had only been about eighteen months since I had taken the old stuff out. I had painted the hallway and a room off our kitchen. The old molding was cracked and worn, so I had bought new. It was out in one of our out-buildings, and now, since it was so damp, I wasn't sure when it would dry. Oh well, maybe a second coat tomorrow.

Charlie and I went and got some pellets for our pellet stove (for heat). Yep, it was April and still cold. I was really ready for warm weather. It was too nasty to even try to get Jack interested in going outside, and he said he was too weak anyway. But it would have been nice if it were warm enough for him to try.

I offered to make him sausage and gravy with biscuits today, and he said that did not even sound good. *That* was a serious clue as to how bad he felt. If he turned down biscuits and gravy, he definitely had a problem. Growing up in the South, that was a breakfast staple. To turn it down . . . well, it left me wondering.

I had tried to make fudge out of the maple sap we had left, or rather that I held aside, and mostly it was just sugary. Today I put it back in the pan to boil some more. I figured it wouldn't hurt it, so I heated it up again. It worked. We had some fudge. I needed to see if there was actually any left or if three kids and an adult went home on a sugar high.

Today had been a gray, ugly day. I didn't feel like I accomplished anything. Looking back, though, I realized I had stained some molding, went to the store and bought pellets for the pellet stove so Jack could stay warm, worked on schoolwork with the kids, and made fudge out of leftover sap/syrup. It wasn't a wasted day after all.

Wednesday, April 10, 2013—Not Much Change

Today was frustrating in that I had been booted three times from the Internet while trying to get something done. The storms knocked out the router, and I had a hard time getting some work done. Needless to say, I was frustrated and done for the day. I used to have a fair amount of patience, or at least I thought I did. Maybe it was the stress, but I could get so frustrated so easily, and that did scare me a bit because I did not want to become angry over simple things. When I needed to get something done, though, and kept having issues, it really made my day worse.

There was not much news today, but the accumulated stress was causing me some problems. It's a good thing it was a relatively quiet day. I spent most of the day researching something and had written a long post about it—just to get booted as I was finishing up. There was no way to save it either. When you are in the middle of typing and suddenly you see a blank screen, you know whatever you were working on was gone. Because of the rain and cold I had aching hands. Rheumatoid does that to you. I decided enough was enough.

Thursday April 11, 2013—A Better Day

Saying it was a better day was not saying much because anything would be better than the past few days had been. It was not the rain that causes the pain—it was the cold rain. Ugh! Sure made the RA hurt.

I knew people were praying for us. I was so thankful, and I posted that in my emails. I did feel better. I was still aching but I had a better attitude this day, or at least I hoped I did. At least I was not so frustrated.

Last night I was the one taking pain meds to go to sleep. They worked too, because I slept through the night. I knew I'd never sleep with the aching hands, so I broke down and took something. You are probably thinking I was dumb to not take it all the time. I did. I had to take something every morning to get through the day. I just did not want to overload.

That said, I would measure good days by whether Jack would eat. He did eat a yogurt, and then I got him to eat a piece of sausage and some scrambled eggs with some gravy on them (I made the

162

gravy with the sausage, which he liked). For dinner he actually ate a couple of bites of chicken leg and some black-eyed peas. It was a good day, food-wise.

It had been a busy day, and I knew the next day would be another busy one. I had some reports for the company that had to be done before end of April. I also needed to get some paperwork done as the boss had seven loads scheduled between now and the end of May. He would only be in two days next week and then would be gone again. Everything he needed had to be done by then. I had to file a federal report and a state report also. Those take some focus, and I needed to pay attention when I worked on them.

We wrapped up this day with a visit by Pastor Garry and Martha. Jack was happy to see them. He always was comforted when they stopped by. Suzanne stopped by also to visit before her trip to Mexico. We all had a good prayer session. I told Suzanne I would miss her next week while she was on her trip because she helped with the kids schooling at least once a week.

The kids were staying the night, so after everyone left, I let them put a movie in the DVD player in the bedroom they were using, and we all went to bed.

Friday, April 12, 2013—A Special Errand

Today was an exciting day for me. I was making a run to the airport to pick up Rich. He was making a quick last minute trip to Michigan. He had an interview scheduled for Monday morning at 8:00 A.M. with a company in Michigan. If the offer was good, they would relocate to Michigan. We had been praying for this to happen. Rich had several interviews and contacts, but so far nothing had worked out, and no offers had been made. We were getting discouraged.

Jack was cranky today and ate very little of the sausage, eggs, and biscuit I fixed. I could fix it; that was no problem. I just wished he'd eat more than just a few bites. I know when your stomach shrinks, you can't put much in it, but the body needs fuel to survive. It was a constant battle to try to get him to eat even a few bites. I didn't nag at him, but I did try to encourage him to at least try to eat. Sometimes he did and sometimes he didn't.

I knew he'd be alone for about six hours, and I was praying he wouldn't fall or anything. I was praying he would fall asleep just before I left and that he would sleep most of the time I was gone. Dave had to make a trip across state, and he would be even later than us coming back. I alerted Charlie so he could be ready to check on his dad if the need arose. All went well, and even though we were back home late, Jack had done well by himself.

Saturday, April 13, 2013—Some Cleanup Done

First, let me say this was a good day in that Jack actually ate some food. I judged a good or bad day by the quantity he ate. He had a small amount of a breakfast casserole I made; some chicken and dumplings (if he would have turned down the dumplings I would really have been worried), and a cup of chicken broth. All portions were tiny in comparison to what everyone else ate, but he did eat.

Since I had a "captive" here in that Rich flew in for an interview, I put him to work. Actually he and Charlie did a lot of work around the yard. Rich and I filled—and I mean filled—the pickup with trash and took it to the dump. Then later, Rich and Charlie filled—and I mean filled—the pickup with metal and took it to the scrap yard. We made $50 on the scrap metal.

They stacked some old tires that had been scattered about on a cement pad, cut a limb out of a tree, and moved some yard equipment off the grass so it can be mowed if it ever stops snowing and has a chance to grow. It was beginning to look a lot neater.

Then, because it was so cold and windy, they came inside to work. They caulked the kitchen floor under the windows so we could put the new molding down. That cut down on the draft across the floor. I was amazed at the difference.

Rich had already requested chicken and dumplings, so I figured if he was going to do all that work, I could honor that request. It was simple enough. Jack ate two dumplings and wanted more. He had a few more and said they were better than at Cracker Barrel. Now, that was saying something, although he probably said that to make sure I'd make them again.

He would talk with Rich and Charlie between jobs. Then he would fall asleep, and they would go back to work. Then he would wake up and accuse me of overworking them so that he could not spend time with them. I'd send them in to spend time with him, and then when he would fall asleep, I'd give them another job. And so went the day.

A toilet seat in our back bath was broken; it was not even usable. The sink in that room was leaking, and there was water in the clothes basket under the sink. The septic was full and needed emptying, or at least I thought it was because nothing was draining properly. Yep, the toilets kept backing up. What fun we were having at the Shelton farm. Oh yes, we did need a lot of prayer!

Sunday, April 14, 2013—More Done; More to Do

First, the good news was that Jack ate a decent breakfast. Rich got him an omelet from town while I went to church. In the afternoon he had a small amount of a Cold Stone Ice Cream—salty caramel, the only flavor he would eat. He also had a cup of chicken bouillon. Like I said, a good day was when he would eat

Well, there really wasn't any bad news—it was all pretty good. Things seemed to be draining well. The ground water was receding, and that helped. I bought two new toilet seats, and Rich installed them. We found the leak in the bathroom sink. We were not sure how repairable it was since the sink was at least fifty years old. It was hard to find parts for things that old (including people).

We also worked in our mini barn sorting and organizing stuff that came out of the semi. We made some good headway. We were getting there. The yard was looking good. The house was pretty well organized and sorted. If it would ever warm up, the old outbuildings would be next.

We had to quit early enough for Rich to clean up and prep for the interview the next day.

Monday, April 15, 2013 I Hardly Know What to Write

With what happened in Boston today, it was hard to even focus on what was going on at home. What we were facing was nothing compared to what hundreds, or possibly thousands were dealing with in Boston. How do you even wrap your head around such utter evil?

It was a pretty "normal" (our new normal) day at home until Jack turned the TV on and we saw what had happened. I was having a hard time reading about or looking at pictures of what happened. It wasn't that I didn't care or have sympathy for all those affected—victims, families of victims, police, fire, EMS, doctors. I just could not drain myself by focusing on it. My physical, mental, and emotional state were already depleted, and seeing this just took a lot out of me. I'm not sure how Jack felt about it, but neither of us could watch for very long.

It had been a pretty positive day up until that point. Rich had not one but two interviews today. They had asked him to come back at 11:30 A.M. for a follow up after the 8:00 A.M. interview. He had to race back home, pack his things, and race out again. Dave drove him to that interview, and then to the airport. Rich said if they were interested, he would get another call for the third interview—probably within a week.

Jack had yogurt and a little corned beef from a sandwich today. He then had chicken broth and said it seemed to help him sleep. I had not slept well the previous night; I had tossed and turned from about 3:30 A.M. until I finally got up at 5:00 A.M. When I did get up in the morning, I felt lightheaded and dizzy, as though I had vertigo, which I didn't. I was sure it was just lack of sleep. A good six hours (I hadn't gotten eight hours in a really long time) would be nice and would refresh me, I thought.

Tuesday, April 16, 2013—Alternative Cancer Therapy?

I was looking for feedback from anyone who had used or knew anyone who had used alternative therapy for cancer. I was, and am, a believer in "natural" products as much as possible. However, all that I was reading about any alternative therapy indicated they did not work on brain tumors.

A friend had told Jack about Cantron (my brother had also used this product) and said he should try it. What he didn't do was research it because everything I read about Cantron said it was not effective for brain tumors. Jack wanted to try it anyway, and I told him he could, but what I had been reading said it would not be effective. I did not want to discourage him, but neither did I want to give him false hope. Also, with Cantron and other therapies it was critical that the patient eat and drink regularly. He was doing neither.

There was another website about a different product that stated they had success with brain tumors with their product. However (there was always a "however"), they said it was not always effective. Well, that was to be expected. No one could ever guarantee their product would cure cancer. They also stated you must adhere to their program of what to eat and drink and how much of each. With Jack's eating and drinking issues, I just did not feel any therapy would work for him. I was not trying to curtail any therapy that could potentially help him, but I could not realistically promote or try any of these programs if he would not follow them to the letter. To do otherwise would be a waste of money and he would be discouraged because he would feel it didn't work. It was a catch-22.

The problem was the blood brain barrier, which one therapy claimed they could get past. Then they said you had to take other supplements to rid the brain of the now dead cells and toxins. Then you had to take yet something else to keep the liver from being impacted by these toxins. The expense varies and would not be covered by insurance, obviously. I didn't doubt some things worked, especially if you caught the cancer early (we were stage 4 at diagnosis). If it worked, the money would be well spent. However, I could find no testimonials past 2010 and very few past 2006. There should be a boatload of testimonials if these things worked. Why the silence?

This was getting to be an issue, and I really needed wisdom to know if it was an avenue we should pursue. I was not so much concerned about the cost as much as the fact that if it didn't work, he would be very, very discouraged and also that if he didn't follow the regimen, he could actually have far worse problems. All of the therapies I investigated called for drinking at least forty ounces of fluid a day, and I was lucky to get him to drink twenty.

We were at a standstill. I was going to a meeting in the evening and needed some time to think it through, so I put it on a back burner for a few days. I was not trying to avoid doing something that might potentially help him, but it had to be the correct choice. Doing something that would not help, or that he would not follow through with would be worse than deciding to continue as we had been—just keeping him comfortable.

Wednesday, April 17, 2013—Praises

Sometimes in the middle of the storm, we forget there are things to be thankful for. I decided to go backwards—starting with the evening's events and then moving back toward morning.

After a meeting I went to Tuesday evening, I stopped at a store to get some groceries. When I was ready to leave, it was pouring rain and lightning literally lit up the sky. I decided to wait it out. I hate lightning. As I was standing there, a voice behind me said, "You afraid of a little rain?" I turned and there was a friend, Kim G. from church. I told her it wasn't a little rain and, yes, I was afraid of lightning. As we talked, it started raining even harder. She had her son go get my truck, pull it up by the door, and load my stuff. Bless them, Lord.

Kim had two baskets of groceries; I had about a half basket. What were the chances we'd be in the store at the same time and that she would be checking out in another aisle and be done at almost the same time as me? I don't think it was a coincidence; I think it was God providing for me in a rainstorm. Praise Him!

The meeting I had attended was the first Stephen's Ministry meeting I had been able to attend in six weeks. Shannon shared again that if we don't praise Him, the rocks will. Thanks, Shannon, for that reminder. Bless her, Lord for her testimony.

Also at that meeting, Pastor Mick spoke on having a "Day Alone with God" (D.A.W.G.). I had done this in the past as part of a Laborer's Network program that I had done years ago. I had been lax lately. Thanks, Pastor Mick for the nudge to get back at it. Bless him, Lord.

Charlie had agreed to stay late at the house so I could go and not fret about being away from home Bless him, Lord. Finally, I had to say "Thank you, Lord, for a great evening out."

Backing up to earlier in the day, I have to explain something. I previously mentioned that we had applied for a refund of Jack's commercial license plate. There was a prayer and a praise here. The prayer was that we would get refunds from more states. Several had sent "reject" notices stating (for various reasons) that they would not refund any portion of the "apportioned money" that Michigan had already sent them. Some states had refunded all the money   not just a portion. Thank You, Lord. We had already received enough back to cover the postage I had paid to send letters out to forty-five states and had some extra, so we were ahead by a few dollars.

Backing up even earlier—in the morning Jack said he was hungry, so I made him some bacon, eggs, and biscuit. He ate almost all of it. Thank you, Lord.

I had all the paperwork current in the office. I had to order a permit from the State of Michigan and would then be caught up. Whew! That was a load off my mind—for a couple of weeks anyway. Thank You, Lord.

The weather had warmed up, which had been a relief in that my hands were not hurting as much. Praise You, Lord.

It was good to focus on other things and realize there was much to be thankful for. Thank you, Lord, for being interesting in, and helping me with, even the smallest things, like Kim being there to help with my groceries.

Thursday, April 18, 2013—The Storm Passed Us By

I was praising again—this time because the storm that came through Michigan was pretty tame in our neck of the woods. I was so glad. Charlie had finally put the generator on the back porch "just in case."

It was not just the electricity going out that could have been an issue. Another issue was how would I get an almost bedridden man out of the house if the storm was really severe? I was just glad God had protected us all winter and spring. I could take the rain; it was the wind I worried about. We had already had huge limbs fall during storms in the past. Thankfully, they had all fallen away from the house.

It had warmed up, and the pellet stove made it like an oven in the house. Because Jack had no "meat on his bones" and his immune system was compromised, he wanted it warm. Today even he admitted it was too warm. It was over 90 degrees in the living room. I could not stay in there in that heat. It made me groggy so that I could not stay awake. I was looking forward to the temperature cooling off so the house would be a little bit cooler.

The girls were staying overnight, so we picked out a movie to have with some brownie refrigerator cake that I found a recipe for online. I made it with gluten-free brownie mix. It had been a hit the previous night at Stephen's Ministry, and I had a little left over to bring home.

Friday, April 19, 2013—On Overload

It was quiet at the house today. The girls did some schoolwork. Jack was about the same. He had been eating some breakfast every morning and said he felt a little stronger. I was glad to see him eating more and glad he felt stronger. I was hoping he would feel good enough to get out of the house soon.

The overload was what was going on in Massachusetts. It was just too much to process and about the time you did, something else would happen. We had to turn the TV off again because it got to be more than we could watch.

Fortunately at this time there was no crisis with Jack. It would have been hard to deal with if there was.

Saturday, April 20, 2013—Moving On

That's what all of life is about—moving on. There was a TV show a while back called *Life Goes On*. That is so true.

For us, we were moving on, slowly as usual. Not much had changed. I could see small signs the brain tumors were causing problems but nothing significant. When I looked back before the diagnosis, I could now see things that were indicators that we had missed. Knowing what I knew now, I could see some things developing. It was so slow and so minor you would miss it or think it was something else. I could not even describe it because at the moment it was not an issue—just a subtle "something was not quite right" in his reasoning and memory. As usual, he was weak but still able to get to the bathroom—about twenty feet away. He still did not want to try to go outside—not that I would have taken him out in the bitter cold.

I saw things on the East Coast slowly coming back to normal. People would go on with their lives, and we would eventually not be as distracted by what had happened. Unfortunately, those families who don't have that option, whose lives are forever changed, would be distracted by this forever.

You could not, however, continue on in the same mental and emotional state as you were right when a crisis happened and right after. The human mind and body just cannot sustain that level of trauma for a long period of time without coming apart. So, even though it would fade from the news, I asked my prayer team to continue to pray for those folks. This was far from over for them.

We also needed continued prayer. While things had settled somewhat, it was far from over. Our lives had changed, and things still went "bump in the night." I still knew who held tomorrow, and I was still trusting in Him.

Sunday, April 21, 2013—Alternatives

Some people asked if I had looked into the alternatives. My answer was yes, I had been, and still was, researching. In fact, I was reading a book on nutrition in regards to cancer and other diseases. Let me say I was and am an advocate of nutrition and anything other than medicine. I know meds have their place, but for me, mostly they were, and still are, a disaster.

That said, I was reading and realizing that I had gotten sidetracked on my own diet in regards to the rheumatoid arthritis. I needed to get serious again. I was having too many flare-ups. I knew it was part stress and part weather, but I needed to get my own diet regulated to minimize the problems.

To understand what I was researching now, I had to go back to December and January. In December, Jack had ten days of radiation on the brain tumors. That ended Christmas Eve. They had told us several times you *must* drink a lot of fluid when doing radiation. Well, getting Jack to drink much on a good day was an issue, so this had become a serious problem. In fact, the day after Christmas we took him to the ER, and they admitted him. He was seriously dehydrated from not drinking enough. If we had not taken him in, I really and truly believe he would not have made it to the New Year.

Fast forward to the third week of January. We had finally started the chemo. They said again you *must* drink a lot of fluid when doing this. Again, getting him to drink more than a couple of cups of coffee a day was a challenge. In less than a week we were almost where we had been in December. In fact, in January Charlie had called his siblings and told them to expect the worst. Josette came out that week and hooked up an IV for him. That stabilized him. Because I knew he would never survive any more treatments, we canceled future chemo. Because of that and his condition, I had called in hospice. At that time, I really felt they would have to take down the bed they brought before he even had a chance to use it. I was sure he would not make it. He pulled through though and had been relatively stable ever since.

It wasn't that we hadn't had nose-dives—we had—but not to the degree we did in December and January. They tried steroids, and after two days he refused them totally. He said they made him nauseous and made his heart irregular. We tried a pain patch, and that was too much and overloaded his system. We also tried a nicotine patch and that did the same, really sending him into a nosedive.

So, when I looked into the Cantron, it said you *must* drink at least forty ounces of fluid a day. I was lucky to get him to drink two cups of coffee (24 oz) per day. Sometimes I could get him to try tea, ice cream, or Vernors but usually not more than one serving in addition to the coffee. He had two sixteen-ounce bottles of water on his table for three days. One had never been open, the other was almost empty

I could not make him drink anything—I could only provide it and encourage him. The rest was up to him, and he would always say he just could not drink that much. I thought part of the problem was that he thought if he drank too much liquid, then he would have to go to the bathroom more, and he was weak enough that was a problem. He was too stubborn to ask for assistance, so, again, we were between a rock and a hard place.

All of that to say that in my research, even in the nutrition book I was reading, they all said drinking a lot of fluid was absolutely necessary. I was guessing it was to wash the toxins out of your body. Whatever course you take, it causes the toxins in your body to accumulate in the kidneys and liver. It is imperative you drink mega amounts of fluids to wash them out or you have other problems.

Since we already had problems with other treatments (radiation, chemo, pain meds, etc.) and those had caused other issues because of his lack of drinking fluids, I had to evaluate each thing to see the requirements. There were no easy decisions.

The other issue was that most other treatments (other than nutrition) gave the caveat that they "might not" work on brain tumors because of the blood-brain barrier. Wasn't God good in providing such protection for our brains? What I could not figure out, though, was how the cancer cells got in there. (From what I was reading—if it was true—they travel through the blood and lymph system and get in that way).

Change of subject. I called in hospice back in January. They were a life saver—mentally, emotionally, and physically for me. I had someone coming out every week to check on things and give me information and instructions. I could call after hours if something went "bump in the night," which I did several times. I felt like it was not all on my shoulders. In short, they had been my lifeline in this. Since Jack was really too weak to be going to the doctor, it was good to have a nurse assigned to us that came out every week and more often if I needed assistance.

Remember the roller coaster? Well, at the moment we seemed to be on the plateau of that roller coaster. I was not sure when we would head down on one of those nosedives, but I had learned to take the quiet time for as long as it lasted. It allowed me to focus on other things and get things done. It also allowed me to get away from the house without worrying about something happening. I was sure it wouldn't always be like that, so I was taking advantage of it.

I still had not made a decision on what, if anything, to try. I had to move cautiously because of the issues we'd had in the past. Causing him to go into a nose dive was counter-productive and while nutrition and holistic therapy should not cause that, it was the lack of daily fluid intake that was an issue even with those therapies.

Monday, April 22, 2013—Interruptions

This day had been a day for interruptions. I wasn't complaining, just stating a fact. I used to get irritated at interruptions because it meant I wasn't accomplishing what I wanted. Notice that—"what I wanted." It may be that some of those interruptions, or maybe all of them, were blessings in disguise. I had learned, however, to be flexible. In the past five months, that lesson had been driven home countless times. So when I say there were interruptions, I am not saying it was a bad day—just a day that didn't go as I had planned.

Dave had to take his car uptown for repairs. We had planned that. I decided to stop at two banks and the post office so as to not waste a trip. Well, one bank didn't open until 9:00 A.M. and we were there about 8:35 A.M. I was not going to wait that long for it to open. That necessitated another trip into town. It's not that it was so far— it's only two-and-a-half miles; but it was another trip, one I hadn't planned to make.

The hospice social worker called and wanted to come out to visit. All well and good, except I had to get the kids started on schoolwork and return some calls for the company—just about the time she came.

Somehow I managed to get all that worked out and, gee whiz, it was lunch time. Where did the time go? Well, it was a nice day out for once, and I wanted to work outside with the kids. That didn't happen. Those plans were interrupted when Charlie called to see if I could take Reina to the eye doctor for a 3:00 P.M. appointment; which was the only one they had this week. That took care of the afternoon plans.

I did schedule a dinner with a wonderful friend and former co-worker and that did not get interrupted. We had an awesome time and talked and talked. I didn't get to do that too often, so I left Charlie in charge and put all thoughts of home on a back burner.

As I said before, I needed to do that when things were relatively "normal" here because I never knew when things would go "bump in the night."

I could do that today because Jack had a pretty good day. He ate all his breakfast for once. That consisted of one egg, one piece of sausage, one biscuit, and sausage gravy to put over it all. Considering where we were a month ago, that was a lot of food.

As I looked at the calendar, I was again amazed that this had all started five months before (November 23). It seemed like forever ago, and yet it seemed like yesterday. Does that make sense?

I could not even try to list all the things I had learned in the past five months. Hah! Did I say learned? I was still learning. I was not there yet. I was still working on patience and flexibility. I would not even touch on some of the others. I'm sure if I asked family and friends who would dare to be honest with me they would say that there were times they really weren't sure they wanted to be around me. I know for sure I was hard to get along with.

I had pretty much come to grips with the fact that *I was not in charge*. I was glad too because it relieved me of the responsibility of trying to make things happen. It was so much easier to hand it over to God and say, "carry it, please" or "carry me while I carry it, please." No, I decided I'd not do the second, just the first. I could not carry it. It was too big a burden. I could not change it, could not fix it. Those were hard lessons to learn, but I was getting there.

Tuesday, April 23, 2013—Getting Things Done

I finally got a good night's sleep. I went to bed about 10:00 P.M. and didn't get up until almost 6:00 A.M. today. That was a good night's sleep, and that was after I could not settle down at first.

I had to thank those who had prayed for a refund on Jack's commercial plate. With the four checks we got yesterday, we had received nearly half of the cost of the plate, which is all I had expected to get. We had thirty states we hadn't heard from yet. I was sure several of them would not refund because they were under $10. I was still looking for a "yea" or "nay" from about twenty. Every day Jack would ask if we got any "pennies from Heaven," which is what he called the refund checks. I would cash them and then give him the money so he could have his own cash when he went to breakfast with friends. He always felt like he should be able to pay his own way, and since that was important to him, it was important to me.

Today Charlie and I took out a section of fencing in the pasture and fixed it so Rica's dog, Molly, couldn't get out. While he worked on that, I picked up a lot of trash that had accumulated in that area. It looked much better. Things like that help because I would feel better when clutter was eliminated. We also did a very small amount of cleaning in the barn (it was overwhelming in there) and had a pile ready to be loaded in the pickup on Saturday for delivery to the dump.

I was glad we got all that done before the rain moved in. And it was supposed to be cooler the next few days—so, yes, we were "making hay while the sun shines," so to speak.

Enough about what I was doing. Jack ate a good breakfast again and actually had gained two pounds. He said he felt a little stronger and only had headaches late in the evening. He was still not feeling like he wanted to try to get out of the house but he was able to get around inside a little easier. His sleeping also seemed to be a little better. He was getting about four hours a night and was able to nap during the day—really nap, not just catnap a few minutes at a time.

Wednesday, April 24, 2013—Another Calm Day

I began to think I did not need to journal every day since things were somewhat "normal." There really was not much to say. Then, again, every time I thought that, something went "bump in the night." I decided that I needed to journal anyway because down the road it would remind me that not every day was a crisis. I needed to remember that.

Jack was now eating two small meals a day, his mental alertness seemed to be about the same, and energy-wise, he was able to get to the bathroom without any problems. I asked if he wanted to try to get out of the house soon, and he said there really was no place that he wanted to go. I would think just getting out would relieve the boredom, but it was his call.

In the meantime, I finished a scrapbook I had been working on and made another pass through several boxes and broke them down even more as to what category of items was in each box. Now those boxes needed to go out in one of the buildings with the rest. Since it had been nasty out, though, I thought it was a good time to do the inside work. The house was definitely not empty, but putting things away and organizing them made it look emptier (and cleaner).

I was about ninety-five percent done on the inside cleaning and organizing. I had a few things to take care of and then it would just be maintenance. I was looking forward to the insane weather to get better so I could start working my way through all the boxes of stuff that had come out of the semi. That was going to take a l—o—n—g time. Like Rich said, "It's like the way you would eat an elephant— one bite at a time." Yep, this elephant was quite huge, and I didn't move all that fast anymore.

There were several reasons I kept working at organizing the things that had come out of Jack's semi. One was that I needed to know what we had as far as tools and truck accessories and parts. Another was that I needed his input on what to do with them. I would not know what could be sold or what no one would want or what was just plain trash. And, I just needed to be doing something some days rather than just sitting and watching him. I needed something else to focus on. It helped me mentally as well as physically to be doing something.

Thursday, April 25, 2013—Connections

I had mentioned that I was thinking of not journaling every day, but I had been asked by some of the friends and family that were reading my journals to continue. So I decided to keep on writing on a daily basis. It was therapeutic for me to put my thoughts and feelings down and was also a stress reliever.

A friend commented that she had met some mutual friends that we hadn't seen in over twenty years. It was like they had never been apart—good friends can feel like that. She passed on our need for prayer and what we are going through. That was an encouragement to me to stick with the journal—I needed the prayer and the connections.

That said, I was truly trying to begin every day by saying, "Thanks God for this great day" and then, "Now take it back and just move me through it."

I quoted something (with modifications) that another woman had written on her journal because, you know, it just says it all. I agreed with her, and it was how I felt, so I felt it was worth sharing. Her quote, with a few changes, is as follows:

> I just want to be His pawn in all of this. I don't want to miss the smallest opportunity to smile or hug or be Jesus to someone who might never see Him any other way.

I realized how important this was because I never knew what a day might bring. As I have said before, I was learning not to let interruptions be a source of stress. If something happened so I had to reschedule my day, so be it.

Any of us can have our lives turned upside down in a heartbeat. Some of you know just what I am talking about.

I had so much to learn in giving my days, hours, and minutes back to the Lord. I never realized how many times, every day, that I did what I wanted—not even really considering what God wanted.

How many times have I avoided eye contact with someone because I was in a hurry to go on to the next task, or felt I "had" to get home right away. We're not the only ones going through a crisis, and sometimes I just needed to get away from my own problems and remember that others had them, too.

I was trying to learn those hard lessons. And because God had given me a faithful "helper," the Holy Spirit, I knew that I had a power beyond human capacity to succeed. Thank goodness! I could never even think about approaching this attitude without the help of God.

That helped me to hold onto all things loosely. Nothing really belongs to me anyway; I am just managing a few things for God.

Easy come, easy go. All the minutes of a day belong to Him—every conversation—every one that moves in and out of my life, both making new friends and renewing old friendships. It's all a part of what He wants for me today.

And if an issue pops up, it's not my problem because the day doesn't belong to me.

Those words were not easy to come by and usually only come when we are stretched beyond our own capabilities. I think I've said before that this had been a learning experience for me. I've learned some valuable lessons. I'm not sure why I always had to learn them the hard way, but at least I was learning.

I told Jack today that in doing research on RA I found out I am at three times the risk of "normal" people for a heart attack—to which he replied, "Don't you even think of leaving me! I could not deal with this without you." Well, that made me feel better—to know I was needed!

Anyway, today he was comfortable. None of us had any idea where we were in this process. I know I've said that before. It's true, though. Anything could happen at any time to turn things around—I had learned that lesson fairly well. It could also be a slow progression. I had read that with his type of cancer, median survival rate was four to six months. We were just past five months. That really meant nothing because there were so many factors involved. I just took one day at a time, making no long range plans and knowing that I might have to change my schedule at a moment's notice.

None of this was easy; it was just necessary. If I really focused and dwelt on it all the time, it would have driven me crazy. So, I just left it all in God's hands and did what I felt must be done as I went along

Friday, April 26, 2013—Going Looney

Got your attention with that title, didn't I? Well, no, I wasn't really going looney—then again, maybe I was. However, Charlie, the kids, and I went to see the migrating loons at Stoney Creek Park just before dark. They usually are long gone by now, but the cold weather up north in Canada had kept them down here in the "tropics."

It was windy and cold, so we didn't stay long. At one point I saw seven of them. Exciting news, I'm sure. Okay, on to something else.

The day was one of those that I mentioned before in that I did not get much accomplished. My boss arrived home this morning, and I did not expect him until this evening. When he was at the house, which is where the office is, I would have to stay in the kitchen and play "gatekeeper" or he would find an excuse to go into the living room and say, "Jack, are you awake?" Well, if he wasn't, he would be after that.

So you are thinking why didn't I just tell him to stay out of the rest of the house and that he only rents one room for an office, which is nowhere near the living room? Well, because Jack had not set that boundary early on. I knew he liked Jack, and this was hard on him also, but I had to make sure he didn't overstep now. On days Jack wasn't feeling good, I needed to make sure he wasn't disturbed by anyone. Therefore, Charlie (if he was here) or I would have to keep him back in the office. I had, on occasion, told him point blank he was not going to see Jack. Sometimes you need to sort that out and then set boundaries. Easier said than done, but it is important to the patient.

It didn't ruin my day in that it did not make me mad. It was just that I could not do anything because if I didn't play the gatekeeper, he would work his way in to where Jack was. There were occasions that I asked Jack if he wanted to talk to him, and he agreed it was okay. In those instances, I would give him the go-ahead to visit with Jack.

Most of the time I could handle it, but sometimes, when I was extremely tired or not feeling well or Jack had had a bad week or whatever, it really would irritate me, and then I could get an attitude. See why I say I needed_prayer? It wasn't just Jack and the illness I had to deal with; it was other people and my own attitude that sometimes got in the way.

Back to the evening activities. I had told Jack I'd be a little late getting back from seeing the loons because I was stopping at the store to pick up a few things. When I got back home a little after 9:00 P.M., I thought he was asleep. He turned on the light, though and asked if I saw the eagle too. There was an eagle's nest and one eaglet at Stoney Creek Metropark. I told him no, we did not see it, but I wished we had. Then he said if he felt up to it would I like to go to breakfast in town in the morning. Well, that was a good ending to a day that had not started out so well. If he actually felt up to going it would be the first time he had been out of the house since his birthday, April 4.

Saturday, April 27, 2013—Giving Thanks

After I posted this journal I felt that I should apologize for my negative attitude on my post for Friday. Sometimes I let it get to me and then I forgot that I really was thankful for things. So I decided to revisit Friday.

I wanted to say thank you to George and Luz for bringing lunch and dinner. Two full bags of Chinese food equaled two meals. I wasn't sure Jack would eat anything, but he had four shrimp and some fried rice. I made up for his lack by eating more than I should—and then doing it again later. Then I still had enough to send the leftovers home with Charlie for Josette.

George also brought about eight or so books on vintage and classic vehicles (cars, pickups, semis). The nice thing was that there were a lot of large pictures and not a lot of writing. Jack looked through some of them right after he got them. Reading a lot tired his eyes, so having the photos to look at was better for him, and he enjoyed the magazines and books.

Today he did feel up to going out. We made it into town, and he was hugged by many friends. He also ate a fair amount of his breakfast of French toast and sausage. When we got back home, he slept for two hours. Even a short trip wore him out completely, but when I asked him if it was worth it, he said, "Yes!"

While he slept, I worked in our old chicken coop sorting through stuff in two rooms. As a first pass, it went well. It was good to be outside and to get something accomplished. I was not a person that could go out and just sit in the sun, so having something to work at was good.

Sunday, April 28, 2013—Even On Rainy Days, Give Thanks

Today was miserable, weather-wise. However, weather wasn't all of life—it just seemed like it sometimes.

Today I had a huge thanks to my friend Bernie for listening to that "still, small voice" and then coming over to pray for me as we were on the balcony at church. I so needed that! For the past few days I'd had some frustration, irritation, and attitude problems. On the way to church I had apologized to the Lord and asked Him to help me with those issues. Well, He answered that in the form of Bernie.

I could always pretend things were fine, but I would only be hurting myself because people would think everything was going well when I really needed prayer. As I looked back over my journal over the past couple of months, I saw so many ups and downs it was a wonder I made sense sometimes. If my journal entries were up and down, it was because some of my days were.

Another thanks—thank you, Bob, for lunch. After church I was invited to lunch and had a good time with George, Luz, Bob, Carol, Amanda, and Emily, and then Josette and Elisha joined us. It was good to talk, and Carol gave me some good ideas that I needed to look into for the girls.

I had fixed Jack breakfast before I left, and he did a good job of eating it. He seemed to have gotten some appetite back. Looking back, I see he started by eating the yogurt early in the month and then was doing some chicken bouillon. Those things seem to have calmed his stomach down so he was doing better at eating. Tonight he had some fish and green beans.

His beard was coming back, although it seemed a big scraggly at first. He was also getting hair back on his head, but it was patchy. I was not sure why it was coming back in such a weird way, and I wasn't sure if it would even all come back in. As I have said countess times, one day at a time.

Monday, April 29, 2013—Cancer Knows No Limits or Age

Today things were calm, and Jack seemed to be stable. So, I decided to step out of our issues for the day and ask for prayer for some other people that were dealing with cancer or other issues.

Hanna Jane—two-and-one-half—dealing with cancer since February 15. Had a tumor in her kidney that ruptured just as they were beginning to do surgery. She had chemo scheduled every month for six months (until August). She had a meltdown every time she put on the "chemo" shirt. Yes, two-year-olds know something is up when they "hurt" every time they wear a special shirt. She wore that shirt so they could access the port in her chest. I can't even imagine!

Jerry K.—age sixty—Similar to Jack in that his was large cell lung cancer that had metastasized to lymph glands and was in his spine. He had radiation and chemo. I asked for prayer for the family as I was sure they were going through a pretty stressful time.

Randa—not sure of her age—She was the sister of a friend. She was a missionary but had to come back to the States for treatment. This was her third bout with cancer and had been told it was Stage 4. It was in her neck—and they were not sure yet if it had traveled anywhere. She was also journaling her thoughts.

Andy—did not have cancer but was seriously injured in an accident. His wife was pregnant. He was paralyzed and could not breathe on his own. The stress had caused a lot of issues in the family. Not only was his wife dealing with all the hormones from being pregnant but now was facing a long-term rehab for her husband, and no one knew if/when he would ever regain use of his arms and legs.

Father of a nephew-in-law—age seventy-plus—leukemia. He was getting weaker every day. He had opted to do no treatment.

I knew about all of these because I had a connection with someone in each family. I truly understood what they were going through even though the circumstances were all different. What was the same was all the emotional, mental, physical, and spiritual upheaval that each situation created. There were probably a million stories out there that I didn't know about, but I heard about these regularly and prayed for each family.

Tuesday, April 30, 2013—An Interesting Day

Let's start with the fact that I got the company paperwork caught up—again. It was an ongoing thing because I would get caught up and then would have to do it all again when all the trip paperwork came in. In addition to that today, I had an interesting conversation with the State of Michigan Trip Permit Department. Let's just say their website is not user friendly. There is absolutely no explanation on how to fill in anything. I called and said, "What do I put in this box?" I explained to the woman who answered what box I meant. I won't explain the details, but the bottom line is that she said, "Well, nothing. I mean, well, just put NA. I'm not sure why they put that box in there because you don't fill it in." Yeah, pure Michigan!

I had a meeting with the attorney to wrap up a legal matter that had been hanging out there for several months. I would be so glad when all issues were settled and completed.

Then I stopped at Kroger to get some things. I started to ask a young man where the eggs were. They were remodeling the store, and I didn't know where to look. He stopped me and indicated he was deaf. He then showed me a list tacked on a shelf. Eggs were not on the list. I shook my head and pointed to the list and faced him (in case he could read lips) and said, "Not on list." At that point he called over a clerk he saw, and I told her the issue. The eggs were where they should be—however, there was a huge pile of boxes on one of those rolling carts that completely blocked the area, and I hadn't walked down that aisle to the end and around the boxes.

Charlie had taken Jack to Richmond to get some cigarette-making supplies. Now that he felt a little better, Jack had been sitting at the kitchen table making them for three days. It was so discouraging to see him doing this when smoking was what had caused this problem. It was hard to have compassion for someone when he did absolutely nothing to help himself and was only interested in doing the very thing that caused the problem. All he wanted to do was smoke and would say, "What does it matter? I'm dying anyway."

Well, we should have mattered. I don't think I had ever read of, or heard of, anyone who had such an attitude. Most people would want to do the best they could so they could spend time with family. Since he couldn't drive truck any more, all he wanted to do was smoke. I had even told him his smoking caused my RA to be worse because I was to avoid smoke. His answer—leave the room. Really—how was I supposed to handle this? I was really getting an attitude, and I knew it. I just didn't know how to get rid of it. I wanted to help him. I wanted to do things for him, but I also wanted him to do something for himself.

I knew my attitude needed changing because Jack wasn't going to change. He had done so well. It had been a month, and he was down to one cigarette a day when they talked him into trying the steroids earlier in the spring.

That was the turning point. He said the craving was incredible. He went from not missing it to smoking one after the other. I was sorry they ever talked him into the steroids. They only lasted two days, and he quit because it was making him so jittery, but the damage was done; the nicotine addiction was back in force. I really had to pray that my attitude would change before it became so bad our relationship crashed. I needed to take care of him, and I needed to have a better attitude while I was helping him go through this.

The one good thing in the day was that Jack ate a decent meal and even joined Dave and me at the table. It had been a while since he had sat in a regular chair long enough to eat. I kept forgetting he had no meat on his bones and those chairs were not comfortable even if you had padding.

Wednesday, May 1, 2013—News from the Nurse

The nurse came out this day, and she only confirmed what we already know—there was a tumor in his right lung. For the first time, though, she actually said there was a difference in the air flow between the right and left lungs. Well, I knew that tumors do restrict the air flow. However, she had never before made mention of the fact that she could detect it. I had asked her before and she had evaded answering specifically. Why was today different? I wasn't sure. It was possible she was hearing more of a difference in the sound. She just would not elaborate. It was a reminder, as if I needed one, that he had a tumor in his lung as well as the two in his brain.

When she was leaving and we were by the door, I told her he had felt good enough to go out Saturday for breakfast. I said I hoped he would want to do that again. Her response was to say that I should try to get him out whenever he felt up to it because we should enjoy the days we have. Well, *that* left me thinking. Was that a hint that she actually feels the tumor was causing, or would cause, some breathing problems soon? I guess I should say, "more" because he already had some breathing problems.

She was a hospice nurse who had gone through this many, many times. Each case was different, but there had to be something that she felt was different, even if it was only a "slight" difference because she had never mentioned hearing a restricted air flow sound before.

It was now three months since any chemo had been done. and that was only one three-day session. so I was thinking it had not shrunk that lung tumor much. Since they told us it was aggressive, I had to believe it was growing again—how much and how fast I had no idea.

All that to say I still didn't know where we were in all this, but it was again a reminder to take each day as it came and enjoy what days we could. We had been on a level plateau for a while now. I knew I should not do negative thinking, but what I was trying to do was realistic thinking. I knew this would change—I just didn't know when. I could not live each day as though nothing was going on when in the back of my mind, I knew things could change quickly or perhaps even slowly, but change they would.

Thursday, May 2, 2013—Finally, Warm Weather

Today was one of those spring days that could go on forever. Not only was it in the seventies, but it was sunny. The sun just helps with everything. There had been way too many cloudy, gray days lately. It felt so good to be outside and not shiver.

This morning I felt brave and asked Dave if he wanted an omelet. I had never tried to make one before, but he was game to try it. It must have been good—he ate every bite. It was made with feta cheese, tomatoes, eggs (of course), bacon, and fresh spinach. I have to say, it wasn't too bad. Jack opted for just bacon and eggs (coward). Well, I thought, I should not be too hard on him. After all, he was eating, and that was a good thing.

The kids wanted to do schoolwork out in the mini barn so we cleared off and moved a table we had out there. While they did that, I sorted some more. Yes, I was still sorting and cleaning. I said before there was a ton of stuff I needed to go through—I wasn't kidding.

They all helped clean up one section of the pasture after school-work was done and then watched part of a movie in the barn—we had set up a small TV out there with built in VCR. The one thing missing was heat. That was why we had to use it in warm weather—it was too cold otherwise.

Charlie had picked up some Chinese food for dinner, and Jack ate four pieces of Chinese fried shrimp. We were going to get that on Friday, but I thought it made more sense to get it when there were more people here to eat. Dave left for Chicago, so I would not have a cook for the weekend. I wasn't sure what I would fix as Jack still wasn't eating much when he did eat, so thought I might just pick something up on Saturday and Sunday. I would use any excuse not to cook.

Friday, May 3, 2013—Ospreys and Eagles

I'll write about the birds in a minute, but first let me say that for the first time in months Jack ate two decent-sized meals. Breakfast was still small compared to how much he used to eat, but dinner was getting better. Thursday night he ate four Chinese fried shrimp and some rice. This night he ate two hot dogs (with buns) and some chips. Those were huge meals for him, so his appetite was definitely better. He said in the morning he wanted to go uptown for breakfast. He had to be feeling better. Maybe the warm weather had something to do with it.

Jack was feeling good enough that I felt comfortable in leaving him for a short while even with Dave gone. So, in the afternoon we did an after-school field trip with Suzanne. We went over to Stoney Creek Park to see the ospreys and eagles. We found both nests. The osprey nest was on the top of a cell phone tower. I hoped it wasn't causing problems for people with phones. I had heard it was at least eight feet deep and at least eight feet across. Not too far away was the eagle nest. It was probably slightly smaller because it was in an evergreen tree.

We didn't see the osprey, but we saw one of the eagles in the nest. Even from the distance we had to be to observe it (about 1/4 mile), it was still spectacular to see. We were hoping to see one of the birds flying back with dinner for the eaglet but no luck—until we left the area and were driving back across the park—then we saw the other eagle flying back toward the nest. Those birds are so majestic.

They both eat fish, so there was apparently a war of sorts going on between the birds over the territory and over the available fish. They were not sure why they had nested so close together.

Anyway, it was good to get out and to see the birds. Charlie took the kids with him when he got off work, so Suzanne and I went to Caribou and had a chai tea and sat for a while. It was good to get away and relax. I stopped at Home Depot to get a part for our outside pump. Now I had no excuse for not getting some yard work done tomorrow. I kept plugging away. There is only so much I could do by myself, but I could do some of the lighter work. It was good to be out, and it was good to see the property looking neater.

We had one hen and one rooster that had survived whatever killed our other birds, and they also survived the winter. I found two eggs in the old coop. I was not sure how old they were, so I threw them away. I forgot about them over the weekend but then found four more and marked them with an "X." Now every day I could collect the one not marked and have at least one fresh egg every day.

Saturday, May 4, 2013—Ribs

Ribs sounded like a good title because it was the only thing worth writing about. The ribs were dinner, by the way

It had been a pretty normal day here today. There were really no updates. Jack was still eating two meals a day. Both were small, but at least he was eating. I got the ribs uptown. I got a full order, but we split a half of that order between us. I suppose I could have gotten the half order, but I wasn't sure just how much was there. So: ribs, half a baked potato, and half the coleslaw. We then had leftovers for Sunday.

After dinner he said he was ready to sleep. He did not understand why he didn't have more energy when he was eating more. I was not sure if he didn't understand or didn't realize, but the cancer was what zapped his energy. It left him weak.

He tried to lift a forty-pound bag of pellets to put in the pellet stove (yes, he was freezing even though it was May) and could only roll it into the bin from a stack we had next to the bin. He was so discouraged about that. He kept saying how worthless he was, and I could not get it through to him that he should focus on what he *could* do and not focus on those things he could not do. I know that is always easier said than done. I understood his discouragement; I just could not do anything about it.

We heard that a long-time friend, Wes Beadle, went to be with the Lord yesterday. Jack always liked Wes, and he said if he felt up to it, he wanted to try to attend the funeral on Wednesday. I hoped he would go because I knew he would feel better for paying his respects to a friend. It would also do him good to get out and see other people.

Sunday, May 5, 2013—Visitors

Visitors—as in more than one. Actually, it all started on Saturday when I got a call from a friend that we had known almost fifty years. I guess you could say he was an old friend. He also was a truck driver. His dad and Jack had been partners in a boat hauling business over forty years ago, so Jack knew him almost as long as I had.

When Charlie B. called, I was surprised because he lived in Florida. He said had a load to deliver in Farmington Hills and one in Warren on Monday morning and wanted to know if he could stop by. Well, sure, except that he was driving his rig. I told him no problem— our drive could handle a truck.

He was at the house when I returned from church. He told me he wasn't sure what he should say to Jack, but from the conversation, I'd say he got pretty comfortable fairly quickly. We offered to have him stay at the house overnight since there were no truck stops in the area, but he said he wanted to look up a cousin and he'd park in a Meijer parking lot to sleep. He wanted to be near his first stop because he was to drop the load at 8:00 A.M.

It was good to get caught up on news. He tried to talk Jack into going out to eat, but Jack didn't feel up to going. He had planted the idea in Jack's head though.

A couple of hours later, about 4:30 P.M., Jerry came over. He had sent me a text and asked if it was okay. I told Jack that Jerry would be out, and he was okay with it and said he'd nap for a while so he'd feel better when Jerry got there. When Jerry came, he took us uptown to eat. Charlie B. had planted the idea, and by the time Jerry got there, Jack had rested and was hungry, so he agreed to go. I told Charlie B., that maybe on his next trip to Michigan it would work out. However, Charlie B. never did make it back before Jack passed away.

The warm weather was helping Jack to feel more like going out because he didn't worry about freezing. The trips still wore him out, and he still did not want to go further than town, but at least he was getting out of the house.

He told Jerry about not being able to lift the forty-pound bags of pellets, so Jerry carried six in from the entry room. Jack tried to stop him and said he didn't mention it to get him to do it but to tell him how bad he felt that he could not do that simple chore. Jerry said he was glad to be able to help out and he was glad to be able to do something for Jack.

I was just glad they still had a relationship. It was always good to see Jerry and Lori when they came. I told them one of these days I would surprise them and show up at their RV at the campground in Ohio. They went camping every weekend in the summer.

Monday, May 6, 2013—Talking with the Nurse—Again

I didn't expect the nurse until Wednesday, but she called and asked if she could come and visit. She was really late and didn't arrive until after 4:00 P.M. Sometimes her schedule was wacky—sound familiar?

Anyway, sometimes she would not give out much information, and other times she was pretty good about answering questions and trying to help us understand what was going on. I know she didn't have the answer to many things and couldn't fix it. I didn't expect anyone to fix it.

That said, I wanted others to understand that this was a terminal condition we were dealing with. Survival rate for SCLC with mets was, and is, zero percent. No matter what you did, it would come back, if it ever really went away. There was no real remission as the cancer was never really gone. I said that so there would be no false illusions about the fact that we were at the moment in a stable position—it was not remission—it was just that the tumors were not growing rapidly at the moment as far as we could tell from the symptoms—or lack of them.

Specifically, I asked what his lungs sounded like and what she thought of the "plateau" we were on at the moment. She said sometimes his lungs sounded really congested and "murky" and sometimes she heard "crackling." I looked that up–"crackling"—and it meant restricted air flow because of a blockage of some type (in this case a tumor). At the moment, while she heard the "crackling," it was not real severe, just noticeable.

She told him that even though he was feeling better, and even if he gained strength and ate better over the next several weeks, he would still stay in hospice. The only way he would be signed out was if he really progressed and in several months was out and about on a regular basis. That would not mean he was in remission; it would just mean the tumors had slowed their growth.

She was honest enough to say she doubted that would happen because with SCLC, in her twenty-plus years in hospice, she had never seen anyone get well enough to go back to normal living

She told him not to be discouraged but to understand that he should enjoy, and take advantage of, each day that he felt good. She encouraged him to go out, have breakfast out occasionally, walk around the yard, or do whatever. She said she didn't know how long it would be, but when the tumors started growing rapidly again, things would progress accordingly (in other words, he would deteriorate rapidly).

One of the reasons she said that the prognosis for this type of cancer was poor is because it was "metastatic." That meant it had metastasized to other parts of the body. In his case, because it was in his brain, there were no real options. Dr. Doyle had already told us that and had said just make the best of the time he had.

Well, we had been given more time than we originally thought we had. Without treatment the prognosis was two to four months. With treatment it was six to twelve months. We did partial treatment, so who knew what that meant? We were almost to the six-month time. As I've said before, we were taking one day at a time.

He had fallen Saturday leaving the restaurant. I forgot to write about that when it happened. It's one of the reasons I tried to write something every day. I knew there were things I'd forget. Something came up and reminded me that he had fallen. There was a small step just inside the door of the restaurant. He knew it was there. He went up the step on the way in. On the way out, I saw him miss it, but I could not catch him. Down he went in a heap. I was not sure what happened, but my best guess was he was again having an issue with the peripheral vision on the left side. I don't think he realized the step was where it was even though he had to step up going in and had done that for months, even years.

I was taking these days, weeks, and possibly months of somewhat normal living as a bonus. God had been good. We had a chance to connect with people we hadn't seen in years. We had a chance to connect regularly with family. We were able to get some legal and financial issues handled. We were able to get some things in place that would help me in the future. I couldn't ask for anything more. Well, I could have, but that would have been selfish. I was just thanking God for all He had done and allowed to be done so that going forward there wouldn't be so many issues hanging over my head.

Tuesday, May 7, 2013—Ice Cream Is the Answer

Yesterday Elisha fell in the drive and scraped his elbows. He wailed and wailed. Rica was trying to calm him when I whispered in his ear, "Will ice cream make it better?" He immediately calmed down and nodded his head. We cleaned his elbows and later went to Dairy Queen for blizzards because I had a "buy one get one free" coupon. Yep, ice cream is the answer.

Jack did not scrape his elbows, but he was a bit bored, so I asked if he wanted some ice cream as a snack. Well, of course he did. So he had a bowl of mint chocolate chip ice cream. The way to a man's heart in this family was not through his stomach; it was through a bowl of ice cream! My family will get that joke.

Every family does have something, though, as a rule that is a "comfort food." For us it's ice cream, even in the winter. Even when Jack's stomach was bothering him, he could tolerate a small bowl of ice cream.

He said he wanted to try to go to the funeral of a long-time friend, Wes Beadle, the next day. He said we should have breakfast in Romeo and go to the church from there, so that was the plan. I wasn't sure how much of the service he would be able to sit through as sitting was hard for him, but I wanted give it a try.

Wednesday, May 8, 2013—Saying Goodbye to a Friend

Saying goodbye to a good friend was hard. What made it easier to bear was knowing where he was. Just think—fall asleep in your recliner and wake up in the arms of the Lord. I can't think of a better way to go.

We initially were going to go out to eat breakfast, but Jack decided he'd rather eat at home because it was easier for him. He wanted to save his energy for the funeral service. So we had breakfast at home, and he dozed till time to go.

He did fairly well at the service. He was pretty antsy after about forty-five minutes, though. That was about all he could handle sitting, even in a padded chair. I told him we could have sat in a room off the worship center, but he felt he should be with everyone else for the service.

After the service he agreed to stay for the luncheon, but only if he could sit someplace more comfortable. We went into the room I had initially offered. He was far more comfortable in there on the couch where he could lean back and stretch a bit. Several people came in to visit with him, which made me feel better because I had to go get our food. He did really well, and we were gone for more than two hours so he was getting pretty tired.

I had to run an errand after that, so we were later getting home than we had planned on. By the time we got back to the house, it was 2:30 P.M., and he was more than ready to crash on the bed. It didn't take him long to fall asleep.

Since he had eaten at the church, he only wanted a half of a sausage sandwich, the dinner of champions. I really didn't expect him to eat much anyway because he ate after the "home-going celebration" for Wes. He said he was glad he went. He really liked Wes and was glad he felt good enough to go pay his respects.

Thursday, May 9, 2013—Another Thing Settled

I am going to give some advice to everyone reading this, and I don't care what your age is. No one is guaranteed tomorrow, and I don't want to be pessimistic but reality says *no one* lives forever.

That said, do yourself and your family a favor and get some things in order *now* rather than later. Do you think what I went through will never happen to you? Six months ago, I didn't think it would happen to me. I was not prepared for what happened. None of us really are, but we should at least take the time to let people know what we want for our final service and to put some legal things in place to save our survivors a lot of trouble and stress.

Today, we were able to complete one more piece of legal paperwork and put it behind us. You just don't know what a relief something like that is until you have to deal with it. You may not have legal things to take care of, but I'll bet there are things you haven't thought of that need attention.

When you are taking care of someone terminally ill, whether it is for a few months or a few years, there is so much going on that you don't need other things hanging over your head. Take care of them before it gets to be an issue.

For one thing, I am still (yes, still) sorting stuff that was in the semi. Jack was out in the building today and looked at the thirteen bins of stuff I had sorted and said, "How did I ever fit all that in the truck?" How, indeed? I have no idea.

So, if you don't have a will or trust, you really do need to get that in order. We had talked about it over the years and never really did anything about it. In December, it became a priority.

What would you want done if you could not speak for yourself? Think you'll never have a stroke and that won't happen? Well, live in a dream world if you want, but it could happen. Why take a chance? Let someone know (in writing is best) what your wishes are.

Jack and I told Dave and Charlie what we wanted and what we didn't want and put it in writing. They both have a copy, the attorney has a copy, we have a copy, and a copy is in our safe deposit box. I don't want anyone giving either of them a hard time for decisions we have made and told them to carry out. We also discussed this with the other kids.

Did we have it all in order? Not really. Some things just couldn't be handled at the time. Other things I needed to be thinking about for decisions down the road. For the past several months those had been real low on the list, but I needed to update the list and consider what the future might hold. Not knowing what tomorrow would hold, I couldn't plan exactly what to do, but I could have some idea of what I would need to happen going forward. If, for some reason, God called me home before Jack, the whole thing would change. I wouldn't care—I'd be dancing on streets of gold—or playing soft-ball with Wes Beadle.

What I am saying is there are things you can do now to help those who might have to handle things for you later to make it easier on them. Believe me when I say it will be so much easier to have matters taken care of that can be taken care of ahead of time.

I'm writing this because getting that issue settled today was such a relief I could not believe it. One more piece, and I am done as far as I know, with things that have been hanging over my head for months. I am so thankful to God for leading me through all this and clearing my mind when it needed to be clear to handle some things.

When the road gets rocky again, and it will, not having these other issues causing me stress will make things so much easier to bear.

If you don't get what I am talking about, that is fine. I realize that until you are on this road, you will not fully understand what I am saying. Pray you never walk this road!

In the meantime—settle your debts; take a good look around and ask, "Do I *really* need that?" Decide what you want done should you have a serious illness or become incapacitated to where you can't make decisions; let someone know where the important paperwork is; hug your friends and family and tell them you love them; take that trip you always wanted to take; don't put off until tomorrow something you really do want to do; make sure your heart is right with the Lord and that you know where you will spend eternity.

If you can take care of those things, you can relax and enjoy your days. I hope this has helped at least one person—if so, it was worth writing.

Friday, May 10, 2013—More Advice

Who am I to be giving advice? It's not like I had it all together either. However, I felt I needed to give the benefit of my experience to someone—I have no idea who or why. Before I expound on anything, let me say everyone's situation is different, and people have different personalities, so all things may not fit.

That said, I have been thinking about what it has been like over the past several months. When things were crazy and when Jack had some serious nose dives, it was all but impossible to concentrate on anything else. There were days I could not remember what I was supposed to do—thank God for an organized son who kept a calendar for me—and the problem was that even that kept changing. If you can, have one or more people (family or friends, whatever works), help you with schedules, appointments, and even dinner. It's the little things that get lost.

Looking back, I can only tell you I would never had made it early on without Dave and Charlie being able to assist with so many things. There is just no way to handle something like this by yourself. If you try (or are trying) to do it alone, you are following a recipe for disaster. Those first weeks are still a blur to me.

Don't try to do everything at once. There will be some urgent things that need attention. Focus on those. Work on the others as you have time and can take a break from the urgent. Focusing on something other than the crisis is helpful and keeps you from sinking. The caregiver needs a break. Take it when offered.

Laugh at something once in a while. That is not an insult to the one you are taking care of; it's essential for your mental health. You can't take care of someone if you are overwhelmed and depressed.

Don't feel guilty for laughing out loud at a good joke or movie (if you can find such a thing).

You may reach a level place like we were at times. Enjoy the time; take advantage of it; go out and eat; relax; rest; read; scrapbook; walk—whatever works as a stress reliever.

I will repeat one thing because it, to me, is the single most important piece of advice you can give someone—don't try to do it alone!

I didn't do all things well, but I tried to make sure I had "my" time and that I got help when I needed it. I also tried to make sure all the important financial and legal matters were taken care of and were up-to-date.

In our case, we had a lot of business equipment that had to be disposed of. I was still working on that as often as I could. I still had a long way to go.

Okay, off my soapbox. I have just been trying to pass on any helpful hints that may assist someone going through something like this.

And, before I forget, if you must put your loved one in a nursing or rehab home, do not—and I repeat—*do not* put yourself on a guilt trip. You alone know what you can handle. In our case, I opted to keep Jack at home. For me, this was so much less stressful even though it sometimes meant I had 24/7 care. It was actually never 24/7 as I have two sons that have been a blessing in assisting so I could get away—sometimes just for fun and sometimes to run errands.

All right—done now. Hope this allows you a little insight as to what our journey has been like so far.

Saturday, May 11, 2013—A Special Treat

That I can remember, I have never been the recipient of an anonymous gift of my meal being paid for. This day, that changed. Jack and I went uptown for breakfast. It was a weekly treat right now. We had a pickup totally loaded for the dump, so I'm sure we looked like the Beverly Hillbillies, but who cared? It was junk I was glad to be rid of. We were eating when one of the waitresses we know very well came over and said, "You won't be getting a bill. It flew away." Jack knew what she was talking about, but said anyway, "It went where? Who took it?" She smiled and said, "The person does not want to be named. Just enjoy." So we did.

When we left there, we went to the dump to drop off our stuff. Today they had "large item" pickup. It was unbelievable! The guy just rolled his eyes at our dozen windows and pile of carpet. He wanted to know if we had carpeted a mansion. I told him, "No, they were used to pad boats." He asked what I meant, so I told him that Jack had hauled boats and they used pieces of carpet to pad the boats so they would not scrape and get damaged in transit. He thought that was interesting.

Home again and before long Jack was snoozing on the bed. A morning out, and he was whipped. It was nice, so I worked outside for a while. One of our neighbors had a son that had gone to school with our kids and was now doing lawn maintenance. He and I worked out an agreement where he would do lawn maintenance for us for twenty-six weeks in exchange for an old pickup I had. It was a good deal for me because our riding mower was not working, and I had no idea what was wrong with it. I was hoping Charlie and/ or Rich could get it running because I needed it for moving stuff around with a small trailer that went behind it. Anyway, Larry was over and mowed the yard. It looked so good, and it was one more thing I didn't have to worry about.

Dave fixed fish for dinner, and it was delicious. He rolled it in a combination of crushed corn flakes and gluten-free flour. He then fried it in peanut oil. If you ever want fish a different way, it was really good

Believe it or not, I started working on a Christmas gift. Yes, already. It was an album for Luke, and since I had the photos for almost a year, I decided to work at it little by little. It was my downtime, stress reliever.

The past two days with the cold and rain had played havoc with the RA, and I had to double up on the pain meds. I finally got some relief, but my left hand was swollen. I needed my hands! I was trying to find something that worked because the meds went from $10 for a three-months' supply in January to $35 today for a one month supply.

If it wasn't something I had to deal with for Jack, it was something for me. As they say, getting old is not for wimps.

Sunday, May 12, 2013—Mother's Day Treats

I received two gift cards from Cold Stone and two from Kohl's as Mother's Day gifts from the kids. I could go eat ice cream and then buy a larger size—*not*! I planned to spread out the treats from Cold Stone so I wouldn't "spread out."

We were invited to Charlie's in-laws for Mother's Day and birthday celebrations (they have four birthdays in a ten-day period). I took a cake (gluten free) I made from the recipe I got off the Internet. It went over well. It wasn't bad for my first try at something different. I wasn't sure it would turn out, but everyone that had it complimented me on it.

I wasn't sure Jack would come as it was cold and windy out and he had been saying he was freezing. We were sweating. But then, as I've said before, he had no meat on his bones. Anyway, he went with us and ate a little bit of a pork chop, some potatoes, and veggies. He had some coffee and a small bite of the cake I made. We did not stay long as I knew he would be worn out from the trip. I was glad he came, though, and I think George was pleased that he made it.

While he was sitting on the couch, Ethan (Josette's nephew) came over and sat on his lap and talked to him. Then Elisha sat next to him. Alex (the youngest) had to get in on the deal. It was funny how the three little boys just had to sit on his lap. It reminded me of when three of ours were close to that age group (3–6 years) and how they would do the same thing.

I was not looking forward to the freeze warning for tonight and tomorrow, but my hands were feeling better. Unless you have rheumatoid arthritis, you just do not know what it is like to have a toothache in your hands. That is what I called it anyway. I had deepest sympathy for anyone with RA, fibromyalgia, arthritis, or any other chronic disease. I had never understood how much it restricts what you could do. I was so thankful for my children and grandchildren who were such a blessing in helping all they could.

I continued journaling a scrapbook I had been working on for my "Arizona baby," as I called Luke. I loved doing this. I could not sew and could not crochet—so their inheritance would be journals of activities in their lives, or at least those I have been involved in. If I wasn't so nit-picky about how I want each page to look, I'd get done a lot sooner. But, as my grandmother used to say, "Anything worth doing is worth doing well."

Monday, May 13, 2013—Sleepless in Armada (Again)

I was up until 3:30 A.M. today. I have no idea why—I just could not sleep. Rather than toss and turn, which I did enough of anyway, I got up and did some work on the computer. I figured if I wasn't going to sleep, I could get some things done so if I overslept today at least the work would be caught up. That worked and after I did go back to bed, I didn't get back up until after 8:00 A.M., which was late for me.

It had been cool, but I worked out in one of the buildings anyway. There was so much to do, and I needed to do what I could while the weather was somewhat decent. I figured if I worked at it a little here and there, I should make some headway by summer's end. And it was anyone's guess as to where we would be in this process at that time.

I called my insurance company today, and they told me the pharmacy company tripled the cost of my meds. If the cost went any higher I'd have to consider something else to take.

On a better note, I received something in the mail that I hoped would put the last piece of the legal issues behind me. I passed it to the attorney and if it was a "go" before the end of the month, I would not have any of the issues hanging over my head any more. Then I just needed to make sure all the paperwork would be in place for next year's taxes—but that was far enough away that I could relax for a while.

Once again, Jack seemed to be cutting back a little on quantity of food each meal. It was not real noticeable all at once, but breakfast had become one piece of sausage on one piece of bread cut in half. Dinner was a small portion of whatever we were fixing. I had been gauging his good days by how well he ate because he had always eaten a large breakfast and decent dinner. The cancer and treatments had pretty much wiped out his appetite. He would not be able to keep up his strength unless he was eating and drinking enough to sustain him, so this was a daily concern of mine.

His hair was coming back, which we expected. It looked to be more salt and pepper than white now. It was still pretty short, so maybe it was too soon to tell. I had heard that after chemo it was possible for a person's hair to come back in quite differently than it had been before. Other than the change in color, his hair seemed to be the same. It was less patchy looking than it had been but was still pretty sparse. His beard was filling out more also, and that too was more salt and pepper than the pure white it had been.

Tuesday, May 14, 2013—It's a Small World after All

Charlie was planning on coming out after work to visit his dad. I was planning to take Rica to youth group at church and maybe spend some of my Mother's Day gift cards. An evening out to go shopping for myself was something I rarely did. I wasn't sure where to start.

Today Jack had a visitor—a friend he had known for years that also had been a truck driver. When Steve called the previous week, I asked how he had heard about Jack. Well, he and his wife attended church where Pastor Garry's son-in-law was pastor. What a connection, eh? They were at an event, and Pastor Garry told Steve about Jack.

When Steve first called, he said he was nervous about what to say to Jack. I got that a lot from people before the first visit. After the first visit, they were far more comfortable visiting. I told him to just talk about whatever popped into his head. Jack was pretty open about discussing what was going on and would tell people he knew he was terminal. Steve's comment to that was, "You are only terminal when the Lord decides you are ready to go Home." Well said, Steve.

Wednesday, May 15, 2013—Changes

I had thought again to journal less often. I wasn't sure putting down our daily routine had any value. Some days seemed so boring, and I would just ramble. Then I thought that it still might help others to know that some days would actually be like that—boring. That is hard to believe when you are the caregiver to a person who is ill, but it's true. Not every day is a crisis.

Charlie and I had a talk with the hospice nurse, and while she could not make any predictions, she did say he was on a plateau at the moment and that it could last a while. She said to get him out and enjoy the warm weather. Go places. Do things.

So I asked him if he knew he had six more months, what would he want to do besides watch TV and be bored? He said he couldn't do anything. Well, that was not entirely true. While he couldn't lift anything heavy, couldn't drive, and couldn't read for long periods, there were things he could do—we just had to find them. Unfortunately, he had never developed any hobbies or interests.

The nurse did say things could change slowly or quickly, depending on where and how the tumors in the brain grew. At the moment, since the symptoms were a lot less noticeable, she suspected the radiation had shrunk them quite a bit. The one in the lung was not an issue for them because it wouldn't affect things the way the brain tumors would.

Thursday, May 16, 2013—Trying to Keep Boredom at Bay

There were still things going on that we were now aware of because now we knew what to look for. There was still a problem with vision and depth perception on the left side; his left hand still curled on its own when he was relaxing; he could not read for very long as his vision was affected somewhat.

What we needed to monitor were those issues plus any unsteadiness in walking, speech issues, memory issues, eating and drinking issues, and extreme fatigue. There would be other things along the way, but those seemed to be the first indications that something was happening.

I had asked for prayer that we find something that would interest him that he could get involved in that did not take too much energy, time, or money. We needed to do whatever it was in small doses because he really was short on energy and would not last long at whatever it was.

Saturday, May 18, 2013—Forty Years!

Today was a special day.

Forty years! Can you believe it? I couldn't. Forty years of marriage! A milestone. In December I did not think we would celebrate this milestone together. I really did not know where the time went. I had heard people say that, and now I knew what they meant.

Our celebration was to go uptown for breakfast. I tried to talk him into Cracker Barrel, but he said he did not want to go further than town.

He said he did not have a good night last night and was not feeling real well today. I didn't know exactly what that meant because he wouldn't, or couldn't, identify what was wrong. It was not a headache or an upset stomach. He just felt lousy. He also said he had been a bit "wobbly" lately. He would never tell me what was going on, so admitting that was telling me he was not doing well at all.

I was not going to push him because there was something we wanted to do on Sunday, and I wanted him to feel good enough to do it. So, maybe after tomorrow I would bug him to get out but not today.

I had said right from the start that I felt the Lord told me He would walk me through all the things that needed to be taken care of. Well, He kept His word. (doesn't He always?) The last piece of our financial issues would be handled on Tuesday, and I could then begin to move forward with just focusing on taking care of him. There was a blessing in that issue too, but I was not at liberty to explain it. Just know that God had blessed in a major way.

While I had never felt trapped or angry or depressed, I had at times been very frustrated. The frustration was usually caused by a lot of little nothings that would build up, and on a bad day, I would get overloaded. Fortunately, that did not happen often.

Rich had planned in January to come and visit, and that would be happening in a week. Michele and Luke would be with him. They were making the trip to help out and so that Michele and Luke could stay on for two weeks after Rich left to fly back. He could only stay a week because of his work schedule. I was looking forward to that. It was Rich's last chance to come home because he was out of vacation time and out of money, so we wanted to make the most of that week. Then, again, if that job were ever to come through . . .

I knew Jack would sleep early, and even though it was our anniversary, I planned to take Rica to a team penning competition. Rica loved horses, and I had promised her this for months. Jack did not mind that I would be away for the evening. He said he would probably sleep the evening away anyway.

Tuesday, May 21, 2013—Update for Today

I had been doing some more research and decided to list some things I had found on the Internet because the symptoms seemed to fit Jack's case at the moment.

Below are some of the symptoms of brain edema (swelling). There were several listed, but I deleted some as they did not pertain to Jack's situation, and I listed only those I had noticed were happening with him over the past few weeks. Below that is the update.

- Headaches that occur daily or several times a day
- Headaches associated with nausea and vomiting
- Any change in strength or sensation (numbness or tingling)
- Clumsiness or coordination problems of a hand or leg
- Vision, hearing, or speech changes or difficulties
- Balance or walking difficulties or dizziness

I decided to elaborate on some. Jack had been saying he had headaches at night and was taking one pill to help him sleep. Then over the past few nights he had increased it to two. The day before (Monday) he told me he had a headache during the night and was nauseated but did not throw up. Then admitted he felt "wobbly" and knew his hearing was getting worse. While he was not dizzy, his balance was off.

I had been watching him because I had noticed some of these subtle changes and was pretty sure the tumors in his brain were growing. The hospice nurse visited and said that it was the edema or swelling around the tumors that was causing the symptoms. As the tumors grew, the edema would get worse. She talked him into going back on the steroids. The last time we tried this he took them for two days and stopped because he was so jittery it scared him. I was not sure he would agree to take them again, but after she explained about the edema, he decided he would at least try to take them again.

She told him he should take them early in the day because for some people they caused sleeplessness. We already had a problem with that. He took one at noon. He seemed okay but it was the second or third day before when he had had a problem so it was just wait and see. She said he could take something to offset the jitters but he did not want to get on the merry-go-around of taking one pill to offset another.

I asked what happens down the road when the tumors keep growing and the steroids don't work anymore. She didn't say anything new — just that "we are trying to keep him comfortable." Jack called her his "pill pusher" because she was always trying to get him to take some meds. However, he was agreeable to trying this, which led me to believe he must have been feeling something because he had been so adamant about not taking any more steroids.

I knew his hearing was affected because even when I looked right at him and talked loud he was having a hard time hearing me. We had gone to Pastor Garry's retirement party Sunday night, and he made it an hour and a half — a long time for him. Even with microphones, he could not hear very well and wanted to leave because he was getting uncomfortable and could not really hear what was going on.

I got some earphones for him to wear while watching TV. We had tried this before with a different brand, but those didn't work with our particular TV, so I got these as an anniversary gift for him. Dave installed them, and I was hoping I could sleep past the 5:30 A.M. news that I could hear all over the house, thank you. Ear plugs were not helping me.

So, yes, indications were that the tumors were growing again. I had no idea if it was the two he had initially or if there were more, or even if it was just one at this time. And there was no way of knowing if the cancer had spread to organs other than the brain and lung. Without tests, it was just a guessing game, and I didn't want to waste time guessing

At this time we were doing what we had been doing—taking one day at a time. What the steroids would actually do for him I had no idea. I knew they gave him more appetite and more energy last time. But the downside is they also increased his desire for nicotine. We would just have to wait and see how they worked this time.

Saturday, May 25, 2013—An Eating Machine

Yep, Jack was an eating machine. The steroids did do that again. He now had more appetite than he had had in a long time. Also, he had been out and about three days this week and was still feeling okay. That was all due to the steroids. The only issue was that I knew this was going to be short-lived and we would be doing the yo-yo thing again. That may sound negative, but I was trying to be realistic. This was not going to heal him, nor was it going to increase the time he had left—it was only going to give more quality for a time, however long that time was going to be.

I would have liked to have been able to relax and take those days without having it hanging over my head that I didn't know when it would change. That made it so hard to just enjoy the time. I was still trying to get things taken care of so I wouldn't have a lot to do later. Jack was complaining that I kept moving things around and thought I was throwing his stuff out. I told him to come look in the barn to see I had not thrown any of his stuff away. I would have liked to because some of it was junk, but it was not worth fighting over.

He complained about the earphones, but at least he was using them. It was so nice to not have the TV blaring at 5:30 A.M. And, again at night, if he wanted to watch TV, he could stay up as late as he wanted. It really helped me. I knew, even if he wouldn't admit it, that he heard better with them on.

I was organizing and categorizing things so I could have someone help me decide what was good and what was not. On Friday my brother-in-law took the day off work so he could come out and help me with some projects. He and my sister came out and spent several hours helping me. We loaded the pickup with trash because today was dump day. Pierre put up a new clothes line for me. It was so frigid and windy it was hard for him to tie it up. I felt so bad for him and tried to get him to stop, but he was determined to get it hung. We cleaned out the front bedroom since the kids were done with school for the summer. He put several boxes in the attic for me and trimmed a tree in the laundry area.

Rich called and said they were on the way in. They would be in Sunday evening. Rich would have to leave June 2, and Michele and Luke would stay until June 11. I was putting a list together, but it was hard because some things had to be done before other things could be done. I wasn't sure what should be a priority.

I didn't want to spend my time grocery shopping while they were here, so I went shopping and stocked up. I was hoping that I got enough food.

I talked to a woman from church whose husband had the same cancer—they were now finding out he had four lesions in his brain—after being told in the spring there were none. They gave him two months if he did no treatment. He had already done radiation and chemo. They were trying to talk him into more but said it would only give him four to six months.

But what is the cost (financial and physical) if they were to do that? They had some tough decisions to make. Later I heard from her that they were opting for no treatment. They didn't have the same family support system I had because their family was all in North Carolina except for their two kids, who were taking this hard.

Rob came into town because a good friend passed away, and they were going to visit the family. They wanted to come out in the morning to take Jack to breakfast. I wanted to spend some time with them, so I decided I'd have to skip church in the morning.

Sunday, May 26, 2013—Spending Time with Family

Rob took David, Jack, and me out to breakfast at Papa's Restaurant in town. He insisted he wanted to spend some time with his dad. After breakfast, I decided to go to church so he could spend some time with Jack alone.

While I was gone, Charlie called and said they were going to his in-law's lake house and asked if we wanted to go out. I called Dave, and he asked Jack. Jack said he was too tired but that we should go ahead. I went out and ate with them, and then Luz and I discussed the family party/graduation party we would have there the following week. Just as I was getting ready to leave, Jack called and wanted to know when I would be home as he was hungry. I'm telling you, I could not leave the house for more than two hours or he was calling wanting to know where I was and when I would be back.

He was feeling better but not enough to help me with anything, and I needed some help. I decided when it warmed up, I would drag him out to the barn to go over some stuff with me. I really needed his input.

Saturday, June 1, 2013—Rica's Graduation Party

George and Luz had graciously agreed to host Rica's graduation party at their lake house.

Luz and I had discussed the arrangements and what we needed. I sent out an email to the family and some friends with the time, what to bring, etc. I told everyone it would be a picnic, so they needed to keep it simple.

I was guessing we would have thirty to thirty-five people, depending on who could come. I was hoping Jack would feel up to going because Rica would be disappointed if Papa did not make her party.

I asked the kids to help with getting tables and chairs up to the lake house and for setup and cleanup. We were using paper plates, etc. to minimize the clean-up needed. I wanted it to be special for Rica, but I did not have the time or energy to do any more than a simple party. I was sure she would understand.

Saturday, June 1, 2013—Update

It was a busy week. Rich, Charlie, and I worked on taking fencing down, piling up old scrap metal, and taking it to the junk yard. As of today we had made $194 selling old metal. Jack was happy because he then had "pocket change" to go uptown and see his buddies and eat breakfast. When he came home he took a nap because he was worn out.

He had felt better since being on the steroids but still did not sleep well at night. He went out into both buildings one day after going uptown with his friends. So, although he was feeling better, it still did not take much to wear him out. He went from eating nothing in March, to eating a half of a sausage sandwich to eating a full omelet today. So his appetite really was much better. Other things weren't better, though, and seemed to be getting worse, even if only slightly.

Even with the swelling going down in the brain, there were still effects from the tumors. While he was not having as severe problems with the left side as he had a few months ago, he was having some problems. At this point I thought we were about where we had been back in December. The thing was that we wouldn't be doing more therapy of any kind, so it would just be a matter of how fast the tumors grew and what problems they caused.

While he was feeling better, I had been pushing to get some of things cleaned up and having Rich here for a week had been a major blessing. Jack had given some input, finally, into what some items were and what price he thought they might bring. That was a big help to me because I had absolutely no idea what truck accessories were worth or even what they were.

Because there were some issues now manifesting themselves with Jack, despite the steroids, I decided to journal more often depending on what was happening and how severe it became.

Saturday, June 8, 2013—Another Busy Week

Rich had to leave to go back home to work on June 2, and Michele and Luke stayed with me as we had planned. They would be leaving Tuesday, June 11. We had a great time. Luke and Elisha had worn themselves out playing every time they were together. Michele helped me get some more stuff cleared away outside. Charlie, the kids, and I got the garden planted. I wasn't convinced that was a good idea, but Jack insisted he wanted some tomatoes planted. We also planted corn, onions, and green peppers.

After months of giving me a hard time every time I asked about trying to sell the truck parts we no longer needed, Jack had finally worked with Rich to put prices on them and identify what they were. Now that we had listed them on Craig's List, he wanted me to check it three times a day. We went from him not being interested and arguing about it to wanting to know who has responded and what I said to them.

A good deal of his being more alert was the steroids. The downside was they caused mood swings, so he varied from being somewhat calm to picking on just about everyone. That could also have been from the tumors—it was hard to tell. It was just so up and down, it was stressful. I knew what it was from, so I didn't take it personally, but it was still hard to deal with.

He started saying he had a dull headache almost all day. It was not enough to be real painful, but enough to keep him from wanting to concentrate on anything. So he was bored and kept wanting me to do this and that. Sometimes I just had to escape.

Michele and Luke went to visit a friend of hers, and we planned to meet and go to a campfire program at Stoney Creek Nature Center. It was good for Michele to get away and have some fun time—I had about worked her to death while she was here.

Dave was to drive with Michele and Luke to Denver, where she would visit her sister. Then Dave and Rich would drive to Phoenix (Rich was flying up for a party for his brother-in-law's MBA graduation). On June 22, Dave would fly back to Michigan. I was not looking forward to his being gone. Not only did he cook awesome meals, it was good to have someone at the house when I had to run an errand or just so I could get away. Charlie was going to have to fill in the gap, but he didn't get off till 5:00 P.M., so my time away from the house was going to be limited for a few weeks.

Saturday, June 15, 2013—A Few Bumps in the Road

The steroids were working in that Jack's appetite had increased. He was eating a full meal now. So far he had not had drastic mood changes, and although he was cranky, it was not too bad.

What I had noticed was that while he was alert mentally, there were indications he didn't always process things thoroughly. I could tell him something and later he would remember it, but not always in a way that made sense. In other words, sometimes he would confuse something I said with something else I said and put the two together and then wonder why I did or said such and such. I usually just let it go. He told Charlie once that he was worried about my mental state because of some of the things I was doing. Both Charlie and I knew he was just misreading what I was doing and/or saying.

He told me again that he had headaches during the day but did not want to take more pain meds because he did not want to get on "that merry go around" again. We also discussed what and how much he would have to take later whether he wanted to or not or the pain might become intolerable. He had always told the nurse he only had headaches at night, so this was something new. I knew that when he got miserable enough, he would decide what to take and when. It was his choice, and I wouldn't push it.

He would run out of energy by 5:00 or 6:00 P.M. and then doze off. He then would take pain meds about 9:00 P.M. and said he would wake up at midnight. Because he was sleeping during the day, he didn't sleep well at night. That was going to be an ongoing issue.

By late in the day, I would notice he was dragging his left foot again. It was not as bad as it had been a few months before, but I noticed it because when he was wearing shoes, it made a noise as he dragged the foot instead of lifting it up. There were a couple of other issues cropping up but nothing major.

It was quiet on the home front. After a week with Rich here to help out and then another week and a half with Michele and Luke, we had an empty house. In fact, this weekend everyone was out of town, so I was pretty much home-bound. Dave was gone till June 22; Charlie was out of town for two days, and the others lived out of state.

My niece Suzanne came out with lunch and helped me for four hours cleaning out and organizing the old chicken coop, which was now the garden shed. It was starting to look good, and I could begin to put things where they belonged and actually find them.

I talked to Rob and Ryan, and Ryan asked if he could come June 28 to July 13 so he could help me around the house and earn some "farm dollars" (the farm dollars is a long story).

Tonight was the first Saturday night I was able to relax. I was not going anywhere, and I was not doing anything. Jack was asleep, and I was whipped from working in the yard all day. It felt good to not have to run an errand or take care of something

I was not looking forward to seeing a decline in Jack's abilities and energy level, but the indications were that it would become a reality sooner rather than later. He told me that when he started to fail and when he would not be able to do anything, he'd rather it end quickly. I didn't blame him, but still it sounded scary to hear that.

I knew that God was still in control, and He was still leading, and I was still trusting Him to walk with us through this. Even with all that, some days were just tough.

Monday—June 17, 2013—Rough Night, Rough Morning

I had a call into the hospice nurse.

On Sunday, which was Father's Day, after a BBQ at Charlie's, we made a stop to get some coffee disks, and when I got back in the pickup, Jack asked if I'd hurry home because he was in excruciating pain. He said his stomach and chest hurt. It seemed to come on all at once, and he thought it was the food, but I wasn't so sure. We all ate the same things at Charlie's and Jack ate less than most of us. No one else was sick. Then, again, I had to admit that with his issues, even something that didn't affect the rest of us could cause him some trouble.

When we got home I crushed two Vicodin and gave them to him. I crushed them because I thought they might get into his system faster. It still took an hour for the pain to subside. I crushed four more and put them in two medicine cups. During the night he took both cups.

In the morning when I got up, he was asleep, but a few minutes later he woke up and said he was freezing. He was shaking so bad he could not hold the cup of coffee I made to warm him up. I got a heating pad and put it under him, then warmed towels in the microwave to put over him. It took about thirty minutes of constant switching of the towels to warm him up. Then he took all blankets off and said he was too warm. Then he told me he threw up during the night. He had a trash basket next to the bed, and that was what he used. He did not want to eat anything this morning. He said he was afraid to because of the pain he had the day before.

I left the room for a few minutes. When I returned to check on him he said he fell in the bathroom and had to crawl back to bed. We had a pretty intense discussion about that, and I told him to call me if I was not in the living room before he tried to get up again. He insisted he was okay and he didn't need me to watch him. I knew better. I would have to stay in the living room with him this day to make sure he was okay. I was pretty sure it was from the problems he had had over the previous twenty-four hours.

I alerted the kids as to what had happened and told Dave not to worry and not to try to change his ticket. There was nothing he could do if he came back early, and I would keep everyone informed if there were any more changes.

I had called the nurse and was waiting for her to call me and set a time to come out. As Charlie said, these were quite similar to symptoms he had when he first got sick in November. It was a lot of what he felt when he called me from the road to say he wasn't feeling well. Over the past week or so the headaches had increased even with the steroids, so I was guessing it was the tumors pressing on the brain causing the problems.

Monday, June 17, 2013—Evening Update

Today had been an incredibly stressful day. After Jack took the pain meds Sunday night, he fell asleep. I went to bed and left him some meds as I mentioned.

The nurse came with a PA today (physician's assistant). They both talked to him and examined him. They could not make a diagnosis because they do not have x-rays or MRIs or anything. However, based on where the pain was they both felt the cancer may now have spread to the bones. Because of the pain in his back and stomach and where it was localized, they thought that when he moved in some way it aggravated his ribs and caused the pain.

Or it could be the tumor in the lungs had grown and was pressing against the ribs and in moving he may have pressed it harder against the ribs. Either way, the thought was that it was not a liver issue—yet. That may come, but the pain was not in that area.

They had him stand up to make sure he could get up without getting dizzy. We all could see the difference in his breathing when he stood up even though he said he did not feel short of breath. It was quite obvious the lung tumor was causing breathing issues.

Because of the shaking and freezing this morning, they did think, as I did, that his blood pressure had dropped and that was why he fell (twice) in the bathroom. I was going to take his blood pressure, but he was shaking so bad I could not get the cuff on him, and by the time I could do it, he had gotten up and gone to the bathroom while I was in the office calling Charlie. I needed a bell tied around his neck!

He was feeling better tonight but did not eat much today, which was no surprise. When you feel as bad as he did, you aren't too hungry.

The nurse did talk him into a patch again for the pain because the pain was increasing, and she did not want him to take so much pain med by mouth because it would cause stomach problems. We had that before. Also, I was crushing the meds so they would get into his system faster.

The extreme pain he had Sunday night might have been an isolated incident, but she indicated the headaches would get worse and if it was in the bones, he would have more chest, back, and hip pain. That was one of the reasons she wanted to use the pain patch. The patch would give him a more even amount of medication into his system, which she hoped would help control the pain.

Most of the day I spent working in the office and checking on him every fifteen to thirty minutes, so I did not get much done. Then we had two bad storms. The temperature dropped twenty degrees in a half hour, and everything was flooded. Our yard and house were okay because we don't have a basement, and the yard drained fairly well. We had so much water the corn in the field was sitting in water. I hoped for the farmers' sake it didn't wash away or rot.

I planned to monitor him over the next several days and was hoping I would not be obvious about it because I knew that would make him angry. I was sure he would pretty much stay in bed and just get up when he had to. The falling and shaking episodes had made him quite weak, whether he realized it or not. I had said before that if anything major happened, it would be a turning point for him. Whenever he had a serious downturn he had never come back up to where he had been before the downturn. I could see that even if he did come back a little from these episodes, he would not be as energetic or as strong as he had been even a month ago.

Sunday, June 23, 2013—No News Is Good News

That is to say, no significant news is good news. As I had said before, there were changes, but they were not anything you would notice if you weren't looking for them.

Last weekend was rough, but it had not started out that way. It wasn't until Sunday that we had an issue. We never did know what triggered it, but Jack was in enough pain that when we put a pain patch on him, he did not argue. He did complain later that the nurse was always trying to get him to take one pill or another. I told him to take the patch off then. He said, "No way. I don't want that pain again." So I told him to quit complaining. When I had to put a new patch on, he readily agreed without argument. I was scheduled to change the patch every three days. Even with the patch, he was still taking six Vicodin during the night (not all at once of course).

During the week, I had noticed a lot of small bruises on his arms. His left hand was almost purple from the bruising. I called the nurse to ask what that might be. I had not noticed it because he had been wearing long sleeve shirts because he was cold. She said it could be one of two things. Either it was the steroids causing the skin to become thinner, which made bruising easier, or the cancer was in the bones, and the bone marrow was not producing enough platelets or whatever it produces.

If it was in the bones, he would have other issues because the bones would become more brittle, and he would be subject to falling or breaking bones just walking. Also, coughing could cause ribs to crack. None of this had happened, but she said to just watch for any signs of those kinds of issues. If nothing like that happens, it might just be the steroids, although that dose was quite low.

His appetite, even with the steroids, was a little less than it had been, and that might have been from the patch. I told him that was the trade-off—less appetite but also less pain. If that was the only side effect from the patch, that was minor, and we could live with it.

Mentally, he was still alert, although we saw signs that keeping a conversation going was difficult. He had to take time to process any information that was more than just a few words. Any lengthy visit wore him out.

My brother Allen called and said he and his wife Bonnie would be coming to Michigan for a few days just before July 4th. Rob and Tracy were planning on coming also and dropping Ryan off for a few weeks. Ryan was anxious to come and earn "farm money."

I knew it would be a busy time again, which was okay with me. Dave was back in town now, so I was free to go to church and stop for a few things on the way home. I planned to attend the teen talent show at church in the evening.

Tuesday, June 25, 2013—An Outing

Jack had not been feeling very well for a while, but when I asked if he wanted to try an outing, he said yes. I wanted to do something other than go into town, so I talked him into going to a Cracker Barrel in Port Huron, Michigan, about thirty miles from us. He was okay with that.

It always took him a while to get ready, so we didn't try to make it for breakfast. It was past lunch time by the time we got there, which was okay because you could get breakfast any time of the day anyway.

Since he had had a half of a sausage sandwich for breakfast he decided to get something for lunch. He usually chose the chicken and dumplings or catfish, but he decided to get a pork chop this time. While he didn't eat all of his meal, he did eat more than he had been eating.

216

I was glad he was willing to go out. Ever since the pain problem he had on Father's Day he was very leery of everything, from eating anything to trying to leave the house. I could see changes starting to happen, and I knew that meant we probably did not have a lot of time left. I didn't want to worry everyone and since we had "cried wolf" so many times with his downturns, I just made a note of it and kept moving forward with whatever we could do on any given day.

Saturday, June 29, 2013 — Three Patients

Rob and Tracy arrived Friday night and stayed at Charlie's. Their plan was to bring Ryan out and leave him at the farm. At the moment, though, he was having fun with his cousins.

During the week, I had acquired three patients. I decided to list the patients and their issues because they were all different. I wanted to show how crazy the week had become.

Patient #1 — Last Wednesday evening Rica and I were loading some old rotten wood from out behind our barn to burn in our fire pit. Elisha was running around barefoot. I told him repeatedly to put shoes on or go away because there were nails and screws in the wood. Did he do either — of course not! Rica pulled a board apart, and it fell on the ground, nail side up. Two guesses who stepped on it just as it fell to the ground.

We cleaned Elisha's foot and put a Band-Aid on it. They were spending the night, and he was okay till midnight when Rica dumped him on my bed because he was crying. I gave him some kid's pain meds, and he finally fell asleep. Charlie picked him up took him to the doctor Thursday morning. Elisha got a tetanus shot, the puncture cleaned out, and a Band-Aid. Then it was off to McDonald's, where he got an ice cream treat and played on the play structure (because he could crawl there). He came home with me, and the girls went to work with Charlie. I had to carry him everywhere because he said it hurt too much to walk on it. So we didn't do anything except watch movies.

Patient #2 — me. On Friday, because I could not work outside (rain, rain, and more rain), I decided to clean the front room the kids used for school work. Reina and I had cleaned it up, and she fixed the

217

bookcase since the books were scattered all over. Some of the books kept falling, so I went across the room to get a small jar of rocks to put as a "stop" for the books, and when I turned, I caught my foot in an extension cord that was lying on the floor. A lamp, pencil sharpener, and a TV were plugged into the cord.

I'm always super careful turning and walking because I had a brace on my ankle, and my ankle did not bend normally. For some reason this time I turned and walked without looking down. I pulled the TV off the table it was on, and it and I crashed to the floor. The TV was cracked but still, surprisingly, worked. I called my chiropractor right away. His office told me he was not in because his wife had a chemo treatment (she had breast cancer) and she was having a bad day. Could I see him on Saturday?

Patient #3—Jack. After checking him over and monitoring his bruises, we were sure it was the steroids. His blood did clot. In four places, he had either scraped or scratched his arm/hand because there were four small tears in the skin. The cuts, or tears, appeared to be healing okay. If it got any worse, we would have to cut back or quit the steroids because if the skin was that thin, there would be worse problems down the road. Cutting back the steroids meant more edema in the brain. Well, you get the picture. Either way it was not good news.

He had been complaining of an ear infection, or at least an ear ache. I had been putting drops in his ear every night. Friday night he had the Fentanyl patch and six Vicodin and said he did not sleep because of the pain. I called hospice because if it was not an infection, antibiotics wouldn't help, and I was not sure if it was that or tumor related. They weren't sure either and said he would need to see a doctor for evaluation. I told him we could go to urgent care, and he threw a fit. Why did I call them? We had been over this countless times. I *had* to call them when something changed. He did not want urgent care and said Monday he would see his regular doctor. I told him he may not get an appointment on Monday. He said he would wait. Can you say stubborn? It was his body and his pain, but I had to live with the fallout.

The other thing this week was he asked the social worker about food stamps. I had told him we didn't qualify because we own property. Sure enough, all the paperwork says you can't have assets over $5,000. So his solution was, "Let's sell the property, hide the money, and file for a bridge card." See what I mean by the thought processes. I would say he was kidding but he really was serious. He said other people beat the system. I told him I didn't have the time, energy, or desire to try to beat the system.

I've said it before and I'll say it again—what kept me going (and sane) were the prayers of family and friends and the fact that I knew the Lord was with me every step of the way. You think I could have done this on my own? Think again!

Saturday, June 29, 2013—Evening Crisis

The crisis that evening was not with Jack; it was with me. I had seen my chiropractor about 11:00 A.M. and felt much better after an adjustment. He said my shoulder and neck were knotted from the fall on Friday. Because I had fallen so hard and because I was so knotted up, he told me to come back on Monday for another adjustment.

About 3:00 P.M. that afternoon I started feeling a lot of pain in my stomach and side. The only thing I had eaten was a small breakfast and then some apple cider. I kept saying that I thought I had food poisoning, but I had no idea from what. I could not think of anything else it could be. I was so miserable I did not want to eat. I could now understand what Jack had been through on Father's Day, but did not think I had the same problem.

Rob and Tracy were going to visit some friends and kept asking if I was okay. I told them to go see their friends and I would be fine. Dave fixed pork chops, mashed potatoes, and vegetables for dinner. I had no appetite but thought if I ate, maybe my stomach would feel better. I was hoping the gravy would coat my stomach and bring some relief.

That did not happen. By 5:30 P.M. I was in agony. I ate, but it did not stay down. I was tossing and turning and groaning in a front bedroom when Dave came in about 8:30 P.M. and told me I was going to the ER because I was not only not better, I was worse. As I walked across the living room, Jack said, "If they have to keep you, you better stay." I nodded but thought to myself that I would just get something for the pain and come back home. He told me that at least three times on my way through the house. All I said was, "I'll see you in a couple of hours."

By the time we got to the hospital I was in worse pain and what little I still had in my stomach did not stay down. They gave me something for the pain, and in a little while it was at least tolerable but I still could not keep anything down. They told me I needed a CAT scan and gave me something to drink for the test. The first few sips came right back up. They said to take my time and keep trying to sip it because they really needed the test.

Four hours and several tests later they came in to tell me I had to have my appendix removed as it was seriously inflamed. I was in shock. It was the last thing I would have expected. I was just going to ask if they were going to send me home for the weekend and have me come back Monday when the doctor said I was being admitted and the surgery would be the next morning. By this time the pain meds were working, and I felt better.

I was trying to tell the doctor I could not stay because I had a seriously ill husband at home and Dave was telling him I would stay and what else needed to be done. Since they would only give me meds for pain and since I would have surgery Sunday morning, they wouldn't run any more tests. It was almost 3:00 A.M. by this time. I told Dave to go home and get some sleep. Dave had called Rob and Tracy to tell them what was going on, and they cut their visit with friends short and went back to the house to stay with Jack. They left Ryan at Charlie's because they did not know what was going on with me and wanted to be able to come to the hospital if necessary.

Sunday, June 30, 2013—Surgery Day

They had told us Saturday night that I was scheduled for surgery at 11:00 A.M. on Sunday morning. On Sunday morning at 9:00 A.M. the nurse was in my room saying it was time to go. I told her I was scheduled for 11:00 A.M., and she said I had been moved up to 9:00 A.M. I did not even have time to call anyone and tell them of the time change. Before I could blink, I was being transported to surgery.

When I woke up in my room, the first person I saw was Jack, sitting in a wheelchair by my bed. I was shocked. I had not expected to see him there. He had been so weak and so miserable since getting sick on Father's Day I did not expect him to be up to the trip. Dave told me later they had gotten to the hospital just after I was taken to surgery, and he was very upset that he didn't get to see me before I went down.

Jack had already been there several hours by the time they got me back to my room, and I could see he was really struggling. I told Dave to take him home if he was ready to go because he was already worn out. I told Jack I would be released that day or the next morning.

Late that afternoon they gave me something in the IV for pain, or at least I think it was for pain. At any rate, before long I knew I was in serious trouble. I knew from what I was going through that my blood pressure was dropping. I was pushing and banging on the nurse call button on the left side of my bed. When no one came, I thought of getting up and calling out. When I rolled over I knew I could not get off the bed. I was so dizzy I could not think and felt like I was going to pass out.

Just about then the nurse came back in the room, took one look at me, and started pushing buttons. In seconds three nurses were in the room and were calling the doctor. My blood pressure had dropped to 78/42, and they were worried. I told them I had been trying to call them with the button on the left. They said that button was not connected and I was supposed to use the one on the right—only they couldn't find it. One of them found it—under my pillow. They were all very upset that it had gotten put there because it was supposed to be right next to me on the bed. My nurse told me she had come back in the room just to make sure I was okay. It's a good thing she did that.

By the time everything had calmed down, I was told I would be spending the night and depending on how I responded the next day, they would consider sending me home. I had to let Dave know and told him to tell his dad the news but to assure him I was all right.

Monday, July 1, 2013—Another Day at "The Henry Ford Hilton"

We called the hospital The Henry Ford Hilton as a joke because it seemed like it was a place one or the other of us visited or stayed in a lot over the past year. Today my blood pressure had not come up enough for them to feel comfortable in sending me home. I was disappointed because Allen and Bonnie were in town, and we had planned some outings, or as many as I could make if I had someone to stay with Jack.

Between the pain on Saturday and the surgery on Sunday, I was pretty much wiped out. Having my blood pressure drop did not help the energy situation. I had no strength at all.

They ran some tests and drew some blood. When the results came back, they told me my hemoglobin had dropped from 12 to 7.8 and I would definitely spend another night. I knew Jack had to know I would not be coming home, but I didn't want to tell him. I knew he would really be upset. There wasn't much I could do about it, though, so I told Dave to let him know and if he wanted to talk to me, he could call on my cell phone, which I had with me.

Tuesday, July 2, 2013—Extending My Stay Yet Again

The blood test they took early in the morning showed my hemoglobin dropped to 7.2 and my blood pressure still was not up to 100 so they said they would monitor it during the day.

Four different doctors visited me and all wanted to talk about the rheumatoid arthritis. None of them were interested in the surgery I had because I was healing from that without any problem. The issue was, where was the problem with the hemoglobin coming from?

Finally, some answers. Because of the rheumatoid arthritis and low-dose chemo I was taking for it, my bone marrow did not make enough of whatever blood cells it makes to compensate for the blood loss from surgery. They told me the only way I could get it to where it needed to be was a transfusion. I was asked if I had any reason, religious or otherwise, to refuse the treatment. I signed the papers. They gave me two units and said they would take blood at midnight and 6:00 A.M. to see if things improved. Maybe I'd go home Wednesday.

Wednesday, July 3, 2013—Home At Last!

At midnight it took three tries to get my blood. First, we had a vein "explosion," which means when they tried to take the blood, the vein burst. It wasn't serious, but they could no longer use that vein. Another try and they missed the vein. Finally on the third one they were able to get one small vial of blood. It was now 1:30 A.M. So much for getting some sleep.

At 6:00 A.M. they tried again and got one tiny, tiny vial of blood. At 8:00 A.M. they returned and said the vial at 6:00 A.M. was too small and there was not enough blood to run the test. I could not call anyone and even tell them what was going on or when I would be released because I had no idea. Allen and Bonnie had offered to pick me up when I was released to take me home. I finally called them and said I would be released today one way or another so they could come any time but it would be early afternoon before anything would happen.

I was finally released early in the afternoon. When I got home, Jack was sleeping, and I did not want to wake him up. Allen, Bonnie, and I sat in the kitchen and talked quietly for a while. When I heard movement in the living room, I knew Jack was awake. I went in and sat on the chair next to the bed. He was restless, and I knew he was waking up so I whispered, "I'm home." He opened his eyes, then pushed himself up and grabbed me and almost pulled me onto the bed. I thought he would never stop hugging me. When I could breathe I said, "So, are you glad I'm home?"

Because I had been away for four days and had not been seeing him on a daily basis, I could clearly see things had been changing. When they changed daily it was almost unnoticeable. I knew that he was weaker and that his mind wasn't as clear. His eye was drooping again and was now noticeable. The curling of his left hand was getting worse. It was a struggle for him to get out of the bed even with the help of the rails and his hearing was again getting worse. He had been very upset about my not being released and all the medical issues. That took a lot out of him physically and emotionally.

223

Thursday, July 4, 2013 — A Quiet Celebration

Allen and Bonnie came out to spend the day with us. Bea and Pierre had left on vacation very early in the morning, and Allen and Bonnie were leaving the next day, Friday. I told them if they wanted to go do something while they were here, I would understand. So far they had visited with family and spent time with me in the hospital. It wasn't the vacation they expected to have, but they were okay with it. We had a good visit and late in the afternoon Jack said he wanted Chinese fried shrimp. We could only find one place open, so Allen and Dave went to pick up the food. We talked for a while longer and then Jack fell asleep, and they said they had to go back to their hotel to get packed up to leave early in the morning.

I was glad they came and felt bad about not being able to do some exploring and shopping with them, but there was nothing any of us could do about that, and they were very flexible and had told me repeatedly that it was okay and not to fret about it.

Saturday, July 6, 2013 — Going Forward

Going forward — I was not sure. After each setback Jack did not come back quite to where he had been. Some days he did well, and on others I could not get him awake for any amount of time.

The pain he had felt on Father's Day had been so severe he had agreed to a pain patch. He was still using the patch, and we were considering increasing it because even with the patch and six Vicodin at night he was complaining. The stress of my emergency surgery had also taken a toll, and he was again eating less and not wanting to go anywhere. I could see him beginning to fail more each day.

I was considering asking if we could increase the patch but not so much that it would overload him again. I did not want him to quit using the patch, so I wanted it to be increased in the smallest increments so his body could adjust without any problems.

I was still weak from the surgery and all the issues, so I knew there was not a lot I could do around the house. He kept telling me to not work so hard and to quit waiting on him hand and foot.

Fortunately, it was relatively quiet and I had already done a lot of cleaning and organizing.

Each day I could see very minor changes in Jack. I knew someone who had not seen him in a while would probably notice things, but I still didn't want to panic anyone, so I did not mention any of the changes I was seeing. Mostly it was just more of the problems he had had on the left side becoming more noticeable and his moods would swing from being calm to being irritable. That, I was told, was from the steroids and the tumors. I had to keep reminding myself he didn't mean anything that he said when he was in a crabby mood. He had told me months before that he knew toward the end he would say or do things that would possibly be cruel or hurtful. He said over and over that he would not mean it and was hoping it would never come to that.

Sunday, July 14, 2013—On the Mend

I was finally on the mend. I felt better than I had a week ago. If I hadn't been feeling better, I would have been in serious trouble. We did not do much all week. I had no energy, and Jack did not feel well. Ryan spent most of his time at Charlie's. He did come out a few times and helped out so he could make the "farm dollars." I felt bad that he had not had the opportunity to do more, but I could not do much about it.

Rob came on Friday July 12 and was planning to leave Wednesday afternoon. He helped me with a big project on Saturday even though it was hot, and then, nut that he was, went mountain biking at Stoney Creek Park.

Jack's bruises were bigger now and more purple—in fact, they were almost black they were so dark. In some areas the skin had split and had been bleeding. I was not sure the steroids were worth the problems they were causing. The nurse wanted me to up the dose to three a day, but I had not done that because of the bleeding. The steroids were supposed to aid with appetite and keep edema in the brain to a minimum. I just didn't know if it was worth it. His appetite wasn't good anyway, and I could see problems manifesting themselves, so what were we gaining?

He had three bad days this week. A bad day was when he could barely get out of bed, and then only to go to the bathroom. On the bad days, he did not talk much and was very "droopy." His appetite was dropping again, even with the steroids. Mentally, he was still alert and could hold a short conversation even though it took a lot out of him.

Thursday, July 18, 2013—Six-Month Review

The hospice nurse and the hospice doctor were out today. It was the first visit by the doctor. It had been six months since we had put him in hospice. We had not expected him to live long enough for the six-month review required by Medicare.

Both of Jack's feet were swollen and had been swollen for a few days. We were pretty sure it was from the heat and humidity of the past week. The temperature for three days had been in the nineties with very high humidity. In addition, it was nearly impossible to get Jack to keep his feet elevated, which would have helped with the swelling. I was going to have to keep an eye on them to make sure they didn't get worse.

The doctor checked his ears since he was still having some pain. He had been complaining of earaches about the time I had the emergency surgery earlier in the month. We had put off going to the doctor because of my emergency and never did make the appointment. He had a slight redness and swelling in both ears so the doctor prescribed drops to clear that up. If that didn't help then we would know the ear problems were related to the tumors.

He also wanted to increase the steroids to four a day to help with the edema in the brain. I was concerned about the bruising and tearing of the skin on his arms if we were to increase the dose. The doctor said it should not get any worse than it was, but to keep an eye on it "just in case." I really felt the increase was not worth the problems I knew we would encounter.

Jack was on a pain patch and still was taking six Vicodin a night. I had thought about asking for an increase in the patch if we could do it in increments that would not cause an overload to his system. If the headaches were the issue in not sleeping, the patch should help with that.

I went out on the front porch to have a private talk with the doctor while the nurse checked Jack out. I asked him about the steroids and how much good they were going to do as the tumor grew. He said he would not recommend more than the four a day he was now prescribing because more than four would not be effective as the tumors would have taken over the space in the brain. I didn't argue with him, but I felt we were already there and could see no need to increase the steroids. They were not helping with his appetite, nor were they helping with the issues he was now having with his left side, eyesight, mental alertness, and hearing issues.

The doctor wouldn't give a timeline but said from his experience and with what had been going on Jack "might" have a couple more months. He said we would have an indication that things were changing when he tired more quickly, seemed to have more difficulty walking, and didn't think or respond as coherently. The steroid increase should help with that—temporarily. How long? He would not say.

Once they were no longer effective, his feeling was that we would see changes happening at a faster pace. It would be slow to start and then move more quickly as pressure from the tumor took over and wasn't alleviated by the steroids.

All that is to say we still didn't have answers and never would, but we now knew what to look for. The thing, or things, that could change all this were: he could get a virus, he could get a blood clot, he could fall and hit his head, he could have a heart attack, or the tumor could press on the nerve that controls the message to the heart, and it could stop.

So, yes, normal was out the window. And, as usual, I wasn't planning more than one day at a time. I had learned to just roll with it, do what I could, and not stress about what I could not control. I was sure down the road, it wouldn't be as easy to get through a day, but for now, I would take one day at a time.

Sunday, July 21, 2013 — Prayer for a Family

Today I wrote my prayer team and family on behalf of another SCCC family that had just lost their loved one to cancer. Jerry and Jack were diagnosed a month apart and had almost the same issues. Jerry's cancer did not metastasize to the brain until later in his journey. He did, however, have more extensive cancer in other places — his spine, lung and lymph glands, among other places.

I had talked to Jerry's wife several times and tried on a couple of occasions to have a face-to-face meeting. This morning I had called on my way to church because she had mentioned that things were rough on Friday, and I wanted to meet her and pray for them.

After church I drove over to her house and thought that I might see if she was home even though she hadn't called me back. Just as I pulled in their drive, she called. I could hear the tears in her voice and told her I was actually in her drive. She said, "Please come in! Please, please!" So I went in, expecting the worst.

Jerry had passed away that morning at 2:30 with Kathy at his side. She was still in shock and still reeling from what had happened. We talked for about an hour, and then she had to get ready to go to the funeral home. Just hearing what she had to say made me realize I was not far behind in that journey. I had thought Jerry was in better shape than Jack, but he apparently had more cancer in his body. I thought, and this was only my opinion, that all the radiation and chemo he had did him more harm than good. Even after the chemo she had told me one of his tumors was larger, not smaller.

As she described his final hours, I was reminded of the last three days of my mom's life and the last few hours that we spent by her side. I could so relate to what she was saying. She kept saying she was afraid she was losing her mind because she could not focus on anything or think things through. I told her that she was perfectly normal, and all her reactions were perfectly normal.

I asked for prayer for her and her two children — nineteen and twenty-three. This was very hard on them. I hoped to make the funeral but was having dental work one day and was hoping it was not on the day they were having the service. She asked me to please come if I could make it, and I told her I would do my best to be there.

We had been together on our journeys for six months and had formed sort of a bond. I knew one day soon I would be where she was now. That did not scare me, but it did make me step back and think. I knew where Jack would be, and I knew where I would be someday. It's the process that is not easy.

Even in the midst of her grief, she showed me an album and some pictures and told me an amazing story. Even in our worst times, God can do things that take the edge off our pain. In June, when Jerry was still feeling somewhat good, they decided to have a "daddy/daughter dance." Since they knew he would not be here for her wedding (she's not engaged or anything), they wanted to do something special. A friend loaned a gown; the tux place loaned him a tux at no cost. Someone picked up the tab for the facility at a nearby park. They had several photos and a video taken there, just as if she was actually getting married. What a treasure! Kathy cried as she showed it to me and said when her daughter does get married they will display it and play the video. There will be many tears—but what a precious memory!

As I talked with her, I was thinking of Mick's message that morning and the music. Both spoke volumes to me, and as I visited with her, the words of the songs and what Mick had said became so real. We praise God when things are good but blame Him when things are bad. Kathy and I were not blaming God; we both knew what was coming. I was just so thankful she had such a wonderful memory provided for them. Yes, even in our grief, He is there! He is, after all, The Great I Am!

I hope this story makes sense. I'm sure it's a little rambling. I was a little emotional after spending some time with her and hearing what Jerry's final hours were like. I knew in the coming days and weeks they would need a lot of prayer support. They were taking Jerry to North Carolina for burial because that was where family lived. I asked people to pray for comfort, peace, and decisions that had to be made and that people would come alongside her not just in the next few days, but the next few weeks and even months. This does not end with the funeral, as most of you well know.

We were holding our own at the moment. Jack was sleeping more during the day. When he was awake, he did not know whether it was 6:00 P.M. or 6:00 A.M. I could understand that. For the most part, he was taking four steroids a day for the edema. I was not sure how long that would be effective, but the doctor had said he would not increase the dose because it wouldn't do any good at that point. His feet were still swollen even though it had cooled off and the humidity had dropped.

I've said this before, and it was my theme, so to speak. I don't know what tomorrow holds, but I know who holds tomorrow.

Monday, July 29, 2013—Little Things

It's the little things that add up—or don't. It's the little things that become big things eventually if not taken care of. Our little things would become big things because there was just no way to fix them.

I had done some research looking into Jack's symptoms. I am not a medical person, so I could be wrong. I was not making a diagnosis. I was just looking at some of the little things and wondering if they did add up to a big thing. The big thing would be congestive heart failure or CHF. If it was one thing, I'd say maybe it was just some swelling. However, there were more symptoms than just the feet that made me feel we could be dealing with CHF on top of everything else.

That said, there were other things that didn't relate to CHF. He had what appeared to be a blood blister on a finger. It was not in a place where he would have rubbed it, which is usually how you get a blood blister. So, where did that come from? I had no idea. I had felt all along that the steroids were causing more problems than they were solving. I still felt that way. They were not helping his appetite much anymore, either. But then, that loss of appetite was another symptom of CHF. On and on and on it went.

I could not get a regular pair of socks on his feet because of the swelling, so I found a pair of thermal socks. They were thicker than his regular socks, but they also had more "give" so I could stretch them over his feet better. Besides, his feet were freezing. He was freezing! Yes, my furnace was running—in July! I was way too warm, and he was barely comfortable. I was hoping it would get back into the eighties so I wouldn't have to run the furnace any more. But then, he wasn't warm until it hit ninety.

He was still sleeping a lot. We did not go anywhere to eat today. He wanted an egg/sausage biscuit from McDonald's, so I went and got him one. He just could not get ready to go out. He said it took too much energy just to get dressed and the idea of walking out the back door and the six steps to the truck scared him. For him to feel that much effort was involved told me volumes about where he was in this journey.

He told the aide today that his headache today was about a "6," so he took two Vicodin early this morning. I had doubled the fentanyl patch to two. If that and two Vicodin barely took care of the headache, we needed to find something stronger. I would be talking to the nurse the next day or Wednesday about another increase. They had been talking about giving him morphine, but he refused it. Down the line I knew he would not have a choice.

He had a newspaper yesterday and fell asleep with it on his lap. I'm not sure if he ever did read any of it because he slept most of the day. This afternoon I had picked up a newspaper, and he had yet to look at it. I could not remember the last time he turned the TV on. Since he had been watching the news every day at 5:30 A.M. and 5:30 P.M., this was a big change.

It was increasingly hard for him to concentrate on anything for more than a few minutes at a time. He had tried to look at some magazines but it took all day to get through a few pages.

Wednesday, July 31, 2013 — The Month Finally Ended

I hated to see summer go, but I did have to say I was not sorry to see July end. It had to be up there as one of my worst months ever!

First, my surgery; then Dave had a broken tooth; then I needed dental work; then the guy with the same cancer as Jack passed away; then a dear friend lost her very short battle with pancreatic cancer.

I was not sure August would be much better. We were seeing some definite changes in Jack, and of course none of them were good. A nurse was out to visit. She was not our regular nurse. The regular nurse was off sick this week. This nurse had been here a few weeks before when the hospice doctor made a visit. She said she could see a definite change in him.

I asked about the CHF, and she said they had considered that as a possibility, but it could also be related to the cancer. Both things can cause similar symptoms. It was hard to know, but either way, it just meant things would continue to go downhill.

Jack was alert and talking when the nurse and the aide were here. That was the first he'd been that alert in a couple of days. Yesterday we went out to breakfast, and after we came home, he slept most of the day, only getting up to go to the bathroom. I asked if he wanted chicken and mashed potatoes for supper, and he said he wasn't hungry. He had not eaten anything today. He had asked for some dinner earlier but left it untouched. He said he was hungry but didn't want to eat when he saw the food.

He had been drinking six to eight cups of coffee every day for most of the summer. I had been making him lattes with rich cream and honey. Yesterday he had three cups and today that I know of he had three or four cups. He did not wake up today until about 11:00 A.M. He had his first cup of coffee then. He had been getting me up at 6:00 A.M. and saying "coffee time." So this was a major change. The not eating and cutting back on fluids were indications that the steroids were not working even though we had upped the dosage. I decided it was time to quit giving them.

I knew he was up in the middle of the night because I woke up about midnight and was up until almost 2:00 A.M. while he was restless and kept moving around. I sat on the couch until I was sure he had gone back to sleep, then I went back to bed. I knew he got up after that because the medicine I had left out for him was gone in the morning.

Tonight he was freezing again and told me his toes hurt and that he thought he had gout. Earlier he had said his back hurt. I doubted that he had gout. His feet were swollen, and so were his toes. His back pain could be cancer that had spread or the way he slept sitting up most of the time.

He had been wearing thermal socks because of the swelling and because his feet were always cold. I cut the top ribbing so it would be looser on his legs. He wanted the furnace on again. He was wrapped in afghans and freezing while I was in shorts and t-shirt and sweating.

232

The nurse said as he slept more and ate less he might lose his ability to swallow. At that point she said we should consider liquid morphine for the pain. It could be put inside his cheek, and he would not need to swallow it.

After Charlie got to the house, I ran some errands. Then, after the nurse left, I had the kids paint some trim pieces out in our new building. I was hoping we could get the building finished before bad weather. It still needed a few panels of siding put up and the trim. We were getting there, though. They loved painting, and I was glad because tomorrow there would be more of the same. I was hoping to get it all, or most of it, primed and painted so we could hang it whenever it stopped raining.

Tonight, lack of sleep was catching up with me, so I was planning an early night and hoping Jack would sleep all night.

Thursday, August 1, 2013—Home Alone

Dave had been invited to a friend's cabin for the coming weekend and wanted to know if I would be okay if he was gone for two days. I knew he needed a break and told him to go and have a good time. Things were getting crazy with Jack, but I did not feel he should give up a chance to get away and do something. He had been with us day and night through this whole process and needed a break.

I knew Charlie would not be available on the weekend except for an emergency, so I planned to ask our friend Carol to come out and spend the night with me. That way I would have someone at the house just in case I needed some assistance. Carol was available, so we made plans for Dave to take off; I would be okay for Friday night, and she would be at the house Saturday.

Friday, August 2, 2013—A Roller Coaster Ride

Jack was drinking less and less coffee. He had two cups on Thursday and very little to eat. The steroids were no longer effective, so I had quit giving them to him. I would put them out or hand them to him, and he would not take them. I figured there was no point in

233

trying to pressure him into taking them. We had increased his fentanyl again and had stopped the Vicodin.

I am glad I had two witnesses here to see what I saw this day, or I would think maybe I was going crazy. It had been so up and down lately I could not keep anything straight.

The other day (Wednesday), the nurse and aide visited. Jack said his feet did not hurt when they touched them even though they were badly swollen. The swelling in the left was far worse than the right.

That afternoon about 4:00 he had a cup of coffee. I tried to get him to eat some roast, but he didn't want any. Thursday morning he did not wake up except to go to the bathroom. Charlie was out later, so he can testify to what happened. Jack slept most of the day and was only awake for short times. He did not want the pork chops we had for dinner.

Late Thursday he wanted to go into our bedroom and sleep in there. He could not make it on his own; Charlie had to carry him in there. He said his feet hurt so bad he could not walk. We eased his socks off as he groaned and said it was excruciating pain. We were shocked to see his feet swollen and red. They looked like the skin would burst. The swelling seemed much worse to me than it had been even a few days before.

He slept for a little while in our bed and then woke up and said he wanted to use the bathroom. Charlie had to help him again. Jack thought the coffee table was his bed and tried to lie down on it. We finally got him into his hospital bed. I called hospice because I wasn't sure what to do about his feet. They said to leave the socks off but keep them covered and check them every so often.

Today he did not wake up until almost 1:00 P.M. and then sat up like nothing had happened and asked for coffee. He did not remember sleeping almost thirty-six hours except for short times awake and vaguely remembered the foot pain.

The nurse came out and went over everything. She said there was a possibility there was a broken bone in the foot, or it also could be cellulitis. Jack was sure it was gout. I still doubted that it was gout. At this point, it was anyone's guess but his feet had been swollen since those ninety-degree days we had had in July.

I had doubled the pain meds and that seemed to help with the foot pain. The left one was still bad and was very painful to the touch. Dave and I eased some socks on him when he said his feet were cold. He said the left one hurt when we put the sock on it.

Late in the evening he said he wanted to go to breakfast with his buddy the next morning. At that moment I seriously doubted that would happen because I didn't think he could get his shoes on, and I was not sure he could get in the pickup truck. Only serious determination would get him out of the house.

I never knew when or if I should call the family and let them know what was happening because things could change and the next day could be completely different. Like I said, I was glad I was not the only one seeing this up-and-down roller coaster process or I would have wondered about my sanity.

All I knew is someone had to be in the house at all times, and if he did manage to get out, I would have to let his friends know what to look for and what to do.

Then again, the next day I could post and say everything was back to normal. I seriously doubted it would be that way, but it was so up and down it was hard to say what the next day would actually bring.

Sunday, August 4, 2013—Another Wild Ride

I was glad Carol spent the night. Otherwise, I'd think I was crazy. But, I have a witness—I was not crazy.

Jack was very dehydrated. He was not eating. He had had nothing to eat since Thursday. Last night he was delirious all night. Neither of us got much sleep. He talked all night about truck stops, hauling boats, getting his paperwork turned in, etc. It's not that it was gibberish—it was just so disjointed it made no sense. This, people, is typical of a brain tumor. Should you ever have to take care of someone with this, take notes. It can be very bizarre.

His feet had been swollen to the point that I thought the skin would burst. That was Thursday and Friday. Today, you could see the bones! The swelling was completely gone. I was sure I knew why, but I wanted it checked out anyway. The hospice on-call nurse came out for an evaluation because I had called in. She agreed with my thought that his body was absorbing all the fluid it could from the swollen feet to continue to function. He had not been drinking any fluid to speak of in days, and we both felt he was beginning to shut down. This was just one indication. He was so thin he did not have much reserve to call on. She indicated that if he would not eat or drink in the next twenty-four hours, he might have one to two weeks (or less, depending).

She no sooner told us that and left than he woke up and asked for a cup of coffee. Go figure! Of course, one cup won't keep a body alive, but it does go along with what she told us—that with a brain tumor there are no absolutes! Everything was a guessing game. He might sleep four days, then get up and want to eat and have a coffee. Then he might sleep four more days (or more or less) and do the same. Most of it would depend on what reserves his body had to draw on and what other issues he had.

I got the impression we were not talking months anymore but weeks—or possibly even just days if something were to go bump in the night.

I would have said the problems were medicine-induced issues except for the fact that some of this started to happen even before I added the Ativan and Trans-Scop (or whatever it was called) for congestion. The wild stuff the previous night might have been because of the meds, but he had been restless at night for weeks.

He was awake for a while, and even talked to Carol. Then he fell back asleep, and I had to take what time I could to sleep, so I crashed on the couch as soon as I saw him relax. I needed to catch some rest when I didn't have to worry about him getting out of bed and falling.

Dave would be back late Sunday night, and Charlie said he would be out for part or all of the night depending on what he could work out for his son.

Because of where we were in this journey and the misery I saw him suffering (not necessarily pain, but misery nonetheless), the prayer I was asking for was that the Lord would release him from his body that was no longer responding and fit him with his new body in Heaven.

It was a hard prayer to ask for, but I couldn't ask for prayer for him to stay here like this. If you could see this on a daily basis, you would know what I was talking about. It went without saying that I needed prayer for rest and strength and that we all needed the Lord's peace at this time.

Tuesday, August 6, 2013—The Amazing Human Brain

Think about the amazing brain that God gave to humans. No other animal on the planet has a brain like ours. How can people deny Him and say we were an "accident"? How can an accident produce such a miraculous thing?

You don't have to stay awake to tell your heart to beat, or your lungs to breathe in and out. You don't have to tell your eyes to see or your ears to hear. What an amazing thing God has given to us!

Even when the brain misfires, it is still sending messages to the heart and lungs. As I had been thinking about this, it just was beyond my comprehension.

Even in the misfiring, there is sense—at least to the person with the issue. Jack had been rambling for the past few nights. It was not gibberish—he made perfect sense—to himself. It was a bit disjointed, but by the bits and pieces I did hear (he mumbled a lot), I knew he was talking about places he had been and things he had seen. I didn't know what they were, but they were as clear as day to him. You may think I'm crazy, but I found that amazing. Even though he was not fully aware of the world around him, he was aware of an inner world where he had been.

The brain is better than any computer. And, like a computer, we don't know how to use it to its fullest potential. When it malfunctions, we want to throw it away and get a new one. Well, sorry, can't do that with a brain. It's amazing that with tumors and edema pressing on the brain, it still functioned—even though it was misfiring.

I had not posted some of the things we had been through because I didn't see the point, but I decided to write about last night because someone somewhere might be involved with someone with similar events that happen. I've found it challenging, but not frightening. I just think it's amazing how the brain works. And, on a side note, why is it that the one animal with "intelligence" is the one animal that fights with and denies its Creator? Well, that's another discussion.

Last night I fell asleep on the couch about 8:00 P.M. I woke up to hear Jack moving and talking. Thinking he was trying to get out of bed, I got up to check on him. I was totally discouraged to find it was only 10:00 P.M. I was sure it was at least 4:00 A.M. It had only been two hours? I had the whole night to face yet. Knowing people had been praying for me was the only reason I could keep on keeping on.

I got him settled and went back to the couch. I must have drifted off because next thing I knew it was 1:15 A.M., and he was standing by the bed. I have no idea how he got up because he had been so weak he had not been able to get up without assistance. I went over to him and asked what he wanted. He wanted to sit at the kitchen table. I tried to talk him out of it, but he insisted so I helped him the ten steps to the table, which was no easy feat with someone so unsteady and wobbly and trying to turn in different directions.

I finally got him settled, and he asked where his saw and the blades were. I told him they were in the barn. He wanted to know why I keep moving his stuff (that, folks, was a *huge* issue with us). I told him he was always yelling at Charlie and me to put his tools away so for once we did it and they were put away. He said, "OK."

Then he was pulling at something in the air as though he had a string or something in both hands and asked me to take one end and help him tie it around his head to get rid of the headache. I took one end and "tied" it around his head. He said that felt better, so I suggested he go back to bed and get comfortable.

Getting him back to the bed was trickier. He kept trying to sit on the pellet stove, the table, and the arm of the chair. I finally got him to the bed, but he fell on it before I could turn him around. Since he was kneeling half on the floor and lying half across the bed, I had to lift his legs and put them on the bed. I took down the side rail, rolled his legs up, and put the side rail back up. I covered him with a sheet, and he went back to sleep.

I got back to the couch about 2:30 A.M. I woke up just before 6:30 A.M. when he was restless again. I got him comfortable again, and he went back to sleep.

All indications were that he wouldn't come out of this maze, except for very short periods of time. This was not how he wanted to be. He had said if he ever got to where he didn't know who he was or what he was doing, he wanted to be gone. That was why I was asking for prayers for God to release him from this place and take him to where he would be whole and pain free! Do you know how hard it is to ask that? You will never know until you have to do it.

I thanked my prayer team of friends and family for holding us up in prayer for the eight months we had been on this journey. If it were not for their prayer support and comforting words, I would never, ever have been able to make this journey. I could not find enough words to say thank you, and I could not find the proper words to say how awesome the Lord had been through this whole time. He had been my Sustainer, my Counselor, my Decision Maker, my Friend, and my Lord.

Someday maybe I can find the words to express what it had been like to know I had never been alone. I don't mean family and friends hadn't been there—I just mean I had always felt His presence.

There were tears now and would be more when this journey was over. But they were not the tears of those who have no hope.

Wednesday, August 7, 2013—Sometimes I Borrow Stuff

I copied the hymn below because it spoke (and still speaks) volumes to me. I hope someone reading it is as comforted by it as I was.

"He Giveth More Grace"

He giveth more grace when the burdens grow greater,
He sendeth more strength when the labors increase,
To added affliction—He addeth His mercy,
To multiplied trials—His multiplied peace.

His love has no limit,
His grace has no measure,
His power has no boundary known unto men;
For out of His infinite riches in Jesus,
He giveth, and giveth, and giveth again!

When we have exhausted our store of endurance,
When our strength has failed ere the day is half done,
When we reach the end of our hoarded resources,
Our Father's full giving is only begun.

His love has no limit,
His grace has no measure,
His power has no boundary known unto men;
For out of His infinite riches in Jesus,
He giveth, and giveth, and giveth again!

Lyrics by Annie J. Flint

The hospice nurse said yesterday that Jack was in the "pre-active" dying stage (as opposed to the "active" dying stage.) It made me stop and think, "How do you 'actively' die?"

Go back to my other post about the brain. Is it not amazing the body God created for us? Think about it—you actively are born and you actively die. We don't think much about being actively born because we don't have any conscious recollection of it. Do we have a conscious awareness of our "actively dying"? Why did I ponder such things? Because I saw it up front and personal. I had to deal with it. Since I had to deal with it, I wanted to understand it. The problem is—you can't really understand because both are a miracle. That brings me back to how can people *not* believe in a Creator. Well, we won't go there. That is their problem.

For me, I saw someone I loved slowly slipping away from this life and getting ready to enter another. In some ways it was sad, but in other ways it was a beautiful time because watching someone get ready for a "new life" is a miracle in itself.

The body is designed to fight to the last breath to keep on functioning. We don't tell the kidneys to find fluid somewhere to process. We don't tell the liver to find fluid and waste somewhere to process. The body was designed to do that. What a miracle! Even now, in this "pre-active" stage, his body was doing all it could to maintain life. Our agony was watching someone suffer and knowing we couldn't do a thing about it.

Last night was a quieter night than we had had recently. He was less agitated and a little more verbal. At one point, when I was standing by the bed waiting to see if he was going to wake up as he moved around, he looked at me and said, "Why are you standing there looking at me like a vulture?" I just had to laugh.

I told him I was waiting to see if he needed anything. He said, "How about a coffee?" Then he rolled over and went to sleep. Sometimes his mind was so clear it was hard for me to believe we were near the end. Those times only lasted a few minutes, though. He woke up again a few minutes later and asked where that coffee was. By the time I put it on the table by his bed, he was asleep again.

From what I had read, this could actually go for a few weeks if he did get some coffee in him every day. That fluid would sustain him even if he was not eating. Eventually, though, even coffee wouldn't be enough. Charlie and I were taking bets last night (didn't know I was a gambler did you?). If he didn't drink anything over the next few days and started to really decline, I told Charlie I bet he would hold on until my birthday, which would be the following Tuesday. I said he'd do that—the stinker—just so I'd never forget what day he went to be with the Lord. There you have it—my family's weird sense of humor (and no, I don't really gamble).

Jack was restless and kept calling for me. When I would ask what he wanted, he would not answer. I think he just wanted to know where I was.

Thursday, August 8, 2013—Long Days and Longer Nights

I'm not sure which was worse—the long days or the longer nights! Both had their issues.

Saturday, Sunday, and Monday nights were really wild. He was very restless and talked a lot—mostly about things from years ago. He kept trying to get out of the bed. I finally bungee corded a kitchen chair backward against the bed where the opening was between the rails. I would hear him trying to get that chair loose, and it gave me time to get to the bed to see what he wanted.

Tuesday night was quieter in that he wasn't as restless and the talking was less. Last night was so quiet that when I woke up at 4:30

this morning, I ran to the bed to see if he was still breathing. It was eerily quiet.

Most of today he had been barely responsive. Dave and Charlie helped me situate him on the bed so he was more comfortable. It took all three of us, mostly because I didn't want to hurt him by trying to move him unless we could do it as gently as possible.

Pastor Garry was here, and Jack asked him why he got his hair cut. To understand just how funny that statement was, you would have to know Pastor Garry and Jack. Pastor Garry had beautiful, white hair. It was never out of place and was always precisely cut. He had not had a recent hair cut so for Jack to see something different, if he really did, was funny. For Jack to mention it was so unlike him. I don't remember Jack ever commenting on anyone's haircut so to comment on Pastor Garry's was not only unusual, it was really funny.

Charlie talked to Jack, but he was barely aware of who it was talking to him. When he had called for me earlier, I asked what he wanted. He wanted to know when I got back. I told him I hadn't gone anywhere. He said he thought I went to church. I told him it was 3:00 P.M. and church was over. Those were the type of conversations we were having.

I don't know if anyone has been through this and what their thoughts are, but when he was sleeping it seemed almost normal. I would think he was just taking a nap—even though I knew better. It was sort of unreal.

We were thinking his last meal had been the past Friday morning, but it could have been Thursday. Time was just a blur right now. For sure the last thing he had to drink was Sunday night when Pastor Garry and Martha were here. That was about 7:00 P.M. So now it had been four days without any fluid of any kind.

He complained of a headache, so I asked if he wanted morphine. He said no, so I asked if he wanted me to increase the patch of pain medicine, and he said okay, so I added a patch.

I read back through some of my earlier posts, and there were several times we thought we were close to the end. We were afraid people would think we were "crying wolf" because he would go into such a tail spin and then come out of it. This tailspin, though, was different. He would not be coming out of this one—not on this side of Heaven.

We told the kids what we were expecting to happen. Rob decided to come for the weekend, and Karen was planning to be in the next Tuesday through Friday so they would have their time to say good-bye. Rich had been home in May and June, so all had had a chance to come and help and spend time with him.

The closer we got to the end of this journey, the more I thought back to two hymns I had posted months ago. They made me cry (and still do) and at the same time gave me such comfort. Both were written at times of great pain and loss for the ones who wrote them. Maybe that is why they touched me so deeply. Those people suffered more than I ever have and still could write such comforting words. I wanted to share them again. Hopefully, someone will also find them comforting.

"God Leads Us Along"

In shady, green pastures, so rich and so sweet,
God leads His dear children along;
Where the water's cool flow bathes the weary one's feet,
God leads His dear children along.

Refrain:
Some through the waters, some through the flood,
Some through the fire, but all through the blood;
Some through great sorrow, but God gives a song,
In the night season and all the day long.

Sometimes on the mount where the sun shines so bright,
God leads His dear children along;
Sometimes in the valley, in darkest of night,
God leads His dear children along.

Though sorrows befall us and evils oppose,
God leads His dear children along;
Through grace we can conquer, defeat all our foes,

God leads His dear children along.

Away from the mire, and away from the clay,
God leads His dear children along;
Away up in glory, eternity's day,
God leads His dear children along.

Lyrics by George A. Young

"It Is Well With My Soul"

When peace like a river, attendeth my way,
When sorrows like sea billows roll;
Whatever my lot, Thou hast taught me to know,
It is well, it is well, with my soul

Refrain

It is well, (it is well),
With my soul, (with my soul)
It is well, it is well, with my soul.

Though Satan should buffet, though trials should come,
Let this blest assurance control,
That Christ has regarded my helpless estate,
And hath shed His own blood for my soul.

My sin, oh, the bliss of this glorious thought!
My sin, not in part but the whole,
Is nailed to the cross, and I bear it no more,
Praise the Lord, praise the Lord, O my soul!

For me, be it Christ, be it Christ hence to live:
If Jordan above me shall roll,
No pang shall be mine, for in death as in life,
Thou wilt whisper Thy peace to my soul.

But Lord, 'tis for Thee, for Thy coming we wait,
The sky, not the grave, is our goal;
Oh, trump of the angel! Oh, voice of the Lord!
Blessed hope, blessed rest of my soul

And Lord, haste the day when my faith shall be sight,
The clouds be rolled back as a scroll;
The trump shall resound, and the Lord shall descend,
A song in the night, oh my soul!

Written by Horatio Spafford and composed by Philip Bliss

Saturday, August 10, 2013—Seventy-two Hours

Seventy-two hours—that's what the hospice nurse said today. How do they arbitrarily pick a number? How do they know? Our times are in God's hands, so how can they make that decision?

Well, they don't, not really. They had been careful to not be specific. So, here's how it happened. The nurse was out on Friday. She was the on-call nurse for the weekend, so she called in the morning to see if there were changes, and I said yes, so she said she'd be out.

I told her Jack had nothing to eat or drink for six days—not since the past Sunday when Pastor Garry was here. He had maybe two or three ounces of coffee twice during the week, but that was not enough to sustain someone.

I asked if she thought he would make it to the next weekend— two weeks without food or fluid. She said he would be lucky to make it through this weekend. Then she checked him over and revised it and said he had "up to seventy-two hours." That would be ten days without food or water. Could he make it past then? Stranger things have happened, but she said his condition had changed so much from yesterday that she doubted it.

She also said most people die during the hours of 2:00–4:00 A.M. if they have been ill. The reason is the body slows down in preparation for sleep once it's dark. For the person that is ill, that slowdown can be the turning point. It's not to say someone can't die during the day, but it's usually less likely.

Today his blood pressure was 82/42 and his pulse was 120. Those and the fact that he was barely responsive were major indicators to her. He was in a coma. Bodily functions were down to a bare minimum or had stopped completely. He was on morphine now for the pain. She said to watch his forehead. When it was creased deeply he was in pain. I could administer as much pain medication as was needed. Obviously, I wouldn't be overloading him but comfort was the main goal now.

I said before to watch the body "actively die" was weird. He seemed almost normal. He looked like he was sleeping. He even snored a bit. He would try to respond when talked to but it took so much effort, he would barely get his eyes open. We all had to help move him up in the bed and turn him from side to side. He had no strength to do it at all.

Pastor Garry was out and spoke to him and prayed over him. He did not respond at all. He barely responded to the nurse's voice. She said that was probably because he was afraid she'd push another pill on him. That had been an ongoing joke. He would tell her of a symptom or pain and then say, "I'm sure you have a pill for that." He would ask me "Is the pill pusher coming today?" It was our standing joke.

So what now? I had no idea. I had been going day to day. Now I was going hour to hour. It was still in God's hands. I didn't know His plan. We thought we were prepared. Hah! What a delusion that was—you are *never* really prepared. I expected to cry my eyes out. The only reason I hadn't yet was I hadn't allowed myself the luxury of falling apart. I had to keep it together so I could handle things these next few days. Or so I thought.

I hope somehow, if you are ever on a sad journey like this one that you will let God touch you in some way that will help you face whatever comes your way.

Sunday, August 11, 2013—Escape into Eternity

When we knew on Saturday that Jack's time was at hand, I said a quick prayer that it would be Saturday night since Charlie and Rob were both spending the night. I knew both would want to be here.

Sunday morning arrived, and Jack was still with us, but changes were happening rapidly. I was sure he would not go through another night. What I didn't know was how to prepare for what I knew was going to happen. In reality, there is no way to prepare for it.

Family members stopped during the day, and by late afternoon, when it became apparent he was struggling, Rob decided to stay as late as he could. I was sure Rob would feel awful if he left and got an hour down the road and got the call. I asked how late he could stay as Charlie had called and said he would try to spend the night again. Rob would wait until he came. Charlie had to work until 5:00 P.M. It was now hour by hour.

Josette came and helped turn him and showed us how to situate him for comfort. She also used a machine to get the mucus out of his throat. That unnerved me, and I had to leave the room. I went into the back bathroom and stayed there until I quit crying and pulled myself together. I was so grateful for her nursing expertise. I just could not have done that. I would have been so sure I would hurt him. She kept insisting I would not hurt him and I had to "be aggressive" to get the mucus out. Easy for her to say—she's a nurse! She knew how to do it right.

After she left, his breathing started getting more "ragged." It's hard to describe. Mostly it was that he was struggling for breath. She said it had a name; it was the type of breathing you do when you are dying—as in "actively dying."

I knew we were there, and this was the part I knew I would have the hardest part dealing with. After nearly nine months of struggle, this was the worst part of it! I could take the uncertain days, the sleepless nights; these last few hours and minutes would be the hardest.

We were in and out of the living room and then settled around the kitchen table where we could hear Jack if he moved. Dave kept going into the living room to check on him. After he would leave I would go check on him. I could not make myself sit next to him because that labored breathing was more than I could handle right then.

I would check on him every few minutes and go back in the kitchen. Then Dave would go in and check on him again. And so it went. Every few minutes one of us would go in the room and check him. Neither of us could stay for very long because it really unnerved us. I was giving him morphine for pain every few minutes. The nurse had said to give it as often as needed. She showed me how to tell if he was in pain. I was keeping a log of how often I gave him the meds — not because it mattered but because I needed to know how much pain he was in and keep track of how often I gave him the meds for it.

At 5:45 P.M. I went in the living room to check on him again. I had not given him pain meds the last few times I had checked on him because he didn't appear to be struggling any more than he had been. The nurse had said to give him the morphine every ten to fifteen minutes if I felt he needed it for pain. It was close to that time, so I got a swab because they said to swab his mouth and then give the med orally and try to get it in his cheek and not down his throat. Swab in one hand and med in the other, I went in to him.

As soon as I bent over, I knew he had escaped into eternity. I didn't know what to do. I had my hands full and needed to check for a pulse. If I laid the stuff down, it would then be dirty, and I would have to get new stuff. But as I looked at him, I knew that didn't matter and I laid both things on the bed beside him.

I checked his feet — they were very warm. His hands — they were very warm. His chest — very warm but not moving, not rising and falling. His head — warm but no pulse in the neck. I went around the bed to make sure I was touching the right places. Again, I checked his feet, hands, chest, and neck. By then others had come into the room, maybe sensing something was up.

I told them I could not detect a heartbeat and asked if they would check also to make sure I wasn't misreading anything. I left the room to contact Charlie as he had not arrived yet. When I came back, Dave, Rob, Bea, Suzanne, and Michelle all confirmed what I had said. I then called hospice — and then the tears were free to fall.

Psalm 23 says, "Yea, though I walk through the valley of the shadow of death I will fear no evil for You are with me."

Death was just that — a shadow. There was no bogeyman in a black cape and hood. There was no fear, no agony, no grasping at anything. Jack had simply escaped into eternity.

The Bible says "To be absent from the body is to be present with the Lord."

We look at death as God's ultimate punishment and think it is because He hates us. While death is the payment for sin, that payment was made on the cross. Yes, our bodies die, but our soul lives on. Believing in Jesus takes away the sting of death and leaves us with assurance we will one day be with Him. I can't put it any simpler than that.

Jack's journey was over—he was now on a new journey, one I could not take with him. My journey with him was over—I was now on a new journey, one I would have to take without him. Someday our new journeys will merge when I escape into eternity.

Monday and Tuesday, August 12–13, 2013—Saying Good-bye

Yesterday (Monday) was a very emotional and tear-filled day and evening. I thank God for technology. We had a private family viewing time last night and were able to "face time" Rich with Charlie's iPad. How wonderful that all my kids were able to be there with me. We were sad that Rich was not there physically, but seeing his face on the iPad was so wonderful. It was a tough decision whether to try to get him here yesterday or have the time in September for the memorial. We all felt we wanted more of him later. I am so thankful we could have him with us via technology

I was glad we all got to see Jack looking better than he had at home. I could now remember him better the way he was on Monday. He was in his jeans with a flannel shirt and his Army baseball cap. I expected him to ask for his paper and coffee; that's how "normal" he looked.

I told the funeral home we'd have about twenty family members there and only needed a small room. Charlie said he counted thirty-six. Oops.

George Clarke had graciously offered to take everyone to dinner after our family time. It was so awesome and generous of him. I will never be able thank him and Luz enough for all the support they had given us over the past nine months. How do you ever thank someone enough for renting an RV for a week (back in December) so we could go to Tennessee and then pay for the gas on top of it! May God bless George richly for his supreme generosity.

We began to plan a memorial service for a Sunday in September. Our favorite pastor, Garry, was to be out of town every weekend until Labor Day, so we had to wait because no one else was going to do this service for us.

I thanked everyone that had taken this difficult journey with us. I would never have imagined the intense emotional strain on a person when you watch a loved one who was so strong physically deteriorate to such a degree. It was truly heart wrenching.

If you know someone going through such a time, don't try to "fix it" or tell them "it'll be okay"—just send your love and prayers. It truly is the best thing you can do.

Epilogue

W̲e held a "Celebration of Jack's Life" on September 8, 2013 at Stoney Creek Community Church in Washington, Michigan. There were over 200 people in attendance. Jack's sister Joyce, brother Aubrey, and two nieces (Theresa and Donna) came from Tennessee. My brother Allen came from Florida. There were family members from around the area. Richard, Michele, and Luke had flown in from Arizona on Friday and stayed for a week. Many friends from church were in attendance as well as young people the kids had grown up with. Several of Jack's friends from Armada and some business acquaintances were able to attend.

The celebration began with a Military Honor Guard Ceremony. It was beautiful, emotional, and very touching. Pastor Garry and Martha read several eulogies from family members, and then Dave, Charlie, and Allen spoke. Reina sang "I'll Fly Away," and Rica sang "I Can Only Imagine." Pastor Garry gave a wonderful message about Jack and about their relationship as friends as well as Pastor Garry being "Jack's personal spiritual advisor" and about how to give your life to Christ.

Charlie had asked if the new owner of the Kenworth would allow us to have the truck at the church for the service. John agreed and left the truck there on Saturday. Sunday afternoon Charlie pulled the truck right up to the doors of the building. I don't think anyone has ever gone to a memorial service and found a semi parked in the doorway. It was truly an amazing day!

Two days after the memorial service for Jack, Richard was offered a job in Troy, Michigan, which he accepted. He started the job the

251

first of October and Thanksgiving week in 2013 I flew to Arizona and helped him and Michele move their belongings to Michigan to start a new chapter of their life near family. We were sad that this job, which was a completely different one than he had been seeking, did not come up in time for him to relocate to Michigan while his dad was still alive. We were happy, though, that he and his family were finally back home.

A Final Note

For months afterward I struggled with the fact that there had been no one in the living room when Jack took his last breath. I felt immensely sad and wondered if I had neglected him in the end. I prayed about it and asked that if I had done something wrong, that God would show me that so I could ask forgiveness. I felt that no one should be alone in their final moments.

I shared my feelings with a friend, and she told me that some people wait until they are alone and then they "let go." I remembered then that my grandmother had done just that. My brother had gone to see her and had told her he was going to use the restroom and would be right back. When he got back to her room she was gone. The nurse told him that night that some people just want that last hug or touch or word, and then when they sense they are alone, they let themselves go so the loved one doesn't have to see it happen. That gave me a great sense of relief.

If you are facing that, rest assured that if you did all you knew to do but for some reason were not able to be in the room with your loved one, it is not only okay, it may be the way that person wanted it to be to save you the pain of those final moments. My prayer is that what I have written will help whoever is going through something like this to find comfort, strength, peace, and closure in their own situation.

CPSIA information can be obtained at www.ICGtesting.com
Printed in the USA
BVOW03s1929041114

373511BV00005B/11/P